# Open Architecture for the People



*Open Architecture for the People* explores Japanese architecture and the three different phases of development between the years 1950 and 2018.

Changing ways of life through differing generations have caused fluctuations in the building industry. This book demonstrates how each generation's expectations have resulted in discernible eras in architecture which can be examined collectively as well as in isolation. For example, the sudden increase in productivity from 1950 brought about by the Industrial Revolution flowed to the production of buildings and homes, and designs were influenced by modern ideas.

With over thirty black and white images to illustrate the changes, Matsumura brings to light architectural developments that have previously been confined to Japanese-speaking academics. In doing so, the book broadens the scope for further architectural examinations internationally. It would be ideal for academics, students and professionals within the areas of architecture and urban planning, particularly those with an interest in Japanese architecture.

**Shuichi Matsumura** was born in Kobe City, Japan, in 1957. He graduated from the University of Tokyo (Department of Architecture, Faculty of Engineering) in 1980 and was qualified as a First Class Architect and Engineer by Ministry of Construction in 1982. He earned his doctorate at the University of Tokyo (Department of Architecture, Graduate School of Engineering), completing it in 1985. He has worked as a full-time lecturer (1986–1989), an associate professor (1990–2006), a professor (2006–2018) and a project professor (April 2018–present) in the Department of Architecture, Graduate School of Engineering, the University of Tokyo. He has been engaged in the education and the research activities on housing, building system design, industrialization of building production, building organization, and so on for more than thirty years.

He has been active as a visiting professor in several foreign universities such as Rome University "La Sapienza" (Italy, 1992), Trento University (Italy, 1996), Nanjing University (China, 2004), Dalian Institute of Technology (China, 2005), Montreal University (Canada, 2007), and Loughborough University (UK, 2011–2014).

He has won many prizes for his education, research and writings such as the Prize of Architectural Institute of Japan 2005 (Research Theses Division), the Prize of Association of Urban Housing Science 2008 (Publication), the Prize of

Architectural Institute of Japan 2015 (Book Division), the Prize of Association of Urban Housing Science 2015 (Publication), the Prize of Japan Facility Management Association 2016 (Publication), the Prize of Architectural Institute of Japan 2016 (Education), and the Prize of Association of Urban Housing Science 2016 (Publication).

He has also been socially active. He has worked as a member or a chair of the important committees of the national/local governments as well as academic organizations. For example, he was a vice president of Architectural Institute of Japan during June 2016–May 2018.

He has written many academic papers as well as more than ninety books. Although this book is his first English one, some have already been translated into Chinese and Korean. His most recent book is *Akiya wo Ikasu (Effective Use of Vacant Buildings)*, published in 2018.

*"Too little attention has been paid in English language publications to contemporary developments in Japanese architecture and built environment, aside from the "starchitects" or the embattled vernacular traditions. Yet inside Japan, a lively discourse is ongoing into much deeper transformations of Japanese architecture. At a time of depopulation and resource limits, coupled with a deep cultural reverence for traditional social structures, Japanese architectural production is subtly but inexorably changing. This book makes a significant contribution to understanding these transformations."*

*Stephen Kendall, PhD (MIT'90 – Design Theory and Methods)*
*Emeritus Professor of Architecture, Ball State University*
*Co-Director, Council on Open Building*

## Routledge Research in Architecture

The *Routledge Research in Architecture* series provides the reader with the latest scholarship in the field of architecture. The series publishes research from across the globe and covers areas as diverse as architectural history and theory, technology, digital architecture, structures, materials, details, design, monographs of architects, interior design, and much more. By making these studies available to the worldwide academic community, the series aims to promote quality architectural research.

For a full list of titles, please visit: https://www.routledge.com/Routledge-Research-in-Architecture/book-series/RRARCH

**Visual Spatial Enquiry**
Diagrams and Metaphors for Architects and Spatial Thinkers
*Edited by Robyn Creagh and Sarah McGann*

**Narratives of Architectural Education**
From Student to Architecture
*James Thompson*

**Migrant Housing**
Architecture, Dwelling, Migration
*Mirjana Lozanovksa*

**Architecture, Space and Memory of Resurrection in Northern Ireland**
Shareness in a Divided Nation
*Mohamed Gamal Abdelmonem and Gehan Selim*

**Open Architecture for the People**
Housing Development in Post-War Japan
*Shuichi Matsumura*

**Ruined Skylines**
Aesthetics, Politics and London's Towering Cityscape
*Günter Gassner*

# Open Architecture for the People

## Housing Development in Post-War Japan

Shuichi Matsumura

Routledge
Taylor & Francis Group
LONDON AND NEW YORK

First published 2020
by Routledge
2 Park Square, Milton Park, Abingdon, Oxon OX14 4RN

and by Routledge
605 Third Avenue, New York, NY 10017

First issued in paperback 2021

*Routledge is an imprint of the Taylor & Francis Group, an informa business*



Chapter 2 to 5 published in Japanese by Chikumashobo Ltd., 10 October, 2016.
Chapter 6 published in Japanese by Asahi Shimbun Publications Inc., 30 November, 2018

English translation by: Shuichi Matsumura, Kaori Fujita, Toru Eguchi, Shiro Watanabe, Yuki Takemura and Jessica LeClair

*British Library Cataloguing-in-Publication Data*
A catalogue record for this book is available from the British Library

*Library of Congress Cataloging-in-Publication Data*
A catalog record for this title has been requested

ISBN 13: 978-0-367-78508-6 (pbk)
ISBN 13: 978-0-815-36156-5 (hbk)

Typeset in Sabon
by Swales & Willis, Exeter, Devon, UK

# Contents

*List of figures* viii
*Preface: Why I chose to discuss open architecture* xi
*Acknowledgements* xv

Introduction: Three phases of open architecture – phases of "way to be opened" 1

1 The initiatives of the government and the industry – 1950–1973 9

2 An initiative to pay attention to people – 1973–1986 42

3 The inclusion of customers organized by the industry – 1986–2000 65

4 Connecting with ways of life can give the initiative to the people in the 21st century 90

5 The development of the third phase of open architecture 116

6 Open architecture ahead – to play with vacant buildings 136

*Index* 156

# Figures


1.1 PRECON in around 1950 14
1.2 Sekisui House Type A (Sekisui Chemical Co., Ltd.), which were sold starting in 1960. With impressive shiny aluminum exterior walls, brand new steel sash, and plastic eaves and buttress walls. Source: Sekisui House Co., Ltd. 20
1.3 One of the first prefabricated houses – "Micro House." (Originally called the "*Mizetto House*" in Japanese. "*Mizetto*" is a Japanese loanword from the English word "midget." The name was used to refer to the small size of the home.) (Daiwa House Industry Co., Ltd.) In 1959, it was sold as a study room for children in the garden. It is currently displayed in the research laboratory of Daiwa House 21
1.4 One of the first prefabricated houses – The Matsushita Number 1 model (National Housing Building Material company; currently the Panasonic Homes Corporation). The house was reportedly developed under the sponsorship of Konosuke Matsushita in 1961. Source: Panasonic Homes Corporation 22
1.5 Around 1970, methods utilizing a higher percentage of factory production were also actively under development. An example of the unit construction system, unit factory of Sekisui Heim M1. Source: Sekisui Chemical Co., Ltd. 23
1.6 Diagram showing the change in the size and types of construction method in the new house-building market ("Weather chart of house production") 30
2.1 Yoshimura House. Source: Dr. Nanae Nakao 44
2.2 Imanishi House. Source: Professor Meiji Fujita 45
2.3 Sekisui Heim M1. A preserved version at a research institute in Tsukuba 49
2.4 The composition of a modular unit of Sekisui Heim M1, clearly illustrating Dr. K. Ohno's concept of an "all-purpose box" with attached components. Source: S. Matsumura, G. Hirasawa et al., *3D Zukai ni Yoru Kenchiku Kouhou*

*(Building Construction – learning with 3D drawings)*, Ichigaya Shuppansha Publishing, 2014 51
2.5 Hata House. An example of Dr. R. Kenmochi's "Standardized Component Building System" in 1967. Source: Shinkenchiku-sha 52
2.6 *Gunkyo* 55
3.1 Diagram showing the modular construction grid and division of work in a Japanese-style wooden building 67
3.2 Graph showing the number of new housing units built each year in Japan (based on data from the Japanese Ministry of Land, Infrastructure, Construction, and Tourism) 69
3.3 The first two-story Model 2B built by Sekisui House in 1964. Source: Sekisui House Co., Ltd. 75
3.4 A two-story "Attic House" model built by Sekisui House in 1979. Source: Sekisui House Co., Ltd. 75
3.5 Misawa Home "O Model" in 1976. Source: Misawa Home Co., Ltd. 77
3.6 Misawa Home's original room interiors and fixtures from the 1980s. Source: Misawa Home Co., Ltd. 78
3.7 Diagram comparing the conventional "planned production" manufacturing system, where components are stored in a warehouse, with the new flexible "production by house" system 81
3.8 An automated pre-cutting machine from the 1990s. Source: Miyagawa Koki Co., Ltd. 82
3.9 A photograph showing Tokyo in 2005 full of buildings (taken approximately 10km from the center of the city) 85
4.1 The number of existing housing units by the year built (based on data from the Ministry of International Affairs and Communications) 95
4.2 The change in average total floor area of newly built housing units (based on data from the Ministry of Land, Infrastructure, Construction, and Tourism) 96
4.3 An image showing the conversion of "Offices into Flats" by the Research Team on Conversion in 2001 97
4.4 Mr. Hoshina's House at Echizen Hama in Niigata Prefecture. Sometimes Mr. and Mrs. Hoshina hold workshops with their artist friends at home. Source: Mr. Yasuhiro Hoshina 99
4.5 The library of Comfama de Aranjuez in Medellin 103
4.6 Change in the age of users of "Hometown Migration Support Center" 105
4.7 An old house converted into a company's office in Kamiyama (PLAT EASE Corporation). Source: Professor Kouichi Sato 106
4.8 Reizensou of Yoshihara Jutaku in Fukuoka City. Source: Yoshihara Jutaku Limited Company 111

5.1 The abandoned temple of Saienji was converted from a Buddhist temple into a welfare facility in Komatsu City in Ishikawa Prefecture. Source: Professor Kouichi Sato 120
5.2 A photograph taken at the closing party of the 8th Kitakyushu Renovation School. The man who wore glasses with the white hair reflected at the left side of the photograph is the author. Source: Kitakyushu Yamorisha Co., Ltd. 123
5.3 At the final presentation of the Kitakyushu Renovation School. Source: Kitakyushu Yamorisha Co., Ltd. 126
5.4 "Nagano Monzen Gurashi no Susume" (*Suggestions for Living in Monzen, Nagano City*). Source: MY ROOM Co., Ltd. 127
5.5 One of various human activities at the Tamamusubi Tarrace. Both of the new inhabitants and other people living in the surrounding estates enjoy autumn events organized by the new inhabitants and the management companies. Source: Rivita Co., Ltd. 133

# Preface

## Why I chose to discuss open architecture

### "Architecture" versus Buildings

The Robie House designed by Frank Lloyd Wright, Villa Cook and the La Tourette Monastery by Le Corbusier, Villa Karuizawa by Junzo Yoshimura,[1] Daikan Yama Apartment House by Fumihiko Maki,[2] Sea Ranch by MLTW. It may be puzzling to those who do not specialize in architecture, but these structures are masterpieces designed by world-renowned architects of the 20th century.

When I entered the Department of Architecture at the University of Tokyo, my classmates' and my first assignment was to draw a colored perspective of these masterpieces. However, the plan and elevation, which the professor distributed, did not depict color. As a result, every weekend we would go to architecture bookstores, searching for books with pictures of these architectural masterpieces. Exchanging information among classmates was also critical. Through these processes, we eventually became familiar with each architectural work and the architect who designed it. I brought a huge drafting desk into my small dorm room and drew many colored perspectives. Students living in the same dormitory, who were working with other professors in other departments, regarded me as an "architect." By the time I started sleeping underneath the drafting desk, I felt a surge of pride to have undertaken such a peculiar and specialized profession.

This is only one example, but I think most people who enroll in the Department of Architecture probably have more or less the same kind of experience when entering this world of Architecture. I can easily imagine what happens next. Every day, you learn more and more names of architects and their works. Then, in order to understand those works objectively, you start reading criticisms. You will be living in the world of Architecture. You would naturally start observing and evaluating architecture as "works" by "architects." Eventually, those buildings which are not "works" will become invisible to you. You will walk straight to the target "work" with a camera in hand without looking once to the other buildings.

Such architecture students often do not regard the buildings which form their town as "Architecture." Those buildings do not appear in architecture magazines, and according to what they learned in design courses at university, are not designed at all. However, we live our daily lives in towns made by buildings. The vast majority of us do not live in Architecture.

Sooner or later, students in the Department of Architecture recognize this contradiction. In my case, I may not have come to this realization until I was in graduate school. Buildings were not my concern as I was dreaming of Architecture. However, as soon as I realized this contradiction, I reached the understanding that Architecture and Buildings are made in the same way. Each land parcel has an owner with his/her own circumstances, plans, and preferences. The results corresponding to the taste of each just happened to be Architecture or Building. When I reached this understanding, the distinction between Architecture and Building became inconsequential. More than that, I developed an antipathy, from an architect's perspective, towards the possibility of building anything according to each owner on such cramped plots. I resented the crowds of "Pencil Buildings" competing to be original but each equally ugly. I think this is a typical pattern for architectural students.

My rather conventional sense of aesthetics was totally turned on its head by a single phrase. I was riding a taxi through Tokyo with a professor from the Delft University of Technology, looking at the street full of Pencil Buildings. The professor told me, "This is why I like Tokyo. Buildings can be built according to each person's taste on each piece of land. This is exactly the 'landscape of democracy.' In Europe, this can never happen. We are ordered to make uniform the color, the height, and the wall line. There is no freedom in design. I envy Tokyo so much."

Since hearing these words, my positive feelings have grown towards the chaotic townscape of Japan, made up of freely designed Buildings. This view is certainly a minority within the Japanese architectural community, but I cannot help feeling this way.

The professor's word "democracy" touched my heart, as an architectural student torn between Architecture and Building. By raising the walls of academic, artistic, and technological expertise to guard the world of Architecture, had we not forced a utopian image of architecture onto people outside of the profession?

Let's take "democracy" to mean a system conceived to foster happier and more prosperous lives of the people. In that case, merely because Architecture and Buildings are built according to each owner's taste on each privately-owned piece of land, is it really fair to call that the "landscape of democracy"? Personally, I do not think so. In general, "democracy" seems much more preferable than the forced value created by the fortress of Architecture, guarded by high walls as a specialized discipline. But what can "democracy" in architecture really be?

## A state that can be called "democracy"?

For a long time, I pondered this question. But the answer was not obvious. The walls protecting Architecture as a specialized discipline had been earnestly constructed during the modern era of Japan and, as a result, were tall enough and sturdy enough to withstand attacks. Looking at the lives of people living in Buildings, which were constructed everywhere, there were very few hints of greater happiness or prosperity.

Architecture and Building stood before my simple question. The same social situation established both Architecture and Building, namely modernization.

Modernization was a movement inspired by the motivation to redistribute unevenly distributed goods, energy, technology, and knowledge to every corner of the nation and the world. This movement was accompanied by the vision that everyone could enjoy a modernized life. Architecture was a symbol of this vision. Further, the prevalence of technology and knowledge provided the economic drive to construct a vast number of Buildings. During this grand movement, the opinions and self-motivation of the people, who were the users of architecture, were largely ignored. There were moments, especially after the 1960s, when this kind of attitude was criticized but overall the situation did not change.

However, today more than a decade into the 21st century, the situation has changed dramatically. There is an overflowing stock of technology and architecture accumulated by modern society. It seems to me that society is now ready for people to begin effectively using those accumulated stocks to forge new ways of living and working.

For example, the increasing vacancy rate of old apartment buildings posed a major problem for management. By modifying the contract so that the inhabitants can change the interior decoration and finishing, the uniform units could be colorfully designed according to each inhabitant's taste. New relationships blossomed in the neighborhood when neighbors started helping each other with DIY projects on the weekend, much like sports clubs. In this case, the apartment building was not only full but there was a waiting list of people who wanted to live there after hearing about it. Let us consider another example. In the center of a mid-sized city, where the increasing number of vacant houses and buildings showed no signs of stopping, a number of migrants from the city were able to rent the spaces cheaply and start small businesses. In less than five years, eighty of these small businesses had been created. An artist, who wanted to make an art center and share information around the world, remodeled a closed-down school in Tokyo into an art center where 800,000 people now gather every year.

The efforts by users, not architectural specialists, were able to convert existing buildings into happier and more prosperous living places for people. This movement is becoming apparent all around Japan. I think that people have started following their aesthetic sense to edit the stock of technology and architecture, accumulated in modern society. I can now hope to see a "democratic landscape" – which once existed only in my imagination – built through the efforts of these people.

## Opening the world of Architecture

This book looks ahead to the near future, when the world of Architecture, which was once heavily guarded by architectural experts, will be opened to ordinary people. Further, the future will be marked by efforts to understand the historical significance of this shift and to figure out ways to make this shift result in something better. Many have great expectations that a new world will arise, which is vastly different from the existing closed world of Architecture dominated by professionals.

However, nothing will change by waiting. What can we do to open the world of Architecture and create spaces for a happier and more fruitful life for the people? There should be a "manner" that is fitting to the era. In this book, I will look back on the history of architecture from the viewpoint of "Openness." I will try to find the seeds of the "manner" buried in history. Further, I will consider the examples of activities undertaken by people in various places to find hints for the future, which began developing in this century. In the final chapter, I would like to describe the future "manner" of managing real estate. Please join me for this journey through Japan's architectural history.

## Notes

1 1908–1997. One of the leading modern architects in Japan. After graduating from Tokyo Fine Art University, Yoshimura worked for ten years under Antonin Raymond. Antonin Raymond came to Japan with Frank Lloyd Wright in the 1920s and continued living in Japan, as a pioneer of modernist architecture in Japan. Yoshimura became a professor at Tokyo Fine Art University in 1962.
2 1928–present. One of the leading architects in Japan. While studying in the Department of Architecture at the University of Tokyo, Maki was a disciple of Kenzo Tange. After his graduation, he studied at Harvard University and began working as an architect in the USA. In 1979, he became a professor at the University of Tokyo.

# Acknowledgements

This book is based on English translations of "*Hirakareru Kenchiku – Minshuka no Sahou- (Open Architecture – Manners of Democratization)*" (Japanese) published by Chikumashobo Ltd. in October 2016 and "*Akiya wo Ikasu (Effective Use of Vacant Buildings)*" (Japanese) published by Asahi Shimbun Publications Inc. in 2018. In particular, Chapters 2 through 5 are nearly direct English translations of the original Japanese version of the former book and Chapter 6 is nearly a direct translation of a part of the latter.

In Chapter 1 of the original Japanese version, I did not explain the historical facts related to the production of Japanese houses and buildings from the post-war period through the end of the high economic growth era because I assumed readers were Japanese and would already be familiar with this history. Instead, I explained innovations in building technologies and philosophies from architecture in Europe and the United States after the Industrial Revolution until around 1950, which had more influence on post-war Japan. However, in this English version, the content of Chapter 1 has been significantly changed. I explain mainly the historical facts in Japan concerning the production of houses and buildings during the post-war period until the end of the high economic growth period, assuming that many English language readers would not be familiar with the post-war history and the basic matters of building production in Japan. For readers of this English version, I believe that this history and background on building production is necessary to thoroughly understand Japanese houses, buildings, and architecture.

When I wrote the former Japanese book, Mr. Shiro Nagata of Chikumashobo, Mr. Youji Makabe, who called himself "an architect never built," and Mr. Akihiro Imai, a free editor, supported me in planning and editing the book. In the case of the latter book, Mr. Yutaka Kita of Asahi Shimbun Publications, Mr. Makabe, and Mr. Imai did so. Without their cooperation, the Japanese version would have never been published. I sincerely thank them.

For the English translation, I collaborated with the following people. I cannot thank them enough for translating my difficult-to-read Japanese into English. Following the order of the English translation work process, Professor Kaori Fujita, Professor in the Department of Architecture at the University of Tokyo, Professor Toru Eguchi, an Associate Professor in the Faculty of Urban Innovation at Yokohama National University, Dr. Shiro Watanabe, a researcher at the National Institute for Land and Infrastructure Management in Japan, and Ms. Yuki Takemura, a doctoral candidate in the Graduate School of Frontier Sciences at the University of Tokyo. I appreciate their efforts very much.

The English translations written by the above individuals were good, but it was Ms. Jessica LeClair who made those drafts into truly excellent English. Ms. LeClair also translated Chapter 6. Ms. LeClair lives in the United States and has no formal training in architecture. However, she read other Japanese writings of mine and came to my office in 2018 to ask many interesting questions in Japanese. I appreciated her for her high level of interest in Japanese houses and architecture, as well as her wonderful Japanese ability. As soon as we met for the first time, I asked if she could support our translation of this book into English. Fortunately, her reply was "yes." The English translation took longer than I expected, but thanks to Ms. LeClair, I was able to express exactly what I wanted to say in natural English. I am grateful to her from the bottom of my heart.

Professor Stephen Kendall, Professor Emeritus at Ball State University, also played a very important role for this book. Professor Kendall lives in the United States and has been one of my best friends for a long time. First, he said that he would like to read the English version of my book published in Japan in 2016. That sparked the planning of the publication of this English version. Second, he introduced me to the British publisher, Routledge. Finally, even while he was busy, he read over our English drafts and provided important and relevant comments on the content. I am also grateful to him from the bottom of my heart.

Scholars and individuals who were active in the 1950s, 1960s, and 1970s taught me directly about the actual housing and building technology development, as well as its organizations at that period in Japan. Unfortunately, some of them have already passed away. Even so, I would like to express my sincere respect to them all. Specifically, Professor Kazuo Goto, who was involved in the development of the reinforced concrete building system "PRECON" at the Tokyo Institute of Technology since the 1940s and was in a leading position in the industrialization of Japanese housing production; Mr. Mitsufusa Sawada, who led the national government administration related to Japanese housing and construction after World War II; Professor Yoshichika Uchida, who led the industrialization of Japanese housing production and who was my supervising professor; Mr. Yukichi Fukui and Dr. Tokusaburo Ishimoto, who developed Sekisui House Type A, one of the first prefabricated houses in Japan; Mr. Akio Kobayashi, who developed Matsushita No. 1, which was also one of the first prefabricated houses in Japan; Professor N. John Habraken, who established a new methodology of the industrialization of housing production; and Dr. Katsuhiko Ohno, who developed a unique prefabricated house, Sekisui Heim M1.

Dr. Ohno was also a core member of the journal *Gunyo*, which was periodically published in the 1980s and 1990s. Especially related to the discussion in Chapter 2 of this book, I was very inspired by members of *Gunkyo* from the beginning of its publication. Specifically, I am indebted to the chief editor, Professor Shuji Funo, who was a researcher and an architectural critic; two radical architects, Professor Osamu Ishiyama and Professor Toyokazu Watanabe; the issuer, Mr. Koichi Nobe, who was a consultant on the housing industry; Professor Yoshikazu Fujisawa, Professor Masao Ando, and Professor Tetsukazu Akiyama, who were occasionally involved in editing *Gunkyo*. I learned many insights through collaborating in research with them. I am grateful to them all.

I would like to thank the persons whose activities or ways of life greatly inspired me. I introduce their activities or ways of life in Chapter 4. Specifically, Mr. Yasuhiro Hoshina, a dye artist who emigrated to a small fishing village; the non-profit oraganization (NPO) COMFAMA in Medellin, Columbia, which transformed a big building, that had been ruined, into a beautiful welfare facility for an economically disadvantaged area; Mr. Masato Nakamura, an artist who transformed a former junior high school building in the central area of Tokyo into a lively art center; Mr. Kazuo Kasami, who runs an NPO to support both migrants and local governments that accept them all over Japan; Mr. Nobuya Ohminami, the central figure of an NPO, who has made a great impact by setting up programs for accepting various immigrants in a rural village with a declining and aging population; Mr. Hideki Ikeda and Ms. Saiko Ito, who were enjoying a new lifestyle of immigration from a big city to an old building in a rural area; Mr. Jun Aoki and Mr. Katsumi Yoshihara, who found a new way to manage rental flats, and are pioneers as rental flats owners; Mr. Manjyo Shimahara, who influenced many rental flats owners in Japan with his breakthrough report on the lifestyle in rental flats; Professor Yuko Nishikawa, who specialized in French literature and presents exciting thoughts about family problems in Japan; Mr. Jun Aoki, a world-famous architect, who used to be my classmate at Department of Architecture, the University of Tokyo; and Mr. Yoshinari Ohya, who transformed an unused temple into a beautifully organized welfare facility for the area.

As far as Chapter 5 is concerned, I received much intellectual stimulation from the team who worked together at the HEAD (Home & Environment Advanced Design) study group which I founded with my colleagues in 2008. I would like to thank them, specifically Mr. Yasumitsu Matsunaga, the architect who is the chairman of the HEAD; Mr. Sotaro Yamamoto, an architect who is an executive director of the HEAD; Mr. Yoshitsugu Shimizu, an urban planning consultant who is also an executive director; Mr. Hiroshi Nagaya, an entrepreneur who is also an executive director; Mr. Manabu Shinbori,

Mr. Yoshihiko Oshima, Mr. Masataka Baba, and Mr. Yohei Shimada, who are architects and members of the HEAD; two other members of the HEAD, Mr. Tomohito Yabe and Mr. Hirofumi Uchiyama, who are working in the field of area management and real estate business; another member of the HEAD, Associate Professor Mitsuhiro Tokuda at the Kyushu Institute of Technology; and Mr. Tomonori Kuraishi, Mr. Tsuyoshi Hirose, Mr. Kei Miyamoto, and Ms. Tamami Masuzawa, whom I met at the Renovation School led by HEAD or its relating opportunity. They are promoting advanced renovation machizukuri in Nagano City.

I also deeply appreciate the kindness of the following companies and persons that let me use their pictures and diagrams in this book. Namely, Dr. Nanae Nakano, Professor Meiji Fujita, Professor Kouichi Sato, Sekisui House Co., Ltd., Daiwa House Co., Ltd., Panasonic Homes Corporation, Sekisui Chemical Co., Ltd., Misawa Home Co., Ltd., Miyagawa Koki Co., Ltd., Hometown Migration Support Center, Yoshihara Jutaku Limited Company, Kitakyushu Yamorisha Co., Ltd., MY ROOM Co. Ltd., and Rivita Co., Ltd..

Without the understanding of Routledge, and Taylor & Francis Group, it would not have been possible to publish this book. I am thankful to Ms. Jennifer Schmidt, a senior editor in the field of architecture, Ms. Grace Harrison, an editor of landscape architecture and built environment research field, and Ms. Aoife McGrath, an editorial assistant, who helped me very much in the planning and editing phases of this book. I am deeply grateful to them.

January 4, 2019
Shuichi Matsumura

# Introduction

## Three phases of open architecture – phases of "way to be opened"

When discussing post-war architecture in Japan, the expression "the means of being opened" provides a consistent framework to discuss both the past and future of the industry. I consider architecture as "being more opened," when the autonomy and diversity of inhabitants increase in response to factors of a particular era. In this sense, "the means of being opened" of architecture has several phases corresponding to different eras. In this book, I propose that there are three major phases of "open architecture" in the field devoted to creating the living environment after the modern era. This understanding forms the foundation of this book. First, I would like to explain the overall structure of this book organized by these three phases.

### The first phase of open architecture (Chapter 1 "The initiatives of the government and the industry – 1950–1973")

In Chapter 1, I address the first phase of open architecture. This phase can be regarded as the modern era of architecture. It encompasses the sudden increase in industrial productivity brought about by the Industrial Revolution, as well as the creation of the concept of the modern nation and citizen. This is the phase when these concepts distinctly emerged.

The architecture of this phase was greatly inspired by progress in other fields, especially manufacturing. For example, with the Ford Model T, Henry Ford is said to have achieved the first exemplar of mass production, when he introduced the assembly line method in the 1910s. At a time when cars could only be purchased by people in the upper class, Henry Ford aimed to make a vehicle which was affordable for workers in his own factory. Cars were invented as a replacement for carriages, which had not been in use for long. In contrast, in terms of housing, people had been living in some kind of residence for a long time. However, the residential environment of many people was quite poor. At the same time, the Industrial Revolution and modernization of society had created demand for new types of buildings such as schools, factories, offices, hospitals, libraries, and museums. Much like Henry Ford's vision for the car, the idea of quickly delivering buildings to allow as many people as possible to live healthy and modern lives emerged as a dream for architecture during this era.

The achievements of this era were far from what I would consider "architecture opened to the people." The goal of this phase was to deliver "boxes" universally, where people could enjoy clean, modernized lives. Younger architects such as Gropius and Le Corbusier (also known collectively as "modernist" architects) were symbols of this generation. In addition, engineers and entrepreneurs played key roles. Engineers invented much of the technology fundamental to mass production, such as reinforced concrete structures, steel structures, and light-frame construction (in other words, two-by-four structures). Entrepreneurs used these new construction approaches to create new business ventures.

In Chapter 1, I consider the spirit of the era underlying the first phase of open architecture, as well as the efforts that helped bring the phase to realization. Due to various historical factors, the start of industrialization in Japan lagged behind similar industrialization movements in Western countries. In Japan, industrialization began in the late 1950s, after recovery from post-war damage ended and Japan achieved independence from GHQ.[1] From then until 1973, Japan experienced a period of unprecedented rapid economic growth. During this period, construction began of non-wooden flats and prefabricated houses. In addition, many local builders transformed themselves into entrepreneurs, designing and constructing houses through UKEOI (or "turnkey") contracts.

## The second phase of open architecture (Chapter 2 "An initiative to pay attention to people – 1973–1986")

The shift to the second phase can be described as a reaction to the negative situations that resulted from the mad dash towards modernity in the previous era, namely wars, destruction of the environment, and human disrespect for efficiency.

In Chapter 2, I address the concepts of "Vernacular" and "System." The typical methodology of the first phase centered around proposing a prototype and then attempting to mass produce it. However, people had not only grown tired of this approach, but criticism of it had arisen as well. Within this context, the concepts of "Vernacular" and "System" began to draw attention. "Vernacular" was the idea of re-evaluating and learning from the daily lives of people and their local communities, factors which had been neglected by modernity. "System" encompassed the idea of utilizing the results of industrialization, while seeking to increase the degree of choice and possibility of participation in order for inhabitants to be more actively involved in the creation of the living environment.

During the second phase, young architects and critics took advantage of technological advances in Japanese word processors to begin publishing periodical materials, which they planned and edited themselves. One example is the journal *Gunkyo* (or "group living" in Japanese).

The journal *Gunkyo* introduced many of the theories and practices symbolizing the turning point of the era and representing the shift to second phase of open architecture. The journal discussed the ideas of John Turner, the theorist on housing of the third world who insisted on "freedom to build." It also introduced self-built practices from various places. Readers in Japan learned about the new theory of Christopher Alexander, who presented innovative methodology to open and share the process of architecture in his book *A Pattern Language*. Not surprisingly, ideas about contemporary folk houses from Katsuhiko Ohno, as well as the concept of open technical world by Osamu Ishiyama, were also discussed in *Gunkyo*. Both men were core members of *Gunkyo*.

The ideas discussed in the *Whole Earth Catalog* created by Stewart Brand and his colleagues, as well as the alternative methodology of mass housing proposed by Nicholas John Habraken, also served as important activities and theories of the second phase of open architecture. These were not addressed directly by the *Gunkyo* journal but occurred at the same time and no doubt influenced the writers of the journal.

Even while being in the midst of the first phase of open architecture, Mr. and Mrs. Eames skipped over "System" and proposed "unselfconsciousness." They opened the way to the third phase of open architecture, by showing the possibilities of freedom from system through the design of their own residence. This was also an important practice as a representative of the second phase of open architecture. In this chapter, we will also cover the achievements and practices of Ryo Kenmochi and Katsuhiko Ohno in Japan.

## The point of arrival of the "box delivery industry" in Japan (Chapter 3 "The inclusion of customers organized by the industry – 1986–2000")

In the era of the second phase, the "box delivery industry" took shape, disconnected from struggles with power and concerns about breaking away from modernity by dealing with the tough realities of the market. The industry grew to provide inhabitants with various choices and the possibility of participating in the creation of their own living environment. In Chapter 3, I will discuss the clear example of the housing industry.

The post-war housing industry in Japan satisfied its role of delivering tidy "boxes" to people, who at the time were living in small row houses and rented flats. These tidy "boxes" could be used freely by the inhabitants. This was true for prefabricated houses, wooden houses built by local housing contractors, *danchi* (or "collective housing estates" in Japanese), and condominiums. Various movements worked to realize the dissemination of these tidy boxes to the broader society. These movements include the supply of land by land development, the creation and spread of the housing financing system, improvement in housing quality and production productivity by applying advances in industrialization to the construction industry, an increase of fresh young employees in the construction field, and the entrepreneurial spirit of "I also want to be the owner of my own shop" of local housing contractors and professional construction company owners. The tidy "boxes" delivered by the industry could be used freely by inhabitants. Previously, freedom of use was only enjoyed by the upper class, but after this time it became possible for many more people. I call this era the first phase of open architecture to the people.

However, in the 1970s people became less satisfied with the state of open architecture achieved by the earlier box industry. For example, many of the prefabricated houses created in the 1960s were limited in terms of size and appearance. Many rental flats and condominiums simply repeated the same layout offering little variety. In the housing industry, the question arose: how can we increase our flexibility to meet the specific demands of each inhabitant? This became the key issue facing the housing industry in the 1970s.

In the 1970s, prefabricated houses began to be offered with increased choices in terms of sizes and layout, as well as roof shapes and slope inclination. Some companies even offered fully-customizable "free design" options. In the field of multi-family housing, the public housing authority in Japan, called the Japan Housing Corporation, focused its efforts on "KEP." KEP stands for "Kodan Experimental Housing Project." It refers to a system separating the infill from the support, which allows individual inhabitants to select the layout of the infill. KEP is similar to modern SI housing. At the time, modular coordination systems were "closed systems." For example, in the case of prefabricated houses, the systems were different for each company, meaning that building elements were not compatible with each other. As a result, residents had little freedom in terms of choice and assemblage. During this era, an important shift occurred to pursuing an "open system" by establishing broad compatibility on the basis of a common modular coordination system.

Although not all of these problems were solved during the 1980's, the degree of freedom in the size and layout of the prefabricated houses increased dramatically. In the 1990s, factories introduced the "production by house" system. Some manufacturers even claimed that the number of housing component types under manufacturing control exceeded several million. The variation in the floor plans even within one condominium increased dramatically. In the 2000s, services that accept floor plan arrangements and specifications by residents have become common.

The progress of the second phase of open architecture can be seen in the attitude of the housing industry to expand the freedom of choice for inhabitants in the market. In Chapter 3, I also focus on the importance of understanding the role of salespeople, who worked to form relationships with inhabitants, as well as the tatami module, which is unique to Japanese architecture. These points are related to the development of the third phase.

## The third phase of open architecture (Chapter 4 "Connecting with ways of life can give the initiative to the people in the 21st century")

Thus far, the story of open architecture in the era of the "box delivery industry" can be summed up as increasing freedom of choice for the inhabitants. However, producers led this choice in the market. This begs the question: even if the number of choices increased, would residents be satisfied with relying only on the combination of conventional elements offered for sale?

Perhaps it was satisfying, during the high economic growth period when the way of living was stereotyped to a considerable extent. However, today, family structure, types of employment, and life-work balance have become diversified. Also, Japan is facing a historically unprecedented decrease in population and super-aging society. When each of us is seeking their own way of life and living, clearly conventional housing is not enough. Pioneers of the "place-making industry" found vacant houses and buildings, which were not available for sale on the conventional real estate market. They conducted highly individual renovations of these buildings and started to create new forms of living and working. I think the creativity of these inhabitants represents the way of open architecture shifting to the next phase.

The subject of consideration here is no longer a "box." The important subject is how to deal with the already sufficient supply of "boxes" as spatial resources and how to tailor existing boxes into spaces for a new and vibrant life. Stated more clearly, it is not a challenge of the physical "box" but rather a problem of the software and content, in other words, how people live inside the box.

I dare to say that architecture had not previously involved itself with people's philosophy of life. This might be the reason why leaders of the third phase of open architecture came from outside the existing architectural world.

For example, artists were a key player in the third phase of open architecture. A group of artists renovated an abandoned school building in the central area of Tokyo into the Arts Chiyoda 3331 art center. The young artists were looking for a suitable place to create a new way of living. When their creativity in using existing space met with vacant space resources in the town, a new "place" was created.

Since the United States financial crisis of 2008 and the Fukushima nuclear power plant accident, an increasing number of young people are migrating to vacant houses and buildings in rural areas. This 21st century migration phenomenon was not seen in the second phase of open architecture. It is unique to the third phase, which revolves around people's life philosophy. Although incomes may be lower in rural areas, it is possible to enjoy a much richer life than working for a generous salary in a big city. Some people call this way of living by migration as intentional "high-quality low-altitude flight" (referring to achieving a higher quality of life with lower living costs).

In addition, do-it-yourself renovation emerged as a way to arrange one's own "place" to fit one's own way of life and work. This method spread rapidly due to effective tools and information sharing mechanisms, as well as the appearance of celebrities in the field. DIY renovation is often done as physical activities with friends and neighbors. It is quite different from the former "self-build," which was undertaken as a serious demonstration of a way of life. This new type of DIY renovation represents the third phase of open architecture.

The third phase of open architecture, which started in Japan in the 21st century, is still developing with people's philosophy of life at its core. I do not believe it is important to classify or summarize these movements. Instead, in Chapter 4, I simply report the cases which I know. One common theme can be seen among the cases. Since this commonality is not discussed in Chapter 4, I will take the time to explain it here.

The representing activities of the third phase of open architecture are occurring in the area of rented houses and buildings, rather than owner-occupied houses and buildings. This is a characteristic of the "place-making industry" era. The main battlefield of the "box delivery industry" was owner-occupied houses and buildings. In those days, the goal of people was to own "boxes" which one could use at their own freedom. However, the new phase shows active movement in the area of rented houses and rented buildings. The words of Mr. Yoshihiko Oshima (Blue Studio), one of the pioneering renovators, explain this situation concisely, "Although rental houses were said to be inconvenient, today rental houses have much more freedom, as the customized rentals and custom-made rents have begun to spread. The freedom to move is a large factor, as well as freedom from loans."

In the age of "box delivery industry," the second phase of open architecture, loans which were too heavy, and the same residential form were at times forced on to the inhabitants. One important result of the third phase of open architecture is that people became free from such burdens. The current abundance of spatial resources can be considered the outcome of investments made by people during the seventy years after the war, and thus a gift from all previous generations to all the next generations. In this way, the will of individuals to own their own land and buildings becomes unnecessary.

## The new role of professionals to raise the people's initiative in the future (Chapter 5 "The development of the third phase of open architecture")

In Chapter 5, I discuss actual cases after the third phase of open architecture to address the role of the new type of experts in further developing opportunities for people's independence. In this book, I will refer to this new role as a "manner" to represent the behavior expected from experts.

In Chapter 5, I will explain the concept in the following seven sections: "Visualizing the vast availability of space resources," "Sparking and directing users' creativity to utilize existing space," "Sharing information related to experiences creating places," "Forming a community of allies to act all around the world," "Achieving sustainable town management," "Teamwork between businesses and organizations", and "Open architecture for the people." In conclusion I will discuss the manner required in the future.

## Open architecture ahead – to play with vacant buildings (Chapter 6 "Open architecture ahead – to play with vacant buildings")

As Japan entered the third phase of open architecture, a phenomenon began to emerge where forward-thinking individuals started to play with vacant buildings. In the final chapter of this book, I will consider the factors in modern Japan which allowed such "playing" with buildings to be possible.

As discussed by Dutch historian Johan Huizinga in his book *Homo ludens*, the free and voluntary nature of "play" makes it quite different from the act of "work." For Huizinga, "play" is an essential act for humans. He writes that "play is older than culture." For architectural professionals, like myself, we have long been engaged in constructing new buildings and renovating old buildings as "work." However, modern-day Japan has become a place where non-experts from outside the field of architecture can freely use vacant buildings based on their own creativity. As a result, buildings have become the object of "play" by such non-experts.

Consider the example of a group of contemporary artists and a former factory manager, who worked to remodel a factory, which had stood empty for over a decade. The action of these people, who continued working on the building with no clear final purpose or plan, certainly cannot be called "work." It can only be called "play."

Another example is the case of events announced through social media, where non-experts can gather to learn from professional carpenters. Practicing self-renovation, one group worked together to improve an old building's thermal insulation and then ended the day with a party. This "play" can be likened to a kind of sport activity enjoyed on the weekend.

I expect that this phenomenon of playing with empty buildings will be especially common in places like Japan, which is experiencing an aging and declining population, inevitably leaving a trail of empty, yet still serviceable buildings behind. It should be no surprise then that similar phenomena can also be seen in nearby Asian countries.

When architecture is opened to the people, the natural desire of humans to "play" is widely provoked. It brings a new sense of hope to the relationship between architecture and people, buildings and human beings. I will briefly touch on this topic to close the final chapter of this book.

If after reading this book, you come to understand the historical background to where we now find ourselves architecturally in Japan and see that there are still wonderful treasures within it, I would consider it a success.

## Note

1 General Headquarters, the Supreme Commander for the Allied Powers. It was an Allied Army institution which implemented occupation policy in Japan to enforce the Potsdam Declaration accompanying the end of World War II. The staff was a large number of US soldiers and American civilians, along with British and Australian soldiers.

# 1 The initiatives of the government and the industry – 1950–1973

## Post-war urban housing shortage

Due to air raids during World War II, over 200 Japanese cities were damaged. Approximately 2.23 million houses were damaged, which amounted to 20% of all the houses on the Japanese archipelago, according to the *Recovery from War Disaster – Memory and Heritage of Japan Revival* (morning edition of Nihon Keizai Shimbun,[1] August 10, 2011). Including Japanese repatriates living overseas, the shortage of houses was assumed to amount to over four million houses at that time. In September 1945, immediately after the end of the war, the Japanese government announced the construction of 300,000 emergency winter housing units. By the following year, however, only 83,000 units had been completed.

Amidst the severe housing shortage after the war, in October 1946, the "Association for Factory-Produced Housing" was established with the aim of mass producing high quality standardized houses. The member companies – twenty in total – originally manufactured housing in response to military demand. The houses they produced were made of wood and, in terms of construction system, can be roughly grouped into the following three types:

1) Post and beam frame type: components were pre-cut in the factory with remaining work completed on site.
2) Panel type: houses were assembled from factory-produced panels.
3) Frame and panel combination type: factory-produced panels were attached to pre-cut frame components.

Among these factory-produced houses, the most standard type was 2), the panel type. In fact, the Housing Corporation[2] had developed a similar prototype for housing before the war. The prototype was assembled from wooden panels, based on ideas and discussion that started in 1941. The Housing Corporation scrutinized and analyzed mass produced structures around the world under the guidance of Ken Ichiura,[3] who was strongly influenced by the writings of Albert F. Bemis. Bemis wrote a book on the theory of factory-produced housing in the United States during the 1930s.[4] The Housing Corporation concluded that the panel-type assembly structure was the most appropriate construction system, and then started trial production. Four prototypes were made early in 1942. About 200 houses were constructed by the end of the war.

The most representative factory-produced houses of 1946 are "Premos" (San-in Industry) designed by Kunio Maekawa,[5] and "Kraken" (Kurashiki Silk Fabric) designed by Shizutaro Urabe.[6] The architect Kunio Maekawa was a classmate of Ken Ichiura in the Department of Architecture[7] at the Imperial University of Tokyo and later worked under Le Corbusier. Shizutaro Urabe later became known as a famous architect. Factory-produced houses achieved only temporary success and mostly vanished by 1950, due to a shortage of material distribution, inadequate organization of production, and a mismatch with national government policies.

The reconstruction of war-damaged areas reached its peak after the activities of the Association for Factory-Produced Housing ended. The primary goals of their work were to eliminate the massive housing shortage, along with fireproofing the city. As mentioned above, most factory-produced houses developed after the war were conventional wooden houses (to be discussed in detail later in this chapter). In the meantime, a number of groups, including the War Damage Reconstruction Institution Technical Research Institute, advanced the research and development of simple concrete houses, as a type of fireproofed pre-assembled building. Research and development of these simple concrete houses was not only due to demands for fireproofing but also strongly connected to deforestation caused by wartime military demands that exhausted resources. The War Damage Reconstruction Institution was an organization established in November 1945, in an attempt to centralize and promote government war-damage recovery efforts through unifying relevant departments.

In 1947, with cooperation from both academic and business partners, the War Damage Reconstruction Institution prepared and released the "Housing Standards for Simple Concrete Structures." Based on this standard, the concept of "Simple Concrete Structure Housing" was developed. This type of housing is fire and earthquake resistant. Plus, the housing is designed to be built quickly, using less labor and less materials, in order to save as much material as possible for reconstructing war-damaged areas.

Looking at examples of simple concrete construction from the time shown in *Concrete Block Construction and Lightweight Concrete Construction* (Kenzaburo Takeyama et al., 1952, Kyoritsu Publishing), various types were developed. According to the classification of the time, the types were largely classified as follows: (1) cast type (simplified cast on-site concrete), (2) masonry type (brick, block, etc.), (3) assembled type (post and beam assembled), (4) combination type (combining two of (1), (2), or (3)). Among them, block masonry construction was the most commonly used. Blocks of various sizes and shapes, which can no longer be found today, were developed at the time.

In the initial stage, even public housing developments, as will be discussed later, utilized now unusual simple concrete construction. Indeed, the number of public housing buildings created using block construction was less than 1,000 units in 1951, but reached 9,000 units by 1953.

## The new ministry of construction and three important laws

On November 5, 1945, three months after World War II ended, the national government of Japan established the War Damage Reconstruction Institution, as a unified agency to lead recovery efforts. The mission of this institute was focused on urban planning in war-affected areas, the construction and supply of houses, the processing of real estate property, and the improvement of stability of life for war victims.

By 1947, the Ministry of the Interior had been eliminated and dismantled. Further, the War Damage Reconstruction Institution and the Land Infrastructure Bureau of the Ministry of the Interior had been integrated into the so-called "Dualistic Construction Administration." On January 1, 1948, the Department of Construction was newly established. Although this Department of Construction was established as an external Bureau of the Prime Minister's Office, it was actually a Ministry from the start. The Ministry of Construction Law enacted on July 10, 1948 promoted the Bureau to the Ministry of Construction, through a merger with the Ministry of Transport's Transportation Construction Headquarters. The Building Bureau was established within the Ministry of Construction, along with the General Affairs Bureau, River Bureau, Road Bureau, Urban Bureau, and Special Construction Bureau. The Building Bureau was responsible for coordinating and planning the use of residential land, managing the administrative work for land property rights in areas affected by war or other disasters, administering affairs related to the improvement of deteriorated residential areas, promoting building development and improvement, supervising buildings, managing construction, and improving the supply of housing ("Ministry of Construction, 50 Year History," Ministry of Construction, 1998).

The Building Standard Law, preceded by the Urban Building Law of 1919, was established on May 24, 1950 and encompassed all operations by the Building Bureau. As specified in Article 1, the Building Standard Law established minimum standards related to building sites, structures, facilities, and use of buildings with the aim to protect the life, health, and property of citizens, and therefore to contribute to the promotion of societal welfare. The law had a major influence on the quality of buildings, including houses, in Japan.

Further, a new law – the Public Housing Law – was enacted in 1951 to deal with the affairs of the Building Bureau, such as housing construction, improvement of the supply of housing, management, subsidies, and supervision of houses and other buildings. Article 1 of this law called for the national government, as well as local authorities, to cooperate in preparing sufficient housing to ensure a healthy lifestyle. By offering reduced rents to low-income individuals in need of housing, the law aimed to improve the stability of people's lives and to promote social welfare. Even today in the 21st century, public housing, constructed and managed nationwide based on this law, contributes significantly to the housing supply safety net.

The Public Housing Law was created for the government to directly provide housing to low-income earners in need of housing. Whereas for higher-income citizens in need of housing, a "self-support system" for the acquisition of owner-occupied houses had already been established a year earlier in 1950. This support system encompassed the Government Housing Loan Corporation Law, enacted in May 1950, as well as the related Government Housing Loan Corporation. Article 1 of this law described the purpose of this system as follows:

> The Government Housing Loan Corporation provides funds necessary for the adequate construction and purchase of houses, in order for the public to enjoy a healthy and cultural life (including the acquisition of land or the leasing of land for housing, as well as the preparation of the housing site).
>
> The Corporation itself will invest funds, when banks and other general financial institutions are unable to provide financing. In addition, the Corporation will support investments by banks and other general financial institutions by substituting loan claims, as well as by providing collateral to guarantee bonds.

The Government Housing Loan Corporation was abolished on March 31, 2007. Its operations were handed over to the Incorporated Administrative Agency Japan Housing Finance Agency (JHF) on April 1, 2007. However, from the 1950s even until today, financial support from these national agencies has been highly effective in promoting private-sector housing construction in Japan. From the viewpoint of construction technology, public housing functioned as an opportunity for the government to develop and experiment with new building technologies. Plus, the sheer size of orders meant that the government could guide the development of private technologies. Further, the Government Housing Loan Corporation had the ability to set its own building specifications, beyond the minimum standards outlined by the Building Standard Law. Thus, the agency could exert control to raise the quality of housing as desired by the government.

For example, precast concrete construction was widely used in public housing projects from the 1960s to the 1970s. This promoted private investment in panel manufacturing factories and other related manufacturers. At the same time, the Government Housing Loan Corporation also played a role in promoting prefabricated houses, by making a separate "Factory-Produced Housing Approval System" and providing preferential financing to prefabricated houses.

## From vulnerable wooden cities to fireproof cities

Given the many massive fires that have occurred since the Edo period (1603–1868), it is obvious that Japanese cities crowded with wooden buildings are extremely vulnerable in terms of disaster prevention, especially fire protection. However, technical developments in the field of housing aimed at addressing fire protection only started in earnest in the 1930s, after the experience of the Great Kanto Earthquake of 1923 and as the sense of war grew stronger.

One standard example is the reinforced concrete structure "PRECON" (named in 1949 as an abbreviation of "Precast Reinforced Concrete Truss Construction"). The structure was developed by Professor Heigaku Tanabe[8] and others, starting from the latter half of the 1930s. (See Figure 1.1.)

As Professor Tanabe later wrote in his book *Nonflammable City*, he experienced a fire in Germany, while studying in Berlin after graduating from the Imperial University of Tokyo. He saw that the fire burned only one unit in a multi-story housing development and was quickly extinguished. From that experience, he came to strongly believe that no matter the cost, such fireproof construction must be implemented in Japan.[9] In 1939, Professor Tanabe commissioned the Air Defense Research Institute of the Ministry of the Interior to study reinforced concrete construction methods. Basic research was completed in 1944.[10]

We can only imagine Professor Tanabe's bitter regret when he saw the vast stretches of land burned by American military bombing during World War II. Shortly before he passed away, Professor Tanabe wrote an article titled "Appeal to all young architects", published in the Architectural Institute of Japan's *Journal of Architecture and Building Science* (JABS). An excerpt from the article published in the August 1953 issue of JABS reads as follows:

> Thirty years have passed since I graduated, but neither the dream of reconstructing Tokyo and Yokohama after the 1923 Kanto Earthquake nor the dream of improving fire resistance has been realized. We plunged recklessly into the Pacific War with our wooden cities; and 120 of them, large and small alike, including the capital Tokyo were turned to ashes. I was infuriated to see the

*Figure 1.1* PRECON in around 1950

American news movie *The Last of the Men without Science,* where they showed the world the devastation of war-damaged Japanese cities. I vowed to 'Construct a Non-Flammable City'! After the war, I desperately traveled around the country north to south, and east to west giving lectures with this title on determining fire protection with the goal to influence authorities. Sadly, there is a limit to the physical capacity of human beings. Just before completing the lecture tour of one hundred cities, I became totally exhausted and collapsed.

The lecture tour referred to above was implemented under the sponsorship of an insurance company. The insurance company had been instructed to do so by the US occupying forces, who were vexed by the complete lack of progress with efforts to fireproof Japanese cities (according to verbal evidence from Professor Kazuo Goto at the Tokyo Institute of Technology, who was a disciple of Professor Tanabe). In 1947, the company Taihei Industry was also established with the support of an insurance company, in order to construct PRECON which had been designed during wartime. At last, the dream of Professor Tanabe could finally come true.

The already completed PRECON was designed to create a nonflammable building which could be built by local carpenters. Towards this goal, Japanese wooden building materials were replaced with reinforced concrete, so that carpenters who had experience working on wooden houses could construct the buildings more easily. However, from the beginning, there were issues meeting the building code, so things did not go smoothly. The new company Taihei Industry fell into financial difficulties, and quickly withdrew its involvement. However, one company was interested in PRECON, namely the Toyota Motor Corporation.

The book *The origin of my industrialization* (Nippon Building Material Newspaper, 1997) was written by Mr. Mitsufusa Sawada, who was active throughout Japan after the war and at the forefront of the housing administration. In his book, he describes the situation at Toyota at that time as follows:

> The day before the end of the war, Kiichiro Toyoda, then president of Toyota, was shocked to see a single bomb damage three factory buildings. He commanded, "From now on, nonflammable buildings are essential. Start research on concrete assembled buildings immediately."

In May 1947, Kiichiro Toyoda met with Professor Tanabe, thanks to being introduced by the building director of Aichi Prefecture. Professor Tanabe honestly advised Toyoda, "You should not proceed with development." He said this based on the many difficulties he had experienced. Kiichiro Toyoda responded, "That is exactly why Toyota will do it" (based on verbal evidence from the late Professor Kazuo Goto). After a few days, a memo was handed to the engineering department of Toyota, reading, "Make a Tanabe-style house immediately."

Over the following three years, Toyota repeatedly conducted trial manufacturing research with the aim of commercialization. In 1950, a new company "Yutaka Pre Con" (later named Toyota Concrete Co., Ltd.; currently known as Toyota T & S Construction Co., Ltd.) was founded to manufacture and sell PRECON. However, Tanabe's PRECON did not last long. It had two major shortcomings. First, given the large number of joints, fastening the bolts was labor consuming. Second, cracks in the exterior walls appeared immediately after the plastering finish was completed, due to the presence of multiple seams. In order to overcome this problem, the width of the wall panel was increased to half the height of the floor, compared to the 20 cm width wall panels of the Tanabe-style houses. Ultimately in 1957, the wall panel had a pillar installed and its size was increased to be equal to the height of the story. The resulting building system was vastly different from the original idea of PRECON, which was to replace wooden building components with reinforced concrete.

## Delivery of RC (reinforced concrete) flats in earnest in the 1960s

The fireproofing of cities and houses was not only a project for which Professor Tanabe advocated, but was a national task in post-war Japan. The government was not directly involved in the construction and supply of detached single family houses but instead focused on collective housing, especially RC (Reinforced Concrete) flats.

Efforts by the Japanese government and public authorities to supply mass housing, through building a large number of RC flats in post-war Japan, started slightly later than similar efforts in Western developed countries in Europe and North America. In 1950, the Japanese government founded the Public Housing Law and the Government Housing Loan Corporation Law, which together formed the pillars of post-war housing policy. In addition, the Japan Housing Corporation (JHC), established in 1955, played a central role in urban mass housing developments. Apartment buildings built by the JHC mainly targeted salaried workers living in urban areas. The buildings essentially functioned as company housing for "Japan, Inc," a nickname for the corporate world in Japan that developed during the 1960s boom in close relationship with the Japanese government. The slogan of "Japan, Inc" at the time was "Catch up and overtake the West." Kozoji New Town,[11] Senri New Town,[12] and Tama New Town[13] are examples of such development projects, constructed in previously undeveloped areas.

The JHC was established with the mission to construct and provide RC flats to urban workers, and with the requirement to design more than 20,000 units in the first year. Given the organization's limited size, it attempted to achieve this requirement by applying the standard design method. This method had also been utilized by the developed countries involved in the mass housing movement such as the Soviet Union. Initially, the application of standard design allowed for flexibility. Each branch office could take into account their own specific situation and modify the standard design, which was designed by the central headquarters. In 1963, the first national unified standard design "Type 63" was created. After that, modification by each branch office was essentially prohibited until 1972.

Similar to mass housing in Europe, the JHC was also active in the adoption of so-called industrialized (factory-produced elements) construction.

The trial production of large panel construction systems for low-rise housing started shortly after its establishment. In 1961, the company succeeded in developing a practical application of large-sized panel construction systems to mid-rise housing. In 1965, the JHC itself constructed a large panel mobile plant (daily production, 2 units) in the Sakusabe Housing Estate.[14] There was a plan to place bulk orders with a view towards producing standard design housing. In addition, private capital investments were encouraged. In 1970, the government established SPH (Standard of Public Housing), a standard design for large-sized panel construction, including public housing, and bulk order plans by the JHC were put into action. However, this type of mass housing only succeeded for a few years. In 1973, the total number of houses exceeded the total number of households across all forty-seven prefectures. Plus, the oil crisis struck. Public housing groups were forced to rethink their approach, a change reflected in the slogan "from quantity to quality." In the latter half of the 1970s, orders for SPH standard design housing dwindled. Private pre-cast concrete factories, which had received investments to capitalize on the SPH standard design housing projects, faced a financial crisis.

Incidentally, the mass housing period in Japan differed from such efforts in European countries. While the supply of public housing increased as previously discussed, the mass construction of privately-owned and individually-built detached housing, similar to the United States, also increased. There are several reasons for this parallel increase in detached housing. First, Japan had long relied on wood construction and did not have a culture of multifamily housing like Europe. Second, Japan was strongly influenced by housing policy and lifestyle culture from America, whose forces controlled Japan for a long period after the war. A final factor was a major change in land policy, namely the release of farmland for new urbanizing development.

The post-war construction of detached houses in Japan was different from the original methods used in the United States. In Japan, the main system of housing developed with individuals acquiring their own land and constructing ordered houses. In contrast, in the United States, speculative builders supplied ready for sale houses in large-scale residential developments. The process of industrialization in this field will be described in detail in the following sections.

## Finding a new market for industries that emerged during the war – examples from the steel industry

Wooden structures long controlled a large share of the Japanese market, in terms of the amount of floor space of new construction. However, steel structures came to dominate the market during the "Bubble Economy"[15] in the late 1980s. In the entire world, Japan is the only country where the market share of steel structures exceeds RC structures and wooden structures to dominate new construction starts. Japan can be considered unique in terms of the importance of steel structures to the country.

In 1964, the year of the Tokyo Olympic Games, the building height limit of 31 meters, previously set by the Building Standard Law, was eliminated.[16] Shortly afterwards, the first 37-story skyscraper "Kasumigaseki Building"[17] was built. This skyscraper, along with the many skyscraper office buildings that followed, may be what people imagine when they think about steel structures in Japan. Others may imagine the mid-rise buildings built with ALC wall panels attached to square steel pipe columns and wide flanged steel beams, which are frequently found around cities. However, these two systems of construction alone could not have boosted steel construction to controlling the top market share in the building market. Another type of steel construction also continued to dominate the housing market, in terms of the amount of floor space of new construction. This third type of construction is low-rise steel-frame prefabricated housing, primarily consisting of detached single family houses and rental apartments.

In Japan, the construction of steel-frame prefabricated housing began in 1955, when the domestic production of light-gauge cold-formed steel started. Before World War II, iron was primarily produced as a material for use in machinery and by the military. As a result, people at the time said "Iron is the blood of the Japanese nation." In 1941, nearly 40% of iron was used for machinery and by the military, and only 3% for construction. During the war, demand from the military for iron increased. Within the period of production starting from the Meiji Era, the production of crude steel in Japan peaked in 1943. After the war, production stagnated, mostly due to the occupation by the Allied Forces. Then, in 1950, unrest in Korea broke out. This drove a renewed demand for the production of iron, which increased to recover in 1953 to pre-war levels. However, the Korean War ended in a truce, forcing the Japanese steel industry to find a new market equal to its production capacity. The building construction market, projected to show great growth, attracted attention as one such promising market.

In particular, light-gauge steel and wide-flanged steel beams were viewed as suitable materials for developing the building construction market during the mid-1950s to the late 1960s. Light-gauge steel was used for non-structural components in any type of buildings as well as structural components in low-rise buildings. Wide-flanged steel beams were primarily used for the structural components of high-rise buildings. In 1955, Nakanoshima, a steelmaking company affiliated with Yawata Iron & Steel Co., Ltd.[18], started the first domestic production of light-gauge cold-formed steel in Japan. In contrast, in the United States, light-gauge cold-formed steel had been used commercially since the 1940s.

Once the domestic production of light-gauge cold-formed steel became possible, the steel industry immediately began to develop new applications for the material. The Kozai Club (which means "Steel Material Club" in Japanese) established the Light-Gauge Steel Construction Association. A wide variety of scholars, from prominent professors to young and upcoming researchers, from different fields of architecture such as structural engineering, architectural planning, and architectural design all gathered in the new association. Together, the members worked rapidly to develop design guidelines for the use of light-gauge steel in structural components in low-rise buildings such as houses and schools, determine building construction methods including the details of joints, and gather examples of previous design and construction prototypes.

After 1960, as the accomplishments of the Light-Gauge Steel Construction Association began to emerge, the housing market started to show signs of rapid growth. Many companies, previously not involved in the construction industry, were attracted to enter this new market. Companies from industries such as the steel industry, chemical industry, and household appliance manufacturing industry, aspired to produce industrialized houses, instead of wooden houses, which relied on traditional carpentry. Not surprisingly, these companies ended up focusing on the potential of light-gauge steel, which had only recently been made commercially viable. At the time, thanks to commercialization by the enormous steel industry, light-gauge steel became available as a structural material.

The specific details of light-gauge steel construction methods differ between steel-frame prefabricated housing suppliers and manufacturers. However, in general, channel steel or rectangular steel pipes are used as columns, and channel steel or light-gauge wide-flanged steel are used to make horizontal and truss components. The earlier precast concrete construction, which utilized a structural system of precast wall panels, had been difficult to market in Japan, a country long accustomed to timber post and beam construction. In contrast, steel construction methods were more similar to conventional building methods, in terms of the appearance and design of buildings. As a result, steel-frame prefabricated housing suppliers and manufacturers rapidly increased their sales volume, as well as expanded the degree of flexibility in home layouts, to rise to their current position in the market.

Many early steel-frame prefabricated houses built around 1960 had a sense of "newness," which seemed slightly strange to consumers accustomed to conventional wooden houses. For example, the joints between wall panels were often clearly visible. In addition, people were sometimes surprised to see aluminum as an exterior finishing material (see Figures 1.2–1.4). In addition, at that time, the factories of steel-frame prefabricated housing suppliers and manufacturers had not reached mass production capabilities. As a result, not many types of building components were being produced. Therefore, each company could provide only a limited number of layouts, in terms of the exterior dimensions of the home. Indeed, looking at catalogs from the time, some makers offered only one or two floor plans.

*Figure 1.2* Sekisui House Type A (Sekisui Chemical Co., Ltd.), which were sold starting in 1960. With impressive shiny aluminum exterior walls, brand new steel sash, and plastic eaves and buttress walls. Source: Sekisui House Co., Ltd.

However, by the late 1960s, the style of steel-frame prefabricated houses started to more closely resemble conventional wooden houses. The system of "ready-made" plans with only a few types to choose from was overhauled to create an "easy order" system, which could flexibly adapt to the requirements of specific inhabitants. The practical dreams envisioned by individual inhabitants for their own houses became emphasized over the ideal residences drawn by professionals such as architects and engineers. As a result, steel-frame prefabricated houses became accepted in the Japanese housing market and established in society as another type of housing in addition to conventional wooden houses.

In 1970, only ten years after companies began to enter this new market, some steel-frame prefabricated housing suppliers and manufacturers reached over 10,000 units sold per year. In the 1980s, after enduring the economic shocks of the Oil Crisis, the number of large-scale steel-framed prefabricated housing suppliers and manufacturers (i.e., those with more than 10,000 units sold per year) further increased. In addition, there were advances in the development of systems to create houses over three stories using heavier steel members. After 1970, housing construction systems

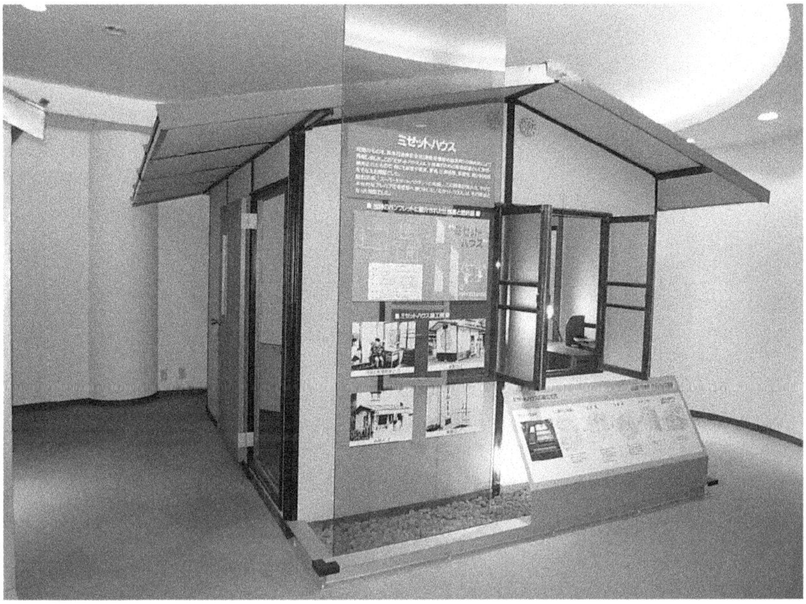


*Figure 1.3* One of the first prefabricated houses – "Micro House." (Originally called the "*Mizetto House*" in Japanese. "*Mizetto*" is a Japanese loanword from the English word "midget." The name was used to refer to the small size of the home.) (Daiwa House Industry Co., Ltd.) In 1959, it was sold as a study room for children in the garden. It is currently displayed in the research laboratory of Daiwa House

using room-sized panels and preconstructed modular units were developed in succession, enabling rooms to be manufactured in a factory. These systems were developed with the goal of increasing the degree of factory production in order to achieve the cost effectiveness required for industrialized housing (see Figure 1.5).

## The emergence of prefabricated housing suppliers and manufacturers

Prefabricated houses in Japan are unique. It is difficult to find similar products or a comparable system of business management in other countries. One unique aspect of the industry in Japan is that there are several housing suppliers and manufacturers in Japan producing over 10,000 homes a year. Moreover, most of these homes are "ordered houses" (i.e., the houses are designed and built according to the detailed specifications of each individual owner). This scale of production by individual companies and degree of customization is only found in Japan. Most of these housing

*Figure 1.4* One of the first prefabricated houses – The Matsushita Number 1 model (National Housing Building Material company; currently the Panasonic Homes Corporation). The house was reportedly developed under the sponsorship of Konosuke Matsushita in 1961. Source: Panasonic Homes Corporation

suppliers and manufacturers primarily produce prefabricated houses, which are assembled from components manufactured in the company's own factories. More than half of prefabricated houses made by these major players are steel structures, which use light-gauge steel for the main structure. International housing experts who visit Japan, thinking it is a country dominated by timber architecture, are often astonished by the prevalence of steel structures.

In our modern 20th century global society, where products and information can freely cross borders, how such a Japanese-style industry formed is interesting from the point of view of industry, culture, and technology. In fact, from 2011 to 2012, our team spent about two years interviewing engineers who were directly involved around 1960 with the development of early prefabricated houses. Sekisui House Type A (sold starting in 1960 by the former Sekisui Chemical Co., Ltd.) was the earliest prototype developed, among prefabricated houses that are still being produced

*Figure 1.5* Around 1970, methods utilizing a higher percentage of factory production were also actively under development. An example of the unit construction system, unit factory of Sekisui Heim M1. Source: Sekisui Chemical Co., Ltd.

today. Fortunately, we were able to interview Mr. Yukichi Fukui and Dr. Tokusaburo Ishimoto, who both worked on the development from the beginning.

Mr. Fukui graduated from the Department of Architecture at the Kyoto Institute of Technology.[19] In 1953, he joined the Sekisui Chemical Co., Ltd.,[20] a company which descended from the pre-war Japan Nitrogen Fertilizer Company.[21] When he started working there, he hoped to become an industrial designer, not an architect. Dr. Ishimoto graduated from the Department of Architecture at the University of Tokyo in 1957 and began working at a chemical manufacturing company, seeking to distance himself from the field of architecture. However, despite the contrary hopes of Mr. Fukui and Dr. Ishimoto, both were recruited to the "All Plastic House Team," established in 1959 by the unexpected command of the company president. Dr. Ishimoto was involved in the development of new houses from the beginning. Mr. Fukui later joined the new housing project team.

Afterwards, they were transferred to the newly established Sekisui House Co., Ltd.,[22] where they dedicated the rest of their working lives to the prefabricated housing industry.

I will not go into detail about the background of the "All Plastic House Team," since it is extensively detailed in the thirty-year history as well as the fifty-year history of Sekisui House. Ltd. published on the company's website. However, the team is an excellent example of how prefabricated houses developed at the time. First, it shows a previously separate industry making a new entry into the housing market. Other examples of similar housing projects are the National Home Project (at present, Panasonic Homes) started by the Matsushita Group,[23] the Hebel House of the Asahi Kasei Corporation,[24] which followed slightly later, and the Toyota Housing Corporation.[25] Second, the team was an attempt to expand the supply channel of new industrial materials into the growing housing market. Other examples include the domestic production of light-gauge steel by major steel production companies, such as Yawata Iron and Steel, and the development of steel-frame prefabricated houses.

Development of the design was inspired by the earlier "All Plastic House," created by the Monsanto Company in the United States in 1956.[26] At an early stage, members of the development team, including Dr. Ishimoto, abandoned the use of plastic for structural components, and instead chose to use light-gauge steel. Further, many industrialized materials, such as chemical products and aluminum, were used for components in order to create a panel-type house, which could be assembled even by non-professionals. At the time, no one imagined the scale to which the industry would eventually grow. As a result, little consideration was given to creating variation in the floor plans. The development team strived to create a construction method with a three-hinged arch making a simple tunnel-like space, similar to the blue and green "Quanset Huts",[27] which were built by US military forces and existed in Kobe city where Dr. Ishimoto lived. In Dr. Ishimoto's business notebook at the time, there is a review of earlier research on calculating the structure, evaluating materials, and arranging rooms, as well as previous planning module research. In his notebook, we can see the experiments of newly graduated engineers at the time.

In the spring 1960, several experimental constructions had been attempted. However, most team members believed the design was still in the process of development. Then suddenly, the new system was put on sale, by an ultimatum issued by President Ueno. This was the birth of the Sekisui House Type A. Approximately 100 Type A houses were constructed that year. However, those early houses were far from modern prefabricated houses. One major technical problem of Type A was that the roof would deform. As a result, Mr. Fukui and Dr. Ishimoto started developing the next generation construction system immediately after the release of Sekisui House Type A. The following year, a completely new construction system using roof trusses was developed and given the name System B. The basic construction system of Sekisui House is still this System B. Without question, it is the most widely utilized prefabricated construction system for housing around the world.

The Matsushita Number 1 model was developed immediately afterwards in 1961. Mr. Akio Kobayashi, who developed Pana Home, recalls spying from the neighboring rice paddies on the prototype building constructed in the Sekisui Chemical factory premises in Nara. The Sekisui House Type A also likely inspired the Daiwa House Industry Co., Ltd.[28] At the time, Daiwa House had already commercialized the prefabricated study room "Micro House." Then in 1962, shortly after the release of the Sekisui House Type A, Daiwa House released Daiwa House Type A. In the case of both the Matsushita Number 1 model and Daiwa House Type A, development was concentrated into a short period of time and conducted by a small team of young in-house architects and engineers. Riding the crest of high economic growth in the late 1960s, the new technology which developed ultimately exerted a significant influence on the Japanese housing market.

## The spread of "ukeoi" (in english, "turn-key") packages by local builders, as well as prefabricated housing suppliers and manufacturers

Japanese houses, especially detached single-family homes, produced by local builders, as well as housing suppliers and manufacturers, are generally built on a "ukeoi" (or "turn-key") contract. In other words, the contract encompasses everything from design to construction to produce a move-in-ready house. Combining design and construction is a traditional approach in Japanese construction. The original roots of the "ukeoi" contract method can be traced back to the 17th century.[29] However, the major transition in building production to the "ukeoi" contract system did not occur until the Meiji era (1868–present). Several sources provide evidence for this later transition.

For example, Gennosuke Yokoyama wrote about the "ukeoi" contract system in his book *The Underworld of Japan*, published in 1899.[30] He described the spread of the system as a shift in the construction industry at the time, writing,

> Although the contract system had been limited to the range of capital, recently payment to construction laborers is also based on contract. Now the master carpenter typically decides the number and payment of workers based on the floor area of the construction project. Each worker then receives payment according to his labor. As a result, the relationship between the master carpenter and his craftsmen has become provisional and based only on money. It is totally different from the intimate apprenticeship of the old days.

Yonekichi Takeda, born in 1889 to a master carpenter in Kanda (a downtown district of Tokyo), reflected on his career, writing,

> While some craftsmen were indifferent to riches and fame, other craftsmen were very attuned to changes happening in society. By acquiring new social skills, such as amassing wealth and networking, they transformed and reimagined themselves into a new occupation, namely "contractor".[31]

These quotes all refer to the building of non-wooden buildings. At least for non-wooden building, the "ukeoi" contract system appears to have become widespread by the turn of the century. Wooden houses took a different path to the contract system. Before the war, wooden houses were typically produced using the direct management system, where the owner provided and managed building materials, such as timber, as well as oversaw worker payments. This system was replaced by the "ukeoi" contract system, which packaged the complete housing construction from start to finish. When did this change occur?

Let's consider an excerpt from *Memories of Craftsmen, Part 2*,[32] written by a master carpenter born in 1889. His text shows that after he established himself as an independent carpenter around 1910 to 1920, he was actually doing "*ukeoi*" contract work with absolutely no capital fund. At the time, payments by the owner were typically divided into three parts: (1) before construction, (2) during construction, and (3) at completion. Shingo Inaba, a literary carpenter enthusiast and author of several books, writes about his earlier "ukeoi" contract work on a one-story building in the 1930s in his book *Kanna-kuzu* (*Wood Shavings*).[33] However, his book also makes clear that the establishment and spread of local builders working mainly on the "ukeoi" contract system did not happen until the postwar reconstruction period. He writes,

> We could earn money from 'ukeoi' contract construction work on military barracks. But from a physical as well as mental health point of view, we were happier and better off, when we worked on intermediate-level housing paid solely based on labor ... Large billboards were seen in town, advertising "Building, Design, and Construction by XX Construction, as if to say those who did not advertise in this way were either foolish or dull."
>
> (Descriptions about societal conditions in the autumn 1947 written by Shingo Inaba in *Kanna-kuzu*)

Among conventional wooden housing contractors established before 1950, over 30% of the 209 surveyed contractors converted to a corporation during 1945–1960, according to a national questionnaire survey of conventional wooden housing contractors conducted by the Sakamoto/Matsumura

Laboratory at the University of Tokyo in 1999.[34] Assuming that converting to a corporation signifies the change from craftsmen carpenters to local builders and contractors, the results clearly show that the post-war reconstruction era was a major turning point in the construction industry.

In fact, the financing system had a significant influence on the spread of the "ukeoi" contract system in the production of detached single-family housing in post-war Japan. The "ukeoi" contract system was a prerequisite of financing by the Housing Loan Corporation, which started in 1950. In other words, the Japanese government financing institution required centralizing responsibility by packaging the complete process of housing construction.

Regardless of government requirements, houses were mainly produced on demand. As a result, it was important from the point of housing production that the relationship between the customer and manufacturer changed from the direct managed system to the "ukeoi" contract system. As a result, the role of the client in housing construction changed. At the same time, the nature of the housing companies shifted dramatically from craftsman to contractor.

In Japan, prefabricated housing suppliers and manufacturers emerged in the late 1950s. It is important to note that at that time, the construction of detached single-family houses was already based primarily on the "ukeoi" contract system.

As discussed previously, many pioneers within the prefabricated housing supplier and manufacturer industry were originally from fields other than housing construction. At the time, houses could not be constructed by simply assembling factory-produced building components. Only structural frame components and exterior wall parts were made in factories. As a result, it was necessary to hire a company to actually construct the houses on-site. Local builders had established their services as construction contractors capable of procuring materials and labor, as well as managing labor. No doubt, the existence of established local contractors significantly impacted the rise of prefabricated houses.

Collaborating with existing companies made it possible to deliver houses as a single package to clients. However, this method could not provide sufficient volume to make factory production by prefabricated suppliers and manufacturers profitable. Instead, prefabricated housing suppliers and manufacturers focused on commercialization, appealing to customers by promoting the value of packaged houses. The marketing approach of directly targeting end users was a major difference in strategy from the earlier focus on building materials and components.

"Micro House" (1959, Daiwa House Industry Co., Ltd), one of the earliest prefabricated houses, was a preassembled study room with a structure built from light-gauge steel. This early prefabricated house already shows the effects of commercialization and resulting differences from the previous style of housing. First, the design of the home was based on market research. Second, it had a catchy name. Third, it was advertised through mass media. Fourth, sales were promoted by displaying the actual product. Pricing was also transparent and easy to understand. Later, as products became full-sized houses, choices increased, and the dependence on on-site construction also increased. Further, the display of actual houses declined. Prices also became less transparent. Instead, the exhibition of model homes and sales by specialized staff advanced rapidly. Until today, the method to commercialize homes has not changed significantly. During the 1980s, commercialization further spread to conventional wooden house construction companies and had a significant influence on the production of detached single-family houses.

There are several reasons why sales have steadily improved in the prefabricated house industry. First, during the 1960s, the housing market experienced a period of expansion. In addition, around the country, similar legal approaches were taken to housing construction. Plus, financing systems by the Housing Loan Corporation had already been put into place. In addition, compared to large countries like the United States, demand for houses in Japan was densely concentrated to a small geographic area. Prefabricated housing suppliers and manufacturers were able to grow to their current scale of producing tens of thousands of houses every year, by constantly experimenting with ways to increase choices and offer greater design freedom in order to meet the demands of individual clients. One critical key to success was the approach of selling "packaged" houses.

Unlike mass-production efforts led by the Japanese government, systematic production based on standard designs was not easy to achieve for built-on-demand housing projects by private companies. However, if companies did not standardize but instead attempted to meet all the demands of specific clients, factory production could never become efficient. Overcoming this dilemma has been a constant challenge for prefabricated housing companies.

## Rapid growth of the building construction market up to 1973

Japanese housing construction statistics announced every month by the Ministry of Land, Infrastructure, and Transport offer a wide variety of classification groupings and superior frequency of publication. From these data, we can easily grasp changes in the quantity, as well as the type, of housing production. However, no definitive data exist showing who is responsible for what kind of housing production. In order to understand this point, we need to effectively use classifications that already exist in the published housing construction statistics and combine them with figures released by relevant industry associations.

A diagram created in 1983 by Mr. Mitsufusa Sawada (then Chair of Japan Building Center[35]) provides an excellent example of this statistical approach. The graphs drawn from data from 1963 and 1973 were created using the diagramming method devised by Mr. Sawada. The diagram allows the structure of housing production to be grasped clearly and immediately. The following procedure dictates how rectangles are combined to produce the figure.

1) The size of the outermost rectangle represents the total number of construction starts per year.
   The numbers in parentheses immediately following the percentage (%) mark indicate the number in each classification. The total number of housing starts is shown in parentheses on the left line.
2) The outer rectangle is divided into two sections: top and bottom. The area of each section represents the ratio of the structure type, either wooden or non-wooden. (For example, in 1973, 58.8% of structures built were wooden, and 41.2% were non-wooden.)
3) Each of the two rectangles are again divided into two sections: left and right. The area of each section represents the proportion of the type of construction, either conventional or prefabricated construction. (For example, in 1973, 92.7% of structures were conventionally built and 7.3% were built using prefabricated construction.) Prefabricated housing did not exist before 1963.
4) Each of the four rectangles is finally divided again into two sections: top and bottom. The area of each section represents the proportion of the type of housing: detached single-family housing or multi-family housing.

By overlaying the names of housing suppliers and manufacturers corresponding to the type of construction represented by each rectangle, we can show the relationship between the various organizations involved in housing production. Of course, the actual situation is far more complicated and multi-layered, given that there are specialized construction workers and vendors who subcontract with prefabricated housing suppliers and manufacturers to create specific components. Therefore, this "weather chart of house production" merely provides one aspect of the total situation. Despite its limitations, I will use this approach to compare housing production in 1963 and 1973. (See Figure 1.6.)

1963 was one year before the Tokyo Olympic Games. The small size of the overall rectangle clearly shows that the number of new housing construction starts was less than 690,000 units. Most of these were wooden houses constructed by carpenters and local construction companies. The rest were non-wooden multi-family housing projects (what we would now call "apartment buildings" or "condominiums"), which had just started to be constructed for public housing. In addition, prefabricated housing construction methods had begun to be utilized for both detached single-family houses and multi-family houses. But still almost 100% of the houses built in Japan were constructed using "conventional methods."

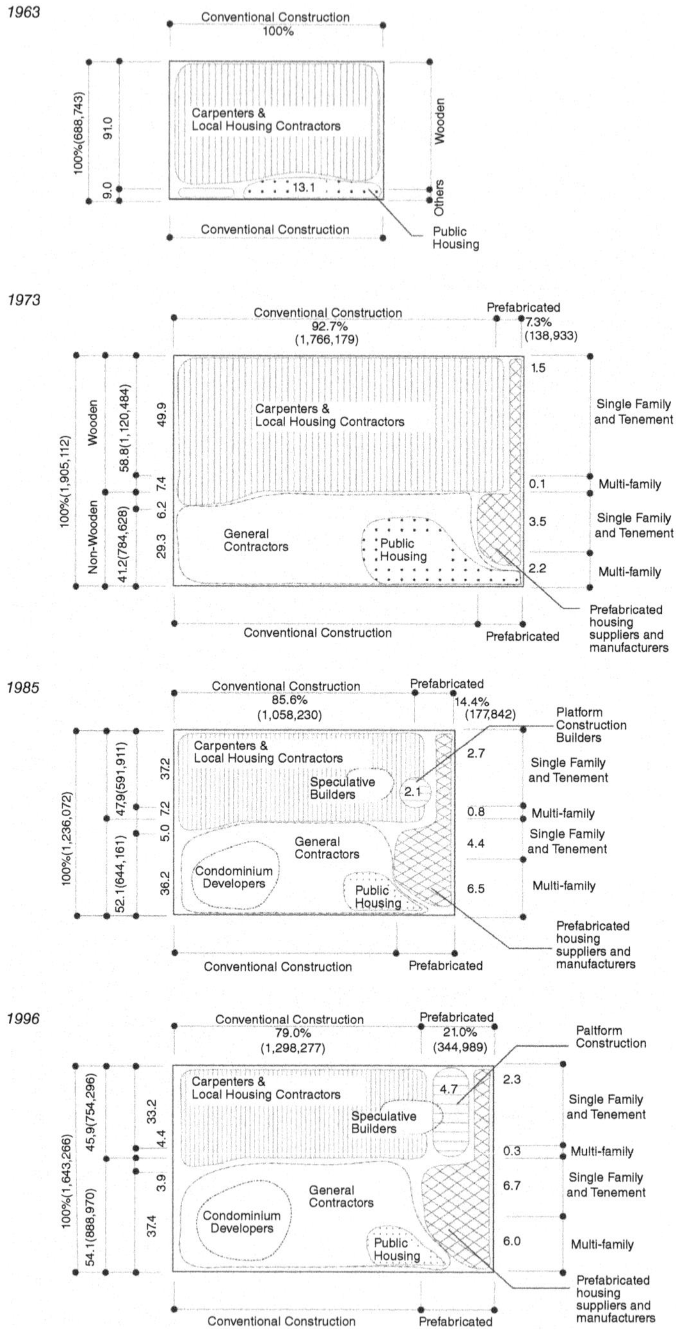


*Figure 1.6* Diagram showing the change in the size and types of construction method in the new house-building market ("Weather chart of house production")

In 1973, only ten years later, the number of new housing starts had almost tripled to 1.9 million units. As the proportion of non-wooden multi-family housing projects increased rapidly, housing construction by general contractors, who played a major role in non-wooden buildings, also increased. The percentage of wooden houses supplied by traditional carpenters and local housing contractors decreased. Although the relative ratio decreased, the absolute number of units nearly doubled in ten years. Based on the increase in the number of carpenters and local housing contractors, we can see evidence for improvements in the productivity of wooden houses, as well as applications of new building materials and components. In addition, prefabricated housing suppliers and manufacturers, who had barely existed ten years before, came to play an important role in housing construction.

In particular, as discussed previously, many companies who had not previously been involved in the housing industry began producing and selling prefabricated houses. During the late 1960s, these companies increased sales by targeting the new population of urban inhabitants who had arrived to newly developed urban areas which were not already controlled by established networks of businesses. Housing shortages continued into the late 1960s. Housing construction continued to increase every year.

Against this historical backdrop, a new way of thinking about the "housing industry" emerged, namely housing construction began to be seen as a new field of production and consumption. As an example, consider "Housing industry – a new leading role in economic growth," an article written by Genkou Uchida[36] and published in March 1968 in the widely-read monthly magazine "Chuo-Koron." First, the article points out that judging from previous eras, the Japanese economy grows steadily when there is a clear industry leader. Further, the leader appears to change every five to six years. At the time, the automobile industry was leading, but he predicted that the industry would stagnate after 1970. The article concludes that by harnessing new technology, the housing industry would rise to be the next leader driving economic growth. Specifically, he proposed creating man-made land by inserting factory-produced housing units into shelves created within a high-rise framework.

The article provides the following reasons for focusing on the housing industry: (1) the scale and reach of the market, (2) the stability of its growth rate, and (3) the greater impact on other industries. In fact, in 1967, housing investment was 3 trillion yen (equal to 7.2% of GNP in Japan). That number was expected to exceed 100 trillion yen in twenty years from 1966 to 1985. Compared to the automobile industry and home electronics industry, the housing industry had a far greater impact on other industries. According to the 1960 input–output table, 100 billion yen invested in the housing industry resulted in 278 billion yen in production by other industries.

As this view of the housing industry became widespread, the industry began to attract attention as the future leading consumer goods industry to replace the automobile and home electronics industries. By 1970, various industries, including large companies of the former chaebol (*zaibatsu*) group, continued to advance their housing-related business enterprises.

Various government strategies further guided and, at times, promoted this trend. The strategies were announced rapidly one after another, for example, the "Basic Plan for Industrialization of Housing Construction" (1966), "A Long-Term Plan for Industrializing Housing Production – Vision for the Housing Industry" (1969), "Guidelines for Promoting the Housing Industry" (1970), by the Ministry of Construction, "Promoting Standardization in the Housing Industry" (1968), and the "Current and Future Prospects of the Housing Industry" (1969), by the Ministry of International Trade and Industry.

The first of these many strategies was the "Basic Plan for Industrialization of the Housing Construction" announced by the Housing Bureau of the Ministry of Construction in December 1966. The plan underscores the necessity to promote the industrialization of all kinds of houses, not only prefabricated houses, citing: (1) the enormous amount of housing that needed to be constructed and (2) the need to respond to the constant increase in construction cost, due to inherent factors of the construction industry. Actual methodologies are proposed by setting three categories: "Factory-Produced Housing," "Semi-Industrialized Housing," and "Housing with Industrialized Components Applied." "Factory-Produced Housing" referred to prefabricated housing and to mid-rise multi-story housing built by the Japan Housing Corporation using precast concrete construction. "Semi-Industrialized Housing" encompassed housing where a section of the structure had been reorganized to make it more standardized, or where some part had been replaced with factory-produced components. "Housing with Industrialized Components Applied" referred to attempts to utilize new construction materials.

As this "Basic Plan for Industrialization of the Housing Construction" clearly shows, the concept and methodology of industrialization was critical to the image of the housing industry at the time. The plan set the goal of reaching 15% "Factory-Produced Housing" of total construction within four years by 1970. However, after four years the percentage had only reached 7.6%, approximately half of the original goal. At the same time, the Ministry of Construction had formulated the "Five-Year Housing Construction Plan, Phase 2," which set the goal of constructing 9.5 million houses in five years by 1975. The industrialization of housing production was pressed forward by such efforts.

Against this backdrop, the Japanese government launched a national competition called the "Pilot House Building Technology Proposal Competition,"[37] in 1970. The competition aimed to promote the development of highly industrialized building construction on a national scale. The government project was modeled after "Operation Breakthrough" (1969–1970)[38] launched by the United States government around the same time.

"Operation Breakthrough" began during the late 1960s, when the housing industry stagnated as growth in the American economy declined. The HUD (Department of Housing and Urban Development) sought to find a fundamental solution to the housing problem by openly inviting new proposals from private companies on how to best industrialize housing production. In 1970, proposals from twenty-two companies were selected as "outstanding proposals" out of the 561 proposals received. Model houses were constructed in ten states. The fact that Mr. Romney successfully served as President of American Motors, as well as skillfully led the project as Secretary of HUD, strikes me as symbolic of the American spirit.

In the case of the Japanese "Pilot House Building Technology Proposal Competition," 145 proposals were submitted by 112 companies. Out of these proposals, seventeen projects from sixteen companies were selected as "outstanding proposals." Then, trial construction commenced, creating both detached single-family houses and multi-family houses. Some of the proposed designs were actually produced and sold with remarkable success. Other designs in the competition served as inspirational "seeds," influencing how industrialized housing later evolved. Many construction methods used in the selected designs for detached single-family homes were widely adopted in industrialized home designs that followed. The project primarily focused on achieving a high comfort of living, inventing quality control technologies for factory production, and improving transportation and on-site construction. These factors were also major concerns in the development of industrialized housing in the decades that followed.

However, even as the housing industry sought to advance industrialization, new industrialized technology did not form the foundation of the housing industry. Instead, the housing industry continued to rely on the skill of carpenters, who had a long history and tradition in Japan.

## The continued importance of carpenters in design and building

In order to modernize Japan as a country, Westernization was essential. Similarly, in the field of architecture, we proactively learned, imitated, and absorbed ideas and technology from pre-modern to modern Europe and the United States. However, unique to Japan was the dominance of wooden architecture, supported by a network of craftsmen around the country.

For example, architectural historian Professor Yasutada Watanabe[39] used historical data to highlight that modernization in Japan was unique because it was supported by traditional carpenters and craftsmen (*The Road to Industrialization*, Fuji Sash, 1962). This occurred just as Japan entered the high economic growth era, and belatedly began to pursue mass production in building construction.

According to Professor Watanabe's article, the original term "carpenter" (*daiku* in Japanese) was once used in ancient times to indicate the top person in the hierarchy of construction engineers in the government bureaucracy. For example, the "Engi Law",[40] compiled in the middle of the Heian period (or the 10th century), provides the following detailed rules for enforcing the law in ancient Japan. Namely,

> the Department of Construction, which was in charge of all the construction work of the court, consists of one 'carpenter' (*daiku*) who is solely responsible for supervising and who is supported by an assistant (*shoku*). Under these two, there are 13 chiefs of engineers (*chojoko*) each specializing in areas, such as woodwork, earthen work, clay tile roofing, pottery, thatching, and lime work, plus several tens of professional engineers (*banjoko*). Under their supervision, there were about 300 workers.

In other words, at the time this law was written, there was only one "carpenter" (*daiku*) in the entire bureaucratic organization of the Japanese Department of Construction.

By the end of the Heian period (or 12th century), large national construction projects began to be supported financially by the leaders of local government groups and aristocrats. As a result, former engineers from the Department of Construction began working as employed engineers (*yatoiko* in Japanese) for aristocrats. However, construction by such high-class engineers was limited to projects for a select few in the upper class.

Watanabe points out that the situation only changed dramatically after the Genna period (around 1620). Until then, carpenters and their supporting craftsmen associations were exclusively employed for construction by the ruling class. However, in the 1620s, the construction of large-scale castles with surrounding towns ended. With the sudden decrease in demand for construction, carpenters expanded their work to constructing urban townhouses and detached houses for relatively wealthy farmers. During this period, the use of advanced wooden construction technology expanded beyond only being used for special national projects. Eventually in the pre-modern era, the technology spread across the country to lower classes in the social hierarchy.

Building production in Japan after the Meiji era (1868–present) developed based on the system of carpenters and wood construction craftsmen associations, both of which had a long history in Japan. Architecture was modernized by expanding the area and societal position, where the society of craftsmen participated actively. Assuming a sufficient number of skilled craftsmen existed everywhere in Japan, it would be possible to deliver a comfortable living environment to many people even without applying mass production methods, such as factory production.

Let's consider the number of carpenters reported in the Japanese National Census. In the census from 1930, the number of carpenters was 456,943. Incidentally, this is the year when data on the number of carpenters began to be gathered. The population of Japan at that time was 64.5 million people. In other words, there was one carpenter for every 140 people in the population. In 2010, an era with much more construction work, there is only one carpenter for approximately every 322 people in the population. It appears that there were enough carpenters before the war to support the modernization of architecture.

Let's next consider the number of carpenters after the war. The 1950 census includes the classification "carpenter and apprentice." That year, the number of carpenters and apprentices equaled 497,896 people (one for every 167 people), 523,967 in 1955 (one for every 170 people), 614,890 in 1960 (one for every 151 people), 692,905 in 1965 (one for every 142 people), 852,745 in 1970 (one for every 122 people), 868,450 in 1975 (one for every 129 people), 936,703 people in 1980 (one for every 125 people). Until 1980, the number of carpenters increased steadily. These numbers represent the first phase of open architecture. Because the major theme of the first phase was to deliver a comfortable living environment to many people, and carpenters had been essential for that.

However, the number of carpenters started to decline after 1980. In 1985, there were 802,700 (one for every 151 people), 734,087 in 1990 (one for every 168 people), 761,822 in 1995 (one for every 165 people), 646,767 in 2000 (one for every 196 people), 539,868 in 2005 (one for everyone 237 people), and 397,400 in 2010 (one for approximately every 322 people).

In particular, the rapid decline in the 21st century is very extreme. I still see the role that craftsmen play in Japanese society. However, when I consider the many long years over which the Japanese craftsmen society formed, I cannot help feeling a sense of impending crisis, seeing this extreme decline in their numbers over such a short period of time. Carpenters' skill is essential for realizing open architecture for the people at any phase.

## Notes

1 Among nationwide newspapers, the most widely read newspaper specializing in economics in Japan.

2 An organization established as a special corporation of the Japanese government in May 1941 as a breakthrough solution to the housing shortage crisis. It was eliminated shortly afterwards in December 1946. However, during that short period, its activities included not only construction of houses but also housing management, brokerage, financial services, administrator training, technician training, and research. It developed activities nationwide as an executing agency of government housing policy. It was established for the first time in Japan to provide housing. At the time when the organization closed, eight branches – Tokyo, Osaka, Yokohama, Nagoya, Fukuoka, Sendai, Hiroshima, and Takamatsu – were established in Japan. Branches were established not only in Japan but also in Taiwan, Korea, and Kanto Province (Dalian), which were then colonies of Japan. (Yoshimitsu Shiozaki et al., *Jyutaku Eidan*

*ni Yoru Jyutakuchi Kaihatsu to Jyukankyo no Keisei (Housing Development by Housing Corporation and Built Environment)*, Memoirs by the Housing Research Foundation, No.36, pp.25–36, 2008).

3 1904–1981. He graduated in 1928 from the Department of Architecture at the Imperial University of Tokyo (currently known as The University of Tokyo). From 1936 to 1948, he did work related to housing construction as an officer in various government agencies including the Ministry of Health and Welfare, the Housing Association, and the War Damage Reconstruction Institute. From 1948 to 1952, he worked as a director of Kajima Corporation, a major construction company in Japan. In 1952, he established his own architectural design office and made a significant contribution to housing policy, as well as to the supply of public housing in Japan. (Reference: Ichiura Housing & Planning website).

4 MIT's "*Guide to the Records of the Albert Farwell Bemis Foundation, 1926–1954*" explains Albert Farwell Bemis's works relating to house-building: "Just before his death, Bemis completed the third volume of his in-depth study of the house, *The Evolving House*. These books described in detail his conception of the history, economics, and rationalization of shelter."

5 1905–1986. A representative architect who helped lead modern Japanese architecture, especially post-war architecture. He was a classmate of Ken Ichiura at the Department of Architecture at the Imperial University of Tokyo. Immediately after graduation from university in 1928, he worked for several years in the atelier of Le Corbusier.

6 1909–1991. After graduating from the Department of Architecture at the Imperial University of Kyoto, he worked as an in-house architect and building engineer at Kurashiki Rayon. In 1964, he established his own architectural design office and brought to realization many prominent buildings in his home town of Kurashiki.

7 The Department of Architecture at the Imperial University of Tokyo (now known as the University of Tokyo) dates back to the Engineering School (in Japanese, *kogakuryo*), which opened in 1873. Within the Ministry of Engineering established in 1870 by the Meiji Government, the school was founded as the first professional education institution for engineering with the aim of promoting the industrialization of Japan. The school had seven departments, including civil engineering, machinery, architecture, telegraphy, chemistry, metallurgy, and mining. Among the original seven, the Department of Architecture is the origin of the current Department of Architecture. In 1877, the Engineering School was dissolved and renamed the Imperial College of Engineering (in Japanese, *Kobu Daigakkou*). It was first managed by the Ministry of Industry and then, after 1885, by the Ministry of Education.

In 1877, the British architect Josiah Condor (1852–1920) was invited to the Department of Architecture to help establish a western-style professional education course of architecture and building. At the time, the department was the first and only architecture and building engineering school in Japan. In 1879, two years after Condor arrived to Japan, the first four graduates from the Department of Architecture – Kingo Tatsuno, Tokuma Katayama, Tatsuzo Sone, and Sichijiro Satachi – graduated. Since then, over 140 years ago, many graduates from the Department of Architecture, the University of Tokyo, have played leading roles as architects, structural engineers, construction managers, bureaucrats, professors, researchers, and businesspeople in the Japanese architectural world. (Reference: the Department of Architecture, the University of Tokyo website).

8 1898–1954. Graduated in 1922 from the Department of Architecture at the Imperial University of Tokyo. From 1929, he worked as a professor at the

Tokyo Institute of Technology. His most famous achievements include research and development activities on buildings and urban incombustibility.

9 Quote from the beginning of *Nonflammable City* written by Heigaku Tanabe (Kawaide Shobo, 1945).

10 According to an interview with Prof. Kazuo Goto (April 1988), who, starting from the 1940s, was involved as a research associate under Professor Heigaku Tanabe's supervision, with the development of PRECON.

11 The first new town development project of the Japan Housing Corporation (currently known as the Urban Renaissance Agency), located in the suburbs of Nagoya city. The decision to develop was made in 1960. The planned population at the time of development was 81,000. The total area is 702 hectares. The development opened to residents in 1968. (Reference: Kozoji New Town website.)

12 The first large-scale new town developed in Japan, completed by the Osaka Prefectural Corporate Bureau. The decision to develop was made by Osaka Prefecture in 1958. The development area was about 1160 hectares. The planned population at the time of development was 150,000 people. It opened to residents in 1962. In 2003, Senri Newtown was chosen by DOCOMOMO JAPAN as one of the 100 Selections of Modern-Movement Architecture in Japan.

13 The first large-scale new town in Tokyo metropolitan area developed by the Urban Renaissance Agency, Tokyo metropolitan government, and others. The basic plan of the development was decided in 1964. The development area was about 2884 hectares. The planned population at the time of development was 342,200 people.

14 A housing estate located in the suburbs of Chiba city. It served as the first step for the Japan Housing Corporation to implement the construction of middle-rise flats using the large precast concrete panel construction method. Eighteen buildings, including 496 housing units, were built from 1965 to 1966.

15 The rise in asset prices and the period of record economic growth that took place in Japan from the end of 1986 until the beginning of 1991; also called the "Japanese economic miracle."

16 Based on Urban Building Law enacted in April 1919, the building height limit was set to 100 *shaku* (about 30.3 meters) in six major cities in December 1920. After that, the limit was expanded to apply to 41 cities. In 1931, the limit of 100 *shaku* was increased slightly to 31 meters. In November 1950, the Building Standard Law replaced the Urban Building Law, but the height limit was carried over into the new law. Finally, in July 1963, the Volumetric District System was established. The height limit of 31 meters, which had been enforced up until then, was abolished.

17 The first building in Japan exceeding 100 meters in height with thirty-six floors above ground and three floors underground. It was completed in April 1968. In 2003, this building was selected as one of DOCOMOMO JAPAN 100 Modern-Movement Buildings in Japan.

18 The predecessor of Nippon Steel Sumikin. It was Japan's largest blast furnace maker from 1950 to 1970.

19 A national university established in Kyoto in 1949. With its origins in the Kyoto Sericulture Training Center, it opened in 1899, and the Kyoto High School of Art and Crafts established in 1902.

20 A major resin processing manufacturer in Japan. Currently, it is also a major housing maker. Established in 1947, following the demolition of post-war zaibatsu (Japanese industrial and financial business conglomerates). The company was renamed to its present name in 1948.

21 Established in 1908. It continued be a leading chemical manufacturer in Japan, until being dismantled after the war.
22 One of Japan's largest housing suppliers and manufacturers, it was established in 1960 from a department of the Sekisui Chemical Co., Ltd.
23 A corporation group centered on a worldwide electronics manufacturer. It began with Konosuke Matsushita manufacturing and selling light bulb sockets in 1917. Matsushita had been extremely interested in the housing business ever since the 1950s. In 1961, the Matsushita Electric Works entered the housing market.
24 A major Japanese chemical manufacturer. Currently it conducts business in areas such as fiber, housing, building materials, pharmaceuticals, and electronics. Like the Sekisui Chemical, it became an independent company due to the dismantling of the Japanese Nitrogen Group after the war.
25 In 1975, the Housing Department was established in Toyota Motor. In 2003, the Toyota Home Corporation, specializing in the housing business, was established as an independent company.
26 H. Ward Jandl wrote in his "*Yesterday's Houses of Tomorrow – Innovative American Homes 1850–1950*" (The Preservation Press National Trust for Historic Preservation, 1991):

"Designed as a collaborative effort between Monsanto's plastics division and the Massachusetts Institute of Technology, this distinctive cross-shaped, single-story house was erected at Disneyland in 1957."

"Without a doubt it was the most celebrated all-plastic house in America."

27 In Japan right after the end of the war, a number of simple semi-cylindrical-shaped prefabricated barracks were built by the US military who occupied Japan.
28 One of Japan's largest housing suppliers and manufacturers. Established in 1955 by Nobuo Ishibashi after he returned from Siberian detention. He started the business by manufacturing and selling huts using steel pipes and tin plates.
29 Kazuyoshi Endo highlighted the construction of Mino Nanguu Shrine in 1640 as an early example of the "ukeoi" contract method, by providing a contract letter for the Pagoda (S. Matsumura, Kazuyoshi Endo et al., *Kenchiku Seisan (Management and Organization of the Building Process)*, Ichigaya Shuppann-sha Publishing, 2004).
30 A book written by Gennosuke Yokoyama and published in 1899. It was based on his observations of living conditions for the underprivileged and the state of the craftsmen's society.
31 Yonekichi Takeda, *Shokunin – Kenchikuka no Kaisou (Craftsmen – Reflections of An Architect)*, Kosakusha Publishing, 1958.
32 Ryusuke Saito, *Shokunin Shu Mukashi Banash (Memories of Craftsmen, Part 2)*, Bungei Shunjyu Publishing, 1968.
33 Shingo Inaba, *Kanna Kuzu (Wood Shavings)*, Shufu no Tomo Sha Publishing, 1967.
34 Over 1200 wooden conventional housing contractors from across Japan responded to the questionnaire survey.
35 Established in August 1965 as a public institution to evaluate technology related to construction and to do technological development, research, dissemination of information, and international exchange.
36 1925–1996. Technical bureaucracy of the Ministry of International Trade and Industry (MITI) in Japan. While at MITI, he coined the expression "housing industry."
37 A national project conducted by the Ministry of Construction in 1970 to promote the development of highly industrialized building systems on a national

scale. It is said to have been inspired by "Operation Breakthrough" launched by HUD in the United States. 145 designs were proposed by 112 companies. Seventeen designs by sixteen companies were selected as "outstanding proposals." The designs then underwent trial construction.

38 A technology development project that was started in 1969 under the initiative of the US government HUD to develop and disseminate innovative housing production design systems through public and private cooperation. Many companies from various fields such as major manufacturers, general contractors, developers, home builders, and consultants participated in various proposals.

39 1922–2000. An architectural historian. He served as a professor at Waseda University.

40 The detailed rule of the law was completed in 927 and was enforced starting in 967.

## Bibliography


Albrecht, Donald et al., *World War II and the American Dream*, National Building Museum and MIT, 1995

Architectural Institute of Japan, Journal of Architecture and Building Science, December 1937, June 1942, April 1946, and August 1953

Architectural Institute of Japan, *Kougyouka Kodate Jyutaku Shiryou (Industrialized Detached Houses)*, Shokokusha, 1983

Chiel, Chris & Decker, Julie, *Quonset Hut: Metal Living for the Modern Age*, Princeton Architectural Press, 2005

Daiwa House Industry, *Daiwa House Kougyou no 30 Nen (The 30 Years of Daiwa House Industry)*, Daiwa House Industry, 1985

DOCOMOMO JAPAN, *Docomomo 100 Catalogue*, DOCOMOMO JAPAN, 2005

Fuji International Consultant, *Kenchiku Kougyouka eno Michi wo Hiraku – Daiwa House (Towards Industrialization of Building Production – Daiwa House)*, Fuji International Consultant, 1964

Goto, Kazuo, *Jyutaku no Koujou Seisan (Factory Production of Houses)*, Rikoh Tosho, 1977

Housing Loan Corporation, *Jyutaku Kinyu Koko 10 Nenshi (The 10 Years of Housing Loan Corporation)*, Housing Loan Corporation, 1960

Housing Loan Corporation, *Jyutaku Kinyu Koko 20 Nenshi (The 20 Years of Housing Loan Corporation)*, Housing Loan Corporation, 1970

Housing Loan Corporation, *Jyutaku Kinyu Koko 30 Nenshi (The 30 Years of Housing Loan Corporation)*, Jyutaku Kinyu Fukyu Kai, 1980

Housing Loan Corporation, *Jyutaku Kinyu Koko 40 Nenshi (The 40 Years of Housing Loan Corporation)*, Jyutaku Kinyu Fukyu Kai, 1990

Ichiura, Ken, *Nihon Jyutaku Kaihatsushi (The History of the Housing Development in Japan)*, Inoueshoin, 1984

Inaba, Shingo, *Kanna Kuzu (Wood Shavings)*, Shufunotomo, 1967

Jandl, H. Ward, *Yesterday's Houses of Tomorrow – Innovative American Homes 1850–1950*, The Preservation Press, National Trust for Historic Preservation, 1991

Japan Housing Corporation, *Nihon Jyutaku Kodan 20 Nenshi (The 20 Years of Japan Housing Corporation)*, Japan Housing Corporation, 1975

Japan Prefabricated Construction Suppliers and Manufacturers Association, *Prefab Kenchiku Kyokai 20 Nenshi (The 20 Years of Japan Prefabricated Construction*

*Suppliers and Manufacturers Association)*, Japan Prefabricated Construction Suppliers and Manufacturers Association, 1983

Kasumigaseki Building 50 Years Anniversary Committee, *Kasumigaseki Building*, Mitsui Fudosan Co., Ltd., 2018

Katano, Hiroshi, *Jyutaku Seisan no Kougyouka ni Kansuru Kisoteki Kenkyu (A Fundamental Study on the Industrialization of Housing)*, Dr. thesis submitted to the University of Tokyo, 1981

Massachusetts Institute of Technology, *Guide to the Records of the Albert Farwell Bemis Foundation, 1926–1954*, https://libraries.mit.edu/archives/research/collections/collections-ac/ac302.html

Matsumura, Shuichi, *Kougyouka Jyutaku Kou (Thought of Industrialized Housing)*, Gakugei Shuppan-Sha, 1987

Matsumura, Shuichi, *Jyutaku ga Dekiru Sekai no Shikumi (The Structure of the World Where Housing Can Be Made)*, Shokokusha, 1998

Matsumura, Shuichi, *Jyutaku to Iu Kangaekata – 20 Seiki teki Jyutaku no Keifu (20th Century Concepts of House-building)*, University of Tokyo Press, 1999

Matsumura, Shuichi et al., *Hako no Sangyou – Prefab Gijyutusha tachi no Shougen (Box Delivery Industry – Talks with Architects and Building Engineers of Prefabricated Houses in the Early Phase)*, Shokokusha, 2013

Matsumura, Shuichi, Endo, Kazuyoshi et al., *Kenchiku Seisan (Management and Organization of the Building Process)*, Ichigaya Shuppan-Sha, 2004

Ministry of Construction, *Kensetsusho 50 Nenshi (Ministry of Construction, 50 Year History)*, Ministry of Construction, 1998

National Home, *Sougyou 30 Nen Kinen (The 30 Years of National Home)*, National Home, 1993

Nihon Keizai Shimbun, *Sensai Fukkou – Nihon Saisei no Kioku to Isan (Recovery from War Disaster – Memory and Heritage of Japan Revival)*, morning edition of Nihon Keizai Shimbun, August 10, 2011

Saito, Ryusuke, *Shokunin Shu Mukashi Banash (Memories of Craftsmen, Part 2)*, Bungeishunju, 1968

Sakamoto, Isao et al., *Nihon no Mokuzou Jyutaku no 100 Nen (The 100 Years of Japanese Wooden Houses)*, Nihon Mokuzou Jyutaku Sangyo Kyoukai (Japan Wooden Housing Industry Association), 2001

Sato, Kouichi & Matsumura, Shuichi, *The Promotion of Prefabricated Houses by the Government Housing Loan – The Housing Loan Corporation's Contribution to an Improvement in Quality of Japanese Houses*, Journal of Architectural Planning Vol.81, No.722, Architectural Institute of Japan, April 2016

Sawada, Mitsufusa, *Watashi no Sangyouka Kougyouka Genryu Monogatari (The Origin of Industrialization Which I Was Involved in)*, Nippon Building Material Newspaper, 1997

Sekisui Chemical, *Unit Jyutaku no Sekai (The World of Modular Housing)*, Sekisui Chemical Co., Ltd., 1990

Sekisui House, *Sekisui House 30 Nenshi (The 30 Years of Sekisui House)*, Sekisui House Co., Ltd., 1990

Sekisui House, *Sekisui House 50 Nenshi (The 50 Years of Sekisui House)*, Sekisui House Co., Ltd., 2010

Shiozaki, Yoshimitsu et al., *Jyutaku Eidan Ni Yoru Jyutakuchi Kaihatsu to Jyukankyo No Keisei (Housing Development by Housing Corporation and Built Environment)*, Memoirs by the Housing Research Foundation, No.36, 2008

Takeda, Yonekichi, *Shokunin – Kenchikuka no Kaisou (Craftsmen – Reflections of an Architect)*, Kosakusha, 1958
Takeyama, Kenzaburo et al., *Concrete Block Zou oyobi Keiryo Concrete Zou (Concrete Block Construction and Lightweight Concrete Construction)*, Kyoritsu Shuppan, 1952
Tanabe, Heigaku, *Funen Toshi (Nonflammable City)*, Kawade Shobo, 1945
Uchida, Genkou, *Jyutaku Sangyou – Keizai Seicho no Atarashii Shuyaku (Housing Industry - a New Leading Role in Economic Growth)*, Chuo-Koron, 1968a March
Uchida, Yoshichika, *Prefab – Kindai Kenchiku no Shuyaku (Prefab – Main Cast of Modern Architecture)*, Kodansha, 1968b
Uchida, Yoshichika, *Kenchiku Seisan no Open System (Open System of Building Production)*, Shokokusha, 1977
Uchida, Yoshichika et al., *Jyutaku Seisan No 70 Nendai (Housing Production in 1970s)*, Kenchiku Bunka Journal, Shokokusha, April and June 1981
Watanabe, Yasutada, *Kougyouka eno Michi (The Road to Industrialization)*, Fuji Sash, 1962
Yokoyama, Gennosuke, *Nihon no Kasou Shakai (The Underworld of Japan)*, Kyoubunkan, 1899

# 2 An initiative to pay attention to people – 1973–1986

## Revaluation of vernacular architecture

The 1972 publication of *The Limits to Growth*, the first report to the Club of Rome, as well as the publication of *Small is Beautiful* by E. F. Schumacher in 1973, symbolized the major changes that were occurring to the framework of thinking about economic growth in developed countries. In Japan, the period of high economic growth that had lasted over ten years ended with the 1973 oil crisis.

Modernization of architecture stopped in one way but moved forward in another way. In the realm of academic discourse occurring in university departments of architecture and architectural design (in other words, within the realm of "Kenchiku," meaning "Architecture" in Japanese), the previous era's focus on universalization and prototyping as a means of achieving universalization disappeared. Instead, architecture as a masterpiece and "postmodernism" as a style became the sole focus of discussion. In this regard, we see the demise of modernization in architecture.

On the other hand, the mass-production capabilities of modern technology, which had supported developments in the previous era, continued to improve. Further, the industry behind creating "*Tatemono*" (meaning "Building" in Japanese) grew significantly. Developments such as raw concrete, plywood formwork, and fluidizing agents contributed to improving the mass production capabilities of reinforced concrete construction. The production of steel construction using H-beams and rectangular steel tubes was also standardized. Even in an earthquake-prone country like Japan, skyscrapers became common, and even super high-rise apartment buildings sprang up all over the country. The various prefabricated housing suppliers and manufacturers grew into large companies, helping to firmly establish a new industry called the "housing industry." In a way, the modernization of architecture seemed to be advancing.

Unexpectedly, the two worlds of "Architecture" and "Building," which appeared the same from the outside, actually had little direct connection. The world of Architecture treated the world of Building as if it could not be seen. Since Architecture depended greatly on the power of the "public" as a client, Architecture acted similarly to artists working under the funding of patrons in the 19th century. On the other hand, despite suffering from the after-effects of the first and second oil shocks, the world of Building managed to apply mass production methods as a means of business, and thus push forward on the path to modernization.

During this period, that is, around 1980, I was a graduate student of the Department of Architecture at the University of Tokyo. Specifically, I was a member[1] of the Laboratory of Building Constructions and Building Systems led by Professor Yoshichika Uchida.[2] Around this time, the research interests of the lab began to change. From the laboratory's start in the 1950s until the late 1970s, the main research interests focused on new architectural design methods based on industrially produced building components and new construction materials, and on new mechanisms of industrialized building production. Because of the lab's unique position addressing both design and production, the interests of Architecture and Building coexisted within this laboratory. These research themes symbolized the previous era, that is, the modernization of architecture.

However, in the late 1970s, these research themes that had continued from the beginning of the lab nearly disappeared. Instead "vernacular" and "system" replaced them as the main research interests.

First, let us consider the theme of the vernacular. Folk houses built before industrialization, which were strongly tinged with local regional features, were called "vernacular (dialect) architecture." A renewed appreciation for such folk houses had developed since the 1960s, seemingly as a reaction to the so-called "international style" and "functionalism" in modern architecture.

A renewed appreciation for features reflecting the whole life culture, captured by neither Architecture nor Building, emerged. Modern prototypes lacked the charm of designs that reflected the culture of everyday life. For instance, floor plans did not reflect region-specific ways of living, and designs did not incorporate local building materials and details born from the accumulated history and skill of local carpenters. The decoration and structure of the prototypes also did not serve to symbolize the status of the resident family. Further, aspects that allowed for environmental control in response to climatic conditions were not incorporated. The charm of everyday life began to capture the hearts of many architects and people living in modern society.

As early as the late 1950s, the valuable work *Japanese Folk Houses*[3] was published, which introduced private folk houses throughout Japan (Teiji Ito,[4] photograph: Yukio Futagawa,[5] Bijutsu Shuppan-Sha Publishing, 1957–1959). The book was so widely read that Ito (1922–2010), the author of *Folk Houses Have Survived* (Bijutsu Shuppan-Sha Publishing, 1963), reportedly said the book was "selling extremely well" (INAX REPORT no. 177, 2009).

During the same period (i.e., 1964 to 1965), a large event on the subject of vernacular architecture was held in the United States. The event was held at the Museum of Modern Art in New York, where in 1932, an exhibition planned and organized by architectural historian Henry-Russell Hitchcock and architect Philip Johnson was also held. Based on that exhibition, the museum became well known for spreading the concept of "international style," which symbolized the modernization of architecture. Thirty years later in the same museum, the exhibition of worldwide vernacular architecture titled *Architecture without Architects* was held and received much attention. The catalog of the exhibition, planned and designed by architect Bernard Rudofsky (1905–1988), also known as an essayist, was translated into Japanese in 1976 and published in Japan (translated by Takenobu Watanabe, Kajima Institute Publishing Co., Ltd.).

During the 1960s and 1970s, a related national regulation underwent reform. In the pre-war period, only three folk houses, including Yoshimura House[6] (Habikino-city, Osaka; see Figure 2.1), were designated as an "Important Cultural Property." The designation of Important Cultural Property started to be actively promoted with the designation of Imanishi House[7] (Imai-town, Kashihara-city, Nara; see Figure 2.2) in the late 1950s. After that, more than 300 private houses all over Japan have now been designated as Important Cultural Properties. In 1975, the amendment of

*Figure 2.1* Yoshimura House. Source: Dr. Nanae Nakao

*Figure 2.2* Imanishi House. Source: Professor Meiji Fujita

the Protection of Cultural Properties Act allowed a group of vernacular buildings that had formed historic streets to be preserved as a "Group of Traditional Buildings" (commonly called *Den-ken Chiku* in Japanese).

At the end of the 1970s, even in Professor Yoshichika Uchida's laboratory where I was conducting research, there was no one studying mass-produced prefabricated houses. Instead, there was a group energetically working to collect wisdom about ways of living with the natural environment from vernacular architecture. Further, in other labs, many students were conducting field surveys around the world to learn from vernacular settlements.

Interest also focused on organizations of local craftsmen, especially headed by carpenters who had played an important role in vernacular architecture. Of course, the tide of modernization had already reached the world of such craftspeople. New construction materials and industrialized building components had spread during the period of high economic growth. Many carpenters who used to be craftsmen had become managers of local housing contractors. However, researchers were focused on identifying aspects of the vernacular, which seemed likely to remain even during the push towards modernization.

## You cannot design the "ordinary."

From the late 1970s to the early 1980s, the framework of "system" became the focus of intense consideration. Theoretical frameworks, such as the General System Theory proposed by biologist Ludwig von Bertalanffy (1901–1972), as well as system dynamics (a technical approach to deciphering complex social phenomena) and systems approach (a methodology for resolving problems), were viewed as effective concepts and methods for dealing not only with architecture, a complicated combination of many parts towards a single purpose, but also for dealing with the social structure that gives rise to architecture.

"System" was different from the previous era's concept "prototype," which attempted to forcibly spread ideals to the world in a top-down manner. Instead, "system" tried to provide each building with a certain individuality tailored in response to particular requirements. Considering houses as an example, "system" did not refer to Fuller's dream to deliver Dymaxion houses all over the world[8] but rather to using the efficiency of 20th century mass production technologies to allow the dreams of individual inhabitants to be realized in his or her own living environment.

Among those systems, one system, which allowed individual inhabitants to freely select industrially produced housing components and combine the components to create the housing interior and facilities, attracted a great deal of attention in Japan. A paper by N. John Habraken (MIT Professor Emeritus, 1928–present) titled "You cannot design the *ordinary*" (Japanese translation: "Urban housing" September 1972) had heavily criticized the intrusiveness of governments and architects in the previous era.

In the paper, he compared contemporary architects to King Midas from Greek mythology. Having asked Dionysus for a new power, King Midas acquired the ability to turn anything into gold, but he suffered from starvation because he changed any food and drinks he touched into gold. Habraken wrote that just like King Midas, everything the architects touched turned into a special thing, namely "Architecture." Therefore, it was impossible for architects to design a house, referring to an ordinary dwelling where people live. Habraken argued that architects cannot design the "ordinary," although they can create "Architecture." That said,

> Recently, around the 1920s, architects began to notice the whole environment. Seeing people living in their residences and going to factories, architects decided to become involved. However, they approached such efforts as if they were architectural problems, so even ordinary things became special for them.[9]

Habraken criticized the intrusive approaches of such modern architects as Gropius and Corbusier, who tried to offer houses with design,[10] as well as governmental agencies who provided uniform homes.[11] Instead,

Habraken advocated for entrusting the design of the house to the inhabitants themselves.

Habraken used two symbolic illustrations in "*Three R's For Housing*" (Amsterdam, Scheltema & Holkema, 1970). One is a modern architectural prototype, "Dom-ino," allegedly drawn by Corbusier in 1914 and featuring a large X drawn over it (a sign of rejection). The other is a Japanese house floor plan, which was drawn by the inhabitant using the number of tatami mats as a guide. Though the latter was not marked with a circle, it is intended to be a circle. These illustrations clearly demonstrate the suggestion expressed in this chapter, namely that the vernacular point of view overlaps with the gaze of ordinary people.

## Industrialization for the people – N. Habraken & K. Ohno

In contrast to "vernacular," which was not connected to 20th century industrialization technology, "system" was discussed on the premise of applying industrialization methods. Given the importance that Habraken placed on the initiative of ordinary people, he can be regarded as part of the realm of "system."

The fundamental aspects of Habraken's thinking can be understood by reading his first book, which was published in 1961 (N.J. Habraken, *Supports – An Alternative to Mass Housing*, Architectural Press, 1972, original Dutch version in 1961). Habraken repeatedly references the natural relation between people and his or her dwelling as the most important consideration when designing a living environment. Further, he argues that mass housing, referring to large-scale public housing developments in European countries like the Netherlands, have failed to consider this important relationship.

In Japan after the war, the Act on Public Housing was established in 1951 in an effort to solve the housing shortage, later followed by the act establishing the Japan Housing Corporation in 1955. The prototypes of floor plans were designed based on the findings of various architectural studies, such as the "theory of dining-sleeping separation,"[12] based on a survey of people's living conditions led by Professor Uzo Nishiyama.[13] Since houses were repeatedly built following the same design details, the name "Standard Design" was used. From the latter half of 1960s, using the reinforced concrete panel design in use at the time in Europe as a reference, mass production using factory production methods was implemented. The situation in Japan was very similar to mass housing projects in European countries. Thus Habraken's perspective, as introduced by an article describing his thought and methodology in the magazine "Urban Housing," were applicable to Japan in 1972.

Habraken argued that in order to restore the natural connection between people and their dwellings, it is necessary to reaffirm that a dwelling represents the very process of living life and to encourage inhabitants to participate in that process of creating contemporary housing. He proposes that there is a way to effectively utilize contemporary industrialization technology, without reverting to pre-modernization circumstances. In other words, Habraken asserts that mass housing and industrialization are independent events, and that industrialization technology has been incorrectly applied to mass housing.

The core of Habraken's proposal was to separate multi-family dwellings into two parts: "support" and "detachable unit" (the latter came to be known as "infill"). "Support" refers to the spatially supporting parts of each family's residence, in other words, the main structure of apartment buildings as well as facilities shared by all inhabitants. On the other hand, "infill" refers to the amenities of each dwelling unit held up by "support," for example interior finishes, windows, exterior finishes, toilets, bathrooms, kitchens, and air conditioning systems – in other words, everything that the household would control or decide on. In mass housing, the attempts to industrialize "support" were not effective, Habraken argued, because true industrialization depends on re-establishing the role of the individual household as a decision-maker. Instead, "infill" should be industrialized, thereby establishing the participatory role of the inhabitant in the modern age.

In 1972, the magazine "Urban Housing" introduced an apt analogy by Habraken. Support is compared to a road and infill is compared to a car. Support is a public property, while infill is a private one, just as public roads are public properties made by public investments by government and/or municipalities, and cars are privately owned and individually purchased goods. Support also has a longer lifespan than infill, just as roads have a longer lifespan than cars. Therefore, infill can be changed according to changes in the lifestyles of families and individuals. Just as roads are not industrial products but cars are; support is not an industrial product (but can use factory-produced parts to build it) but infill is. Just as neither a road or a car alone can create traffic, a dwelling can be established only when the two different domains of support and infill meet.

Although it may sound somewhat abstract, Habraken proposed that based on his/her decision, each inhabitant occupies his/her desired part of the comprehensive support, and purchases his/her preferred industrialized infill components to be assembled for his/her life. Habraken did not aim for industrialization restricted by the whims of producers but instead "industrialization for the people."

During this same time, an architect in Japan consciously used the expression "industrialization for the people." His name was Dr. Katsuhiko Ohno,[14] known as the inventor of the Sekisui Heim M1 system based on the modular construction method. (See Figure 2.3.)[15] Dr. Ohno regarded "system" as the social structure, which established vernacular architecture, especially focusing on Japanese folk houses. He aimed to reconstruct such

*Figure 2.3* Sekisui Heim M1. A preserved version at a research institute in Tsukuba

homes by using modern industrialization technology. His vision is captured by the expression he coined, "contemporary folk house."

In his original publication *Gendai Minka to Jyukankyoutai* (*A Contemporary Folk House and Living Environment*, Kajima Institute Publishing Co., Ltd., 1976), Ohno mentions, "Japanese folk houses have been built rationally and creatively achieving an extreme balance across space and time between the natural environment of villages, the community, the production capacity of building materials, and the labor force of villagers." Presenting the idea of a system utilizing industrialized technologies, he writes, "As a starting point for today's housing methods and creation of living environments, we should begin by organizing a system of 'contemporary folk houses' based on systems of highly advanced technology." Further, he underscores the necessity of reforming the perception of industrialization, writing,

> Finally, as the polymerization and systematization of industrialization technologies begins, it is possible that depending on how technologies are applied, the benefits of industrialization can be secured, even while maintaining ecological diversity and regional character. We must

recognize that industrialization technologies can potentially exist for the benefit of humankind.

## Freedom of choice – towards an open system

How did Ohno think that "industrialization for the people" could be implemented? In short, he thought that such industrialization could be implemented with a system that disassembles the entire building into units recognizable to inhabitants, industrializes each separate unit, and then combines units, which are selected based on the preferences of inhabitants.

An entire building is divided into units, referred to as "subsystems," such as a wall, a portion of a roof, an interior component, and various housing fixtures. Each subsystem relies on competition between producers. Some producers make subsystems in a highly industrialized way, while others depend on the handiwork of craftworkers. Ohno called this subsystem the "demilitarized zone" between producers and users. The term is rooted in the idea that users can freely choose from the market to exert their power, without pressure from producers. Then, chosen elements can be attached to the post-and-beam structure, which forms the fundamental framework of the building space; and the house is complete. Considering the structure as support and subsystems as infill, the system image of Ohno is similar to that of Habraken.

In 1971, one year before the translation of Habraken's theories into Japanese, Ohno achieved his own vision of "system" in Sekisui Heim M1. (See Figure 2.4.) At the time, Ohno was only 26 years old. M1 is not wooden, but instead constructed from steel, a method more suitable for factory production. The design, modeled after traditional Japanese folk houses, utilized a post-and-beam building structure. It was assembled in a factory in a box shape of the maximum size allowed on roads for transport. At the same factory, workers also installed the subsystems such as walls, roofs, interior finishes, and housing equipment, which had been selected by the future residents. The nearly completed boxes (or "units") were transported to a construction site and joined together to complete the house. The number and arrangement of "boxes" varied depending on each house.

In fact, M1 was actually commercialized through these processes. However, since a single company managed all the processes, the subsystems did not have a lot of variations. Under Ohno's original scheme, he hoped that in the future, subsystems would be provided by the market in a more open manner, going beyond individual corporate frameworks. In other words, he felt that open markets guarantee the freedom of inhabitants to make their own choices, and thus industrialization can become "industrialization for the people."

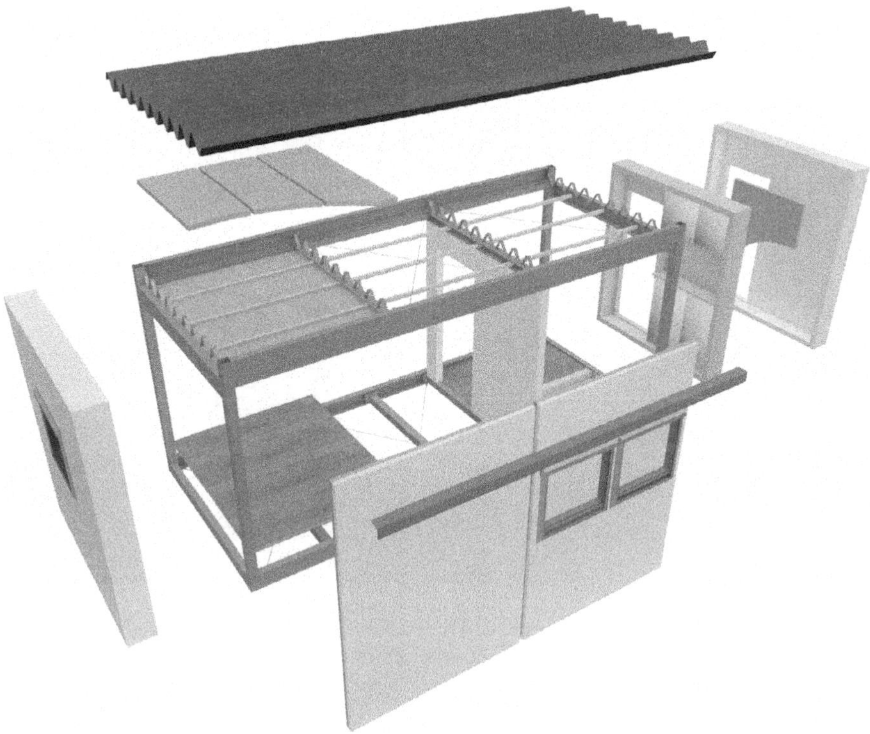

*Figure 2.4* The composition of a modular unit of Sekisui Heim M1, clearly illustrating Dr. K. Ohno's concept of an "all-purpose box" with attached components. Source: S. Matsumura, G. Hirasawa et al., *3D Zukai ni Yoru Kenchiku Kouhou (Building Construction – learning with 3D drawings)*, Ichigaya Shuppansha Publishing, 2014

It goes without saying that Ohno's ideas were patterned after a series of ongoing discussions related to industrialization, which had been unfolding in Japan since the 1960s. In the latter half of the 1960s, Dr. Ryo Kenmochi[16] presented the "Standardized Component Building System," his vision for a new image of industrialization. (See Figure 2.5.) Kenmochi's "standardized components" were designed and manufactured according to dimension and joining method standards, created to allow for the potential of mutual joining. Once parts could be distributed, users could select and freely combine the components to create buildings, like houses, according to their preferences (*Departure to Standardized Component Building System: Manuscript Collection by Ryo Kenmochi*, So Building Research Institute, 1974).

Further, Professor Yoshichika Uchida, advising professor to both Dr. Ohno and Dr. Ryo Kenmochi, applied the general term "open system" to such

*Figure 2.5* Hata House. An example of Dr. R. Kenmochi's "Standardized Component Building System" in 1967. Source: Shinkenchiku-sha

industrialized concepts and frequently discussed the social commitment to expand freedom of choice (*Open System of Building Production*, Shokokusha Publishing, 1977). However, in both cases, the idea of freedom of choice is not clearly defined for inhabitants or users, and an architect is still supposed to be included to make choices. In other words, both Kenmochi and Uchida tried to define a new role for architects in the industrialization era. Habraken and Ohno both struggled with the role of architects in their system. Both Habraken's infill system and Ohno's subsystems completely re-envisioned the architect's role, and especially gave privilege to the user as the key player. The two systems both were at the forefront of the era.

## Freedom from systems – lessons from the radical experiment of the Eames House

Considering industrialization for the people, plus the freedom of choice required to achieve it, in what way was the United States at the forefront of the field?

Actually, around the time of Fuller's Dymaxion Dwelling Machine and Levittown,[17] the husband-and-wife design team, Charles and Ray Eames, were in the process of building an interesting house, which was a symbol of modernization, on a hill outside Los Angeles. The house is known as the Eames House (built in 1949).

A major concern, especially for Charles Eames[18] as an architect, was to achieve low cost housing through mass production. His concern can be easily understood by looking at the special edition of the magazine *Arts & Architecture,* which he edited with John Entenza shortly after his move from Michigan in the Midwest to California on the West Coast. It is also evident in the fact that Charles Eames worked on many mass-produced furniture projects, such as the iconic "Eames Chair." However, he did not intend to develop the prototype for mass production. When constructing his house, Eames tried to implement an inexpensive construction method of diverting industrial products, which were abundantly available in the U.S. market at that time.

The couple mainly used steel components, such as steel window sashes, deck plates, and other building components originally intended for non-residential buildings and available in the US, the most industrialized country in the 1940s. Looking at the patchwork-like details with components fastened to each other by on-site welding, there is no sense of the Japanese or European systems, which attempted to properly design the connection between parts like a machine. Indeed, based on Charles Eames' own explanation, the house seemed to have been made much more cheaply than similarly-sized houses constructed with conventional methods.[19] In the house, one can see the strength of emerging developed countries that lead industrialization in the 20th century, along with a spontaneity unique to the West Coast.

In the Eames house, the previously discussed concepts of freedom of choice and of system have been overcome with ease. The systems of Habraken and Ohno are established on the premise of the existence of infill parts and subsystems produced and supplied according to standard guidelines, such as requirements regarding dimensions and connecting interfaces. However, in the Eames House, there is no such system or rule. Charles and Ray Eames treated industrial products as resources, to be bought and combined creating the living environment without consideration of the original intent of the materials.

The Eames House can be viewed as having achieved freedom from system. The reason such freedom could be achieved was that far more building materials and components had been industrialized in the United States compared to any other country. The freedom achieved becomes very apparent in Charles Eames' short film, titled "House – After Five Years of Living" (1955), which focuses on his house.

This film follows how the appearance of the house evolved over the five years after they started living in it. However, the film does not show lots of architectural photographs, as one might likely imagine. Of course, photographs of sections of the facade, sashes, floors, and stairs are shown, but these architectural elements melt into various favorite objects, which are part of their lifestyle, such as tableware, furniture, stationery, cameras, toys, figurines, flowers, and garden plants. In other words, sections of architecture also function as favorite objects, which serve to shape their living environment. There is no system or rule for arranging and combining tableware, furniture, stationery, flowers, and trees; just as, there is no system or rule for arranging architectural elements like sashes, deck plates, and stairs. The sense of freedom can be immediately felt.

Habraken and Ohno aimed for systems, which would rely on individuals who could somehow envision the whole building, but the Eames house did not presume such people existed. I saw this video for the first time in the late 1980s, and was struck by this fresh perspective, which had absolutely no parallel in the world of architecture. By that, I mean the fresh perspective of being free from imposed prototypes and intrusive systems.

Of course, Eames was also an architect. His professional skills enabled him to achieve this freedom. The house suggests the possibility that inhabitants can achieve freedom in creating their residential environment. This American house in the late 1940s made people realize that compared to industrialization for people, the possibility of open architecture for the people had advanced further.

When talking about the design of his house, Charles Eames used the important word "unselfconsciousness." The concept captured by this word shares something in common with the modern concept of "open architecture for the people," which spread in Japan around 2010.

## "Gunkyo" and "freedom to build"

In the early 1980s, Japanese word processors became available, which enabled journals and magazines with 16-point font size to be published easily. As a result, a group of architects, including Dr. Katsuhiko Ohno, Osamu Ishiyama,[20] Toyokazu Watanabe,[21] and Professor Shuji Funo[22] of Toyo University, who had just started the group "HPU" (Housing Project Union), began to publish the journal *Gunkyo*.

Each of these four architects held completely different positions in the world of Architecture. However, they shared the goal of eliminating the world of Architecture, which had developed along with industrialization to become an elitist world plagued with bureaucracy, and the world of Building, which had contributed to the large consumer culture. Their shared direction pointed to creating new solidarity with local housing contractors and with local craftsmen societies, which had previously had little contact with architects.

The vision is evident in all 52 volumes of *Gunkyo* (see Figure 2.6), published until the end of the 20th century by them, along with Koichi Nobe,[23] Naoyuki Takashima,[24] Tetsukazu Akiyama,[25] and myself. In

*Figure 2.6 Gunkyo*

particular, the first issue, published in 1983, most strongly communicated this vision. For the lead article of that first issue, the chief editor, Professor Funo, chose "*Criteria for Housing Action*" (a discussion paper July 29, 1981. The text here is translated from Japanese text in *Gunkyo* no.2, 1983). The article was written by British architect John F C Turner,[26] known as a practical theorist of housing in developing nations.

Turner worked on slum improvement projects in Peru, starting in 1957, shortly after graduating from the Architectural Association School of Architecture in London. Like Habraken, Turner was critical of centralized housing prepared by the government, and shared the basic idea that a dwelling itself represents the process of living by human beings. However, while Habraken's ideas were based on his experiences and rejection of mass housing in developed countries, Turner's idea was based on housing provided for economically disadvantaged people by governments with weak economies. Therefore, Turner highlighted the inefficiency of the mass housing approach, especially in terms of ensuring financial resources and cost performance.

In his representative work *Freedom to Build: Dweller Control of the Housing Process* (1972), which he wrote and edited, Turner argued that professionals like architects should alter their bureaucratic attitude from "working for people" to "working with people." Further, he referred to the centralization of power within the architectural community as a "closed system" and called the ideal future state an "open system."

Turner also respected freedom of choice but suggested an even greater range of options from building materials and components to building site locations, financing options, construction contracts, and construction tools. He divided the entities, making choices into three types: (1) Private (i.e., industry), (2) Public (i.e., government agencies and local government groups), and (3) Popular (i.e., residents). Based on the General System Theory, Turner emphasized that having flexible resident choice leads to the most effective combination, while the combination of the former two is limited (what he called a "closed state").

The "system" devised by Turner does not apply to the building itself. Thus, his "system" is different from the "system" where a specific individual devises the whole idea and establishes various guidelines. Since Turner's system regards mechanisms and objects existing in society as components that can serve as resources for establishing residential buildings, the framework of selection is far more flexible than the systems discussed so far. Thus "freedom to build" is more suitable as the title, compared to "freedom of choice." The chief editor of *Gunkyo*, Professor Funo, viewed the concept of "freedom to build," as understood in the context of slum improvement projects in developing nations, as a critique of residences in Japan, which had been engulfed by mass consumption. "Freedom of choice" had already become popular in consumer societies such as Japan had become.

## The world of "self-build"

Shortly after the first publication of *Gunkyo*, I visited a building known as "Kikkaikan," located on a riverside in the South-Boso area of Chiba Prefecture, along with other members of *Gunkyo*. An elderly man, named Mr. Miyake, was in the process of single-handedly building a structure using whatever material he gathered, such as iron material and lumber. The enormous scale of the building made it impossible to imagine how many years had passed since he started building. Viewed from the opposite riverbank, it looked like a battleship.

When we entered the ground floor of the building, we saw dozens of machine tools which looked like they might not be working anymore. We were stopped in our tracks by the extraordinary sight of all the machines. Then we heard a sound from deeper inside the building. It sounded like iron being hit. As we approached, we saw Mr. Miyake working quietly.

Not surprised by us suddenly intruding, he did not stop working even for a moment. When we ventured inside with his permission, we found two elevators that had been converted from US military cannonball cases, and near the stairs, spaces which appeared to be a kitchen and bedroom. I was surprised again, when I realized, "He really lives here!"

In that building, the arrival of "freedom to build" was evident. Any visitor would have felt that way. Seeing it, I felt that the building represented a man who builds in order to live. From that experience, I could not help sensing the fundamental relationship between building and living. "Kikkaikan" had a completely separate aesthetic sense from architecture created for a patron.

"*Houses as Commodities*," the special feature of the first issue of *Gunkyo*, was edited with the intent to document and criticize the Japanese housing situation. In contrast, the following issue, No. 2, featured "*Self-Build World*" with the intent to think about the "freedom to build" as opposed to the concept of "houses as commodities" that had become established in the modern market. Further, we aimed to propose the possibility of finding a new approach to housing in Japan.

Self-build refers to inhabitants building alone, with friends, or with the support of experts. The approach offered a unique value, which would not be possible when purchasing a fully finished condominium or packaged housing products, or when living in mass housing developments supplied by other people. Further, self-build encouraged a more intimate relationship between living and merely inhabiting. The approach includes not only Habraken-like methods of buying and assembling desired infill components as part of a system, but also methods of continuing to extend residences with whatever kind of material gathered, as seen in slum housing. Finally, the idea that the process of building itself becomes one's existence, as seen in Kikkaikan, is also part of self-build.

After the counterculture movement of the 1960s and 1970s and the publication of *Small is Beautiful* by E. F. Schumacher, the appropriate technology movement (originally articulated as intermediate technology) attracted attention as a substitute for modern science technology. Among the wide variety of self-build types, construction by people influenced by the appropriate technology movement become the most typical.

This form of self-build was influenced by various ideas, technical developments, and historical factors. However, the greatest influence came from the "*Whole Earth Catalog*,"[27] published on the West Coast of the United States, and its surrounding social movement.

Stewart Brand,[28] who studied biology at Stanford University, began publishing the "*Whole Earth Catalog*" in 1968. Reportedly the Catalog also had a major influence on young Steve Jobs. The Catalog was an innovative media, providing an extensive collection of a range of information about products and processes necessary for people to contemplate and assemble their own lives. Among the topics covered, information on self-build was featured. Brand seems to have been inspired by a lecture he heard in 1966 given by Buckminster Fuller. Indeed, "*Whole Earth Catalog*" began with an introductory article on Fuller.

Buckminster Fuller is known for his development of the Dymaxion Dwelling Machine, which served as a prototype of mass-produced housing in the 1920s and 1940s. Later in the 1960s, he presented the concept of "*Spaceship Earth*."[29] In the context of self-build, his dome construction method was used for self-build shelters in the 1960s and 1970s, for example, the artist community "Drop City" built by young artists in 1965. Fuller can be viewed as a hero of the new generation of his day.

Later, self-build utilizing the dome construction method spread around the world. The catalyst was *Dome book 1*, published in 1970, and *Dome book 2*, edited and published in 1971 by Lloyd Kahn,[30] an editor of the shelter division of "Whole Earth Catalog." In particular, more than 100,000 copies of *Dome book 2* were reportedly sold. Kahn established a new publishing company, and in 1973 published a large book titled *Shelter* (Japanese version is World Photo Press, 2001).

*Shelter* is an interesting book with good sales. The book introduced and explained how to create a lifestyle or dwelling, which is different from the residential buildings and facilities commonly created on a commercial basis. Examples came from the houses of various native people in Africa and America, traditional wooden buildings in Europe and Japan, self-build methods using two-by-four lumber and concrete, construction methods using adobe and soil, tree houses, boat houses, and vehicular dwellings. The book even went so far as to address solutions for problems including energy, water, food, and waste. The editorial choice to indiscriminately mix a revaluation of the vernacular with methods of diverting excess industrial materials illustrates the fact that the modernization of architecture had become a thing of the past.

## Opening the fortress of "space" to the people – the new approach of "pattern language"

As previously discussed, Turner's paper was published in the first issue of *Gunkyo*. The second issue published in July 1983 included a paper titled *Architect Builder Principle* by the architect Christopher Alexander,[31] also a professor at University of California, Berkeley (Vol. 4 of the publication by the Center for Environmental Structure).[32]

In the early 1960s, when he was only in his twenties, Alexander had published several books, including *Notes on Synthesis of Form* (1964) and *A City Is Not a Tree* (1965). Later though, he became more prominent in the world of computer science, rather than within the world of architecture. His book *A Pattern Language*, published in the 1970s, helped him achieve prominence in computer science. The book describes how to empirically extract the patterns that make places comfortable for living, and to combine desired patterns when planning houses and towns. The book sets forth 253 "patterns," such as "balcony overlooking a street" and "staircase as a stage" (*A Pattern Language – Towns, Buildings, Construction* (Alexander, Ishikawa & Silverstein, 1977 [Japanese translation, *Pattern Language – Guide to Environmental Design*, 1984])).

Although it did not provide a detailed explanation of Pattern Language, Alexander's article published in the second issue of *Gunkyo* discussed the role of experts. Alexander says inhabitants can think by themselves about what makes a comfortable living environment and questions whether an architect is really needed. For the general public, the issue of whether architects are needed is of little importance, but for those in the world of Architecture it is a matter of life or death. The previously mentioned self-build and DIY carpentry concepts also touch upon the same issue. Alexander writes,

> Although this process (i.e., the process of creating an inhabitant's house using 'patterns') may seem to suggest that an architect is not needed, undoubtedly the result will be better with the guidance of an experienced expert. However, experts, who are able to provide such help and guidance, do not exist.[33]

Alexander does not follow modern architecture in clearly separating design and construction into business and process. He viewed the process of improving the quality of design during construction as a good thing. He used the term "architect builder" to describe this imagined expert, who is able to offer help and guidance based on their expertise with both design and construction. Alexander believed in the absolute necessity of this expert, especially when thinking about the quality of the living environment in multi-building developments. He criticized self-build, which had become popular at that time, saying,

> On the other hand, there are very extreme construction methods, such as hippie-ish wooden buildings, large bubble-like houses of Styrofoam, and Fuller domes. Such strange buildings sacrifice order and show an ignorance of patterns. Even though the builders straddle the roles of architect and designer, they are only responsible for individual buildings and have no motivation to make the concept work for the entire society.[34]

Clearly, Alexander is more interested in the quality of the resulting residential environment than the relationship between people and the act of creating a living environment. Of course, *A Pattern Language* is conceived focusing on the final results. However, even though he criticized self-building, the question of whether experts are needed or not is not settled. This is a fundamental question that arises when people in the world of Architecture attempt to open building activities to common people: "Are experts still necessary?"

A particularly contested idea was "space," which deep and shallow thinkers alike in the world of Architecture had long chanted like a mantra and upheld as a mystical art. The book *A Pattern Language* gave people the autonomy to consider "space." Thus, naturally, Alexander, who trained within the world of Architecture, tried to address the question regarding the necessity of architects. Even now though, a persuasive conclusion has not been reached. Indeed, in new ways of thinking opened to people by the internet (i.e., the world of "collective intelligence"), *A Pattern Language* seems to be more influential than in the world of Architecture. In collective intelligence, the distinction between experts and non-experts has become even less meaningful.

Regardless of Alexander's new opinion on the role of experts, *A Pattern Language* appeared destined to throw open the fortress of "space" to all people.

## Notes

1 In academic departments at Japanese universities, like the Department of Architecture at the University of Tokyo, each professor and associate professor organizes a laboratory. Members of such laboratories include undergraduate students writing graduation theses and graduate students writing master's theses, as well as doctoral dissertations.
2 1925–present. Professor Uchida is an architect and a researcher of building system design and construction. He is a professor emeritus at the University of Tokyo and a member of the Japan Academy.
3 Photograph: Yukio Futagawa, Text: Teiji Ito (Japanese), Bijyutsu Shuppannsha, 1957–1959. Ten volumes.
4 1922–2010. An architectural historian and architectural critic. Professor Ito used to be the rector and the president of Kogakuin University.
5 1932–2013. A photographer specializing in architecture.
6 A private house built in Habikino City in Osaka Prefecture. The main building was built in the first half of the 17th century and was renovated in the 18th century. In 1937, it was the first folk house to be designated as an Important Cultural Property of Japan.
7 A private house built in Kashihara city, Nara prefecture. According to a sign staked to the building's ridgepole when it was first constructed, it was built in 1650. In 1957, it was designated as an Important Cultural Property of Japan.
8 After Buckminster Fuller invented the 4D House in the 1920s, he started to consider transporting lightweight houses based on American advanced technology all over the world. The idea was the same for his Dymaxion Dwelling Machine, which was actually manufactured and built in 1947. Almost all parts were designed to fit in a cylinder about 3 meters in length.
9 This English text is not the original one but translated from the Japanese version by our team.
10 For example, Walter Gropius, *Programme for the Establishment of a Company for the Provision of Housing on Aesthetically Consistent Principles*, (English

version) Architectural Review, 1961 June and Le Corbusier, *Vers Une Architecture*, 1923 (Japanese version translated by Takamasa Yoshizaka, Kajima Institute Publishing Co., Ltd., 1967).

11 Mass-produced housing started in the 1950s in developed countries such as France and the Soviet Union. From the 1960s to the early 1970s, Japan also applied mass-production methods to public housing and housing constructed by the Japan Housing Corporation.

12 This term refers to the idea of separating where inhabitants eat and sleep proposed by Uzo Nishiyama in the 1940s. It became one of the basic planning principles of Japan's narrow residential floor plans after World War II, when a massive supply of housing was required.

13 1911–1994. An architect and a researcher of architectural and urban planning. A pioneer who scientifically studied housing problems. He worked as a professor at Kyoto University.

14 1944–2012. An architect. He received his doctorate under the supervision of Professor Y. Uchida of the University of Tokyo. He developed Sekisui Heim M1 when he was a graduate student.

15 See Chapter 1.

16 1938–1972. An architect. He received his doctorate under the supervision of Prof. Y. Uchida of the University of Tokyo. He proposed and implemented the "Standardized Component Building System" as a future building system model. His father, Isamu Kenmochi, was a representative interior designer of Japan.

17 The first Buckminster Fuller's Dymaxion Dwelling Machine was built by the Beech Aircraft Company in 1947. Construction of Levittown started in 1948 on Long Island in the state of New York. 17,000 houses were sold in the end. Both projects aspired to deliver better quality houses to more people through mass production methods, and did not emphasize the personality of houses.

18 1907–1978. An American designer, architect, and film maker. The Eames House, co-designed with his wife Ray, is an architectural masterpiece.

19 John Neuhart and Marilyn Neuhart, "Eames Design," Harry N. Abrams, 1989.

20 1944–present. An architect and a professor emeritus at Waseda University.

21 1938–present. An architect and a former professor at Kyoto University of Art and Design.

22 1949–present. An architecture researcher and architectural critic. He has worked as a professor and an associate professor of Toyo University, Kyoto University, Shiga Prefecture University, and Nihon University.

23 1950–present. A business consultant to the housing industry.

24 1951–present. A fine art critic and a professor at Musashino Art University.

25 1951–present. An architecture researcher and a professor at Toyo University.

26 1927–present. An architect who has been involved in developing the theory, practice, and tools for self-managed home and neighbourhood building in the UK, USA, and Peru.

27 A book compiled by Stewart Brand in 1968 with the goal of sharing useful information for people to live better and proposing a better global environment for living. A unique feature of the book is that Brand adopted the style of knowledge books, tool collections, and product catalogs. It was published serially twice a year until 1972, and after that, on an irregular schedule.

28 1938–present. An American writer and editor.

29 A concept advocated by Buckminster Fuller, emphasizing the finite resources of earth and the necessity of using those resources properly.

30 1935–present. Self-build advocate. Also known as the editor of the "Shelter and Land Use" section of the "Whole Earth Catalog."

31 1936–present. A city planner and architect from Vienna. Many people, even in Japan, report being influenced by his publications, including *A Pattern Language*. In 1984, Eishin Gakuen Higashino High School was built in Saitama Prefecture following his design.
32 The text here is translated from the Japanese text in *Gunkyo* no.2, 1983.
33 Ibid.
34 Ibid.

## Bibliography

Albrecht, Donald et al., *World War II and the American Dream*, National Building Museum and MIT, 1995

Alexander, Christopher, *Notes on Synthesis of Form*, Harvard University Press, 1964

Alexander, Christopher, translated into Japanese by Nakano, Hiroshi, *Architect Builder no Genri (Architect Builder Principle)*, Gunkyo no.2, 1983

Alexander, Christopher, *A City Is Not A Tree*, Sustasis Foundation, 2015 (Original Paper published in 1965)

Alexander, Christopher, Ishikawa, Sara & Silverstein, Murray, *A Pattern Language – Towns, Buildings, Construction*, Oxford University Press, 1977 (Japanese version: *Pattern Language – Kankyou Sekkei no Tebiki*, translated by H. Hirata, Kajima Institute Publishing, 1984)

*Arts & Architecture, 1945–54: The Complete Reprint*, Taschen, 2008

Blanc, Sydney Le, *20th American Architecture*, Whitney Library of Design, 1993

Corbusier, Le, translated into Japanese by Yoshizaka, Takamasa, *Kenchiku wo Mezashite (Vers une Architecture)*, Kajima Institute Publishing, 1967

Corbusier, Le, translated into Japanese by Sakakura, Jyunzo, *Kagayaku Toshi (La Ville Radieuse)*, Kajima Institute Publishing, 1968

Ford, Edward R., *The Details of Modern Architecture Vol.2: 1928 to 1988*, The MIT Press, 1996

Fuller, Buckminster, *Operating Manual for Spaceship Earth*, Southern Illinois University Press, 1969

Gargiani, Roberto, *Auguste Perret*, Gallimard/Electa, 1993

Gropius, Walter, *Programme for the Establishment of a Company for the Provision of Housing on Aesthetically Consistent Principles*, Architectural Review, July 1961

*Gunkyo (swarmed dwellings) no.0 (preparation issue) to no.51 (the last issue)*, Gunkyo Publishing Committee, 1982–2000

Habraken, N. J., *Three R's For Housing*, Amsterdam, Scheltema & Holkema, 1970

Habraken, N. J., *Supports - An alternative to Mass Housing*, Architectural Press, 1972

Habraken, N. J., *The Structure of the Ordinary*, The MIT Press, 1998

Halberstam, David, translated into Japanese by Kaneko, Nobuko, *The Fifties*, Shinchosha Publishing, 1997

Herbert, Gilbert, *The Dream of the Factory-Made House*, The MIT Press, 1984

Ito, Teiji, *Minka wa Ikitekita (Folk Houses Have Survived)*, Bijutsu Shuppan-Sha, 1963

Ito, Teiji and Futagawa, Yukio, *Nihon no Minka (Japanese Folk Houses)*, Bijutsu Shuppan-Sha, 1957-1959

Ito, Teiji and Naito, Hiroshi, *Interview with Teiji Ito*, INAX REPORT no. 177, 2009
Jandl, H. Ward, *Yesterday's Houses of Tomorrow – Innovative American Homes 1850–1950*, The Preservation Press, National Trust for Historic Preservation, 1991
Kahn, Lloyd, translated into Japanese by Tamai, Kazumasa et al., *Shelter*, World Photo Press, 2001
Kelly, Barbara M., *Expanding the American Dream – Building and Rebuilding Levittown*, State University of New York Press, 1993
Kenmochi, Ryo, *Kikaku Kouseizai Kenchiku eno Shuppatsu – Kenmochi Ryo Ikoushu – (Departure to Standardized Component Building System: Manuscript Collection by Ryo Kenmochi)*, So Building Research Institute, 1974
Liell, John Thomas, *Levittown: A Study in Community Planning and Development*, PhD thesis submitted to Yale University, 1952
Marks, Robert W., *The World of Buckminster Fuller*, Reinhold Publishing Corporation, 1960
Matsumura, Shuichi, *Kougyouka Jyutaku Kou (Thought of Industrialized Housing)*, Gakugei Shuppan-Sha, 1987
Matsumura, Shuichi, *Jyutaku ga Dekiru Sekai no Shikumi (The Structure of the World Where Housing Can Be Made)*, Shokokusha, 1998
Matsumura, Shuichi, *Jyutaku to Iu Kangaekata – 20 Seiki teki Jyutaku no Keifu (20th Century Concepts of House-building)*, University of Tokyo Press, 1999
Matsumura, Shuichi et al., *Hako no Sangyou – Prefab Gijyutusha tachi no Shougen (Box Delivery Industry – Talks with Architects and Building Engineers of Prefabricated Houses in the Early Phase)*, Shokokusha, 2013
Matsumura, Shuichi, Hirasawa, G. et al., *3D Zukai ni Yoru Kenchiku Kouhou (Building Construction – Learning with 3D drawings)*, Ichigaya Shuppan-Sha, 2014
McCoy, Esther et al., *Blue Prints for Modern Living*, MOCA, 1989
Meadows, Donella H., *The Limits to Growth; A Report for the Club of Rome's Project on the Predicament of Mankind*, Universe Pub, 1972
Neuhart, John, Neuhart, Marilyn & Eames, Ray, *Eames Design – The World of the Office of Charles and Ray Eames*, Harry N. Abrams, 1989
Nishiyama, Uzo, *Korekara no Sumai (Housing in the Future)*, Sagami Shobo, 1947
Nishiyama, Uzo, *Nihon no Sumai (Japanese Dwellings) vol. 1, 2, 3*, Keisou Shobo, 1975–1980
Ohno, Katsuhiko, *Gendai Minka to Jyukankyoutai (A Contemporary Folk House and Living Environment*, Kajima Institute Publishing, 1976
Ohno, Katsuhiko, *Toshigata Jyutaku (Urban Housing)*, Kogyo Chosakai Publishing, 1979
Ohno, Katsuhiko, *Chiiki Jyutaku Kobo no Network (Local Housing Network)*, Shokokusha, 1988
Pawley, Marin, *Buckminster Fuller*, Trefoli Publications Ltd., 1990
Rudofsky, Bernard, translated into Japanese by Watanabe, Takenobu, *Kenchikuka Nashi no Kenchiku (Architecture without Architects)*, Kajima Institute Publishing, 1976
Schumacher, E. F., *Small is Beautiful – Economics As If People Mattered*, Blond & Briggs, 1973

Sekisui Chemical, *Unit Jyutaku no Sekai (The World of Modular Housing)*, Sekisui Chemical Co., Ltd., 1990
*Spectator*, vol. 29 & 30, The Editorial Department Inc., 2013 & 2014
Turner, John F. C. et al., *Freedom to Build: Dweller Control of the Housing Process*, New York: Macmillan, 1972
Turner, John F. C., *Criteria for Housing Action*, a discussion paper, 29 July, 1981
Uchida, Yoshichika, *Kenchiku Seisan no Open System (Open System of Building Production)*, Shokokusha, 1977
*Urban housing*, Kajima Institute Publishing, September 1972
*Whole Earth Catalog*, 1968–1972

# 3 The inclusion of customers organized by the industry – 1986–2000

## The culture of users using the tatami system to participate in layout planning

Ever since the 1970s, Professor Yoshichika Uchida at the University of Tokyo has suggested that the construction system underlying typical Japanese wooden homes is truly outstanding. Such residential buildings are likely viewed as prime examples of vernacular architecture. In other words, the exact opposite of system-based building. However, the buildings do have an underlying system which we should seek to emulate even today. That system is based primarily on the tatami module such as the "Edo Module"[1] and "Kyo Module."[2]

In 1976, I left Western Japan where the old capitals, Nara and Kyoto, were located, to enter university in Tokyo (a city in Eastern Japan). Before I left, my mother warned me, "In Tokyo, the 'Kyo Module' (i.e., the standard tatami mat size commonly used in the region around Kyoto) is not popular. So, a six tatami mat room in Tokyo is barely the size of a four-and-a-half mat room here in Western Japan. Be sure to be careful."

Even as a young high school student, who had no special knowledge of architecture, I knew what "Kyo Module" meant. I even knew approximately how large "six tatami mats" and "four-and-a-half tatami mats" were. In fact, when warning me about the size of rooms, my mother had assumed that I understood such measurements. That is precisely why she said that. In Japan, using tatami mats to understand the size of a room is taken for granted. However, scholars who are interested in architecture as a system no doubt would be astonished by this level of standardization.

First, even ordinary people can imagine the space within a room quite concretely from hearing only the number of tatami mats (e.g., "six tatami mats," "four-and-a-half tatami mats," "eight tatami mats," etc.). By additionally defining the type of room (e.g., "Zashiki"[3] or "Chanoma"[4]), the image of the room becomes increasingly clear. The system is truly amazing and has no parallel anywhere else in the world. The book *A Pattern Language* attempted to tear down the wall separating common people from the specialized world of architecture. However, in Japan, Japanese-style room concepts based on the tatami mat module had already opened architecture to non-experts outside the world of architecture for centuries.

By standardizing the size of tatami mats (even with regional differences), Japanese architecture becomes accessible to all. In traditional architecture, the floor of every room is covered wall-to-wall with tatami mats. Indeed, the first *zashiki* room with wall-to-wall tatami mats, which was built in the Muromachi period in the Tougudou Doujinsai of the Jishouji Temple[5] (known as "Ginkakuji"), still exists today. Amazingly, over hundreds of years, such wall-to-wall tatami mat rooms, reserved in the 15th century for the luxurious living spaces of the upper class, have now become commonplace in ordinary homes. Truly, it is a system unique to Japan.

Habraken, whose ideas were mentioned in the previous chapter, highlighted the ability of Japanese inhabitants to draw the floor plans of their own wooden home, as an excellent example of inhabitants participating in architecture. Indeed, because the system of tatami modules enables someone to precisely visualize the space, inhabitants can easily draw house plans by themselves. For example, someone could imagine a home with "an eight-tatami mat room followed by a ten-tatami mat room next to a six-tatami mat room." Even more amazingly, if you show a carpenter a floor plan drawn freehand on graph paper by an inhabitant, the carpenter can begin construction work without creating any additional drawings. From a mere sketch, a carpenter can immediately grasp the length and number of necessary structural components (e.g., posts and beams), as well as foundation and secondary components (e.g., joists, studs, and rafters). In the same way, craftsmen who manufacture windows and doors can understand how many *fusuma* and *shoji* (sliding doors finished with paper) are needed; craftsmen who make tatami mats can calculate the number of tatami mats; and roofing craftsmen can determine the number of roof tiles needed.

Within the bounds of this book, I would even be so bold to suggest that this system of Japanese-style wooden buildings not only matches, but actually exceeds, the level of openness achieved by open architecture in its second phase.

When thinking about architecture as a system of material objects, it becomes essential to have explicit rules governing dimensions, as well as to clearly divide labor based on those rules. As mentioned earlier, the size of tatami mats is typically standardized within geographic regions. The long side of a tatami mat is roughly about one *ken*[6] and the short side is about half a *ken*. As a result, no matter how many rooms of different sizes are connected, any building will fit within a half-*ken* grid. To follow the grid dimensions, individual components are typically half a *ken* in width and the interval between joists is set to half a *ken*. In addition, each specific part of a building is allocated to workers according to the type of work required. For example, structural work is conducted by carpenters. Fitting work, tatami mat work, and tile work are each conducted by craftsman from those respective fields. (See Figure 3.1.)

As mentioned in the history of carpentry in Chapter 1, this system of wooden buildings has been refined in Japan over hundreds of years and has spread all over the country. The system has become commonplace, and yet impressively influential at the same time.

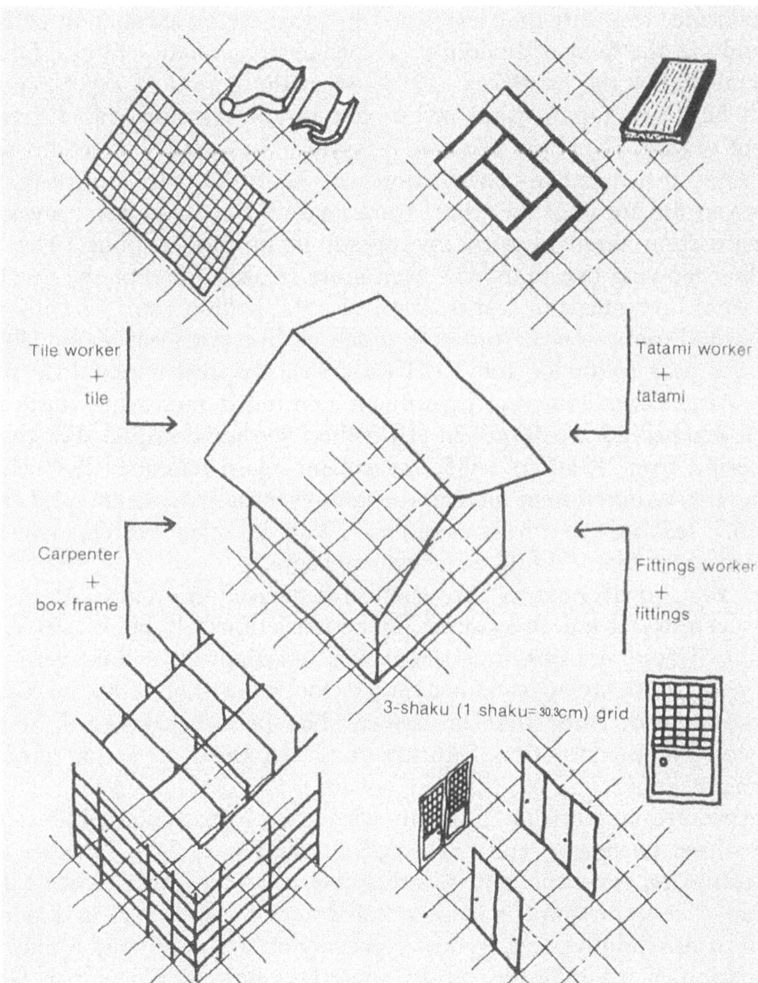


*Figure 3.1* Diagram showing the modular construction grid and division of work in a Japanese-style wooden building

In this chapter, I will discuss the extent to which the industrial world within the realm of Building in Japan especially made advances in opening architecture to be accessible to people, through developing at a distance from the realm of Architecture. First though, I want to highlight the ways in which the world of Building benefited greatly from the unique culture in Japanese architecture of using the tatami module.

## The basis of the "box delivery industry"

Let's consider the shift that happened in Japanese investment in construction (only in the field of building), according to estimates by the Japanese government. For the fiscal year 1960, when the period of rapid economic growth began in Japan, total investment in construction was 1.5 trillion yen (out of that, .7 trillion yen was invested in housing). For the fiscal year 1965, total investment in construction was 3.7 trillion yen (out of that, 2.3 trillion yen for housing). In other words, within five years, total investment in construction doubled with investment in housing tripling. The trend over the following five years was even more remarkable. For the fiscal year 1970, total investment in construction was 9.7 trillion yen (5.2 trillion yen for housing), almost three times as much as five years earlier in 1965. In 1974, the year following the 1973 oil crisis, investment remained mostly stable. After that, however, investment continued increasing until 1980, when it reached 29.2 trillion yen (16 trillion yen for housing). For the five-year period from 1980 to 1985, investment again remained flat. Then in the late 1980s, investment increased again, eventually reaching 52.2 trillion yen (26.7 trillion yen for housing) in 1990. In other words, investment increased more than 30-fold in just thirty years.

After that, investment in construction decreased gradually. At the start of this century, total investment in construction fell below 30 trillion yen (out of that, housing investment was less than 20 trillion yen). Until fiscal year 1990, investment accounted for more than 10% of GDP in Japan. However, after that investment has been below 10% of GDP. Even so, the construction industry has remained a major target of investment.

Consistently, investment in Japan within the construction industry has been focused on newly built construction (see Figure 3.2). In other developed countries, investment in refurbishing and renovating existing buildings can exceed investment in new construction. However, in Japan, the pattern of heavily investing in new construction has continued for decades. The mission of the industry, which constructs new buildings, can be captured by the name "box delivery industry." To create this simple name, I considered both the future of the industry, as well as the mission of the industry thus far. The mission of the industry is to deliver a "box," which can accept the lives of its inhabitants and which fulfills its promise to be solid and secure.

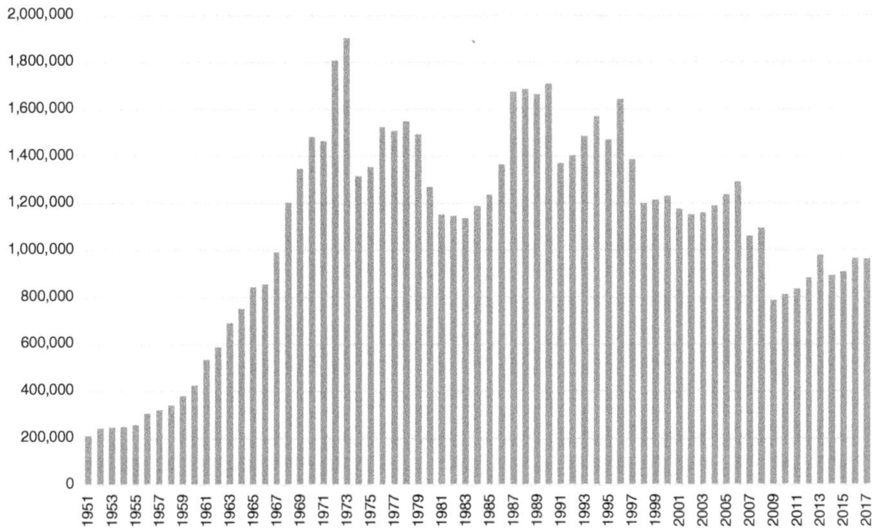


*Figure 3.2* Graph showing the number of new housing units built each year in Japan (based on data from the Japanese Ministry of Land, Infrastructure, Construction, and Tourism)

As reflected in construction investment trends, the box delivery industry grew rapidly after World War II, especially following the period of high economic growth in Japan. Indeed, the industry contributed significantly to delivering "boxes" to people, providing a container where citizens could live modern and healthy lives. In terms of infrastructure, the industry relied on two critical factors: land and funding.

First, let's consider the role of land. Land was supplied by clearing forests, turning over fields, and reclaiming land to create new land from oceans. At the same time, the infrastructure necessary for daily life was also developed.

Next, let's turn our attention to the factor of funding. In modern Japan, it is relatively easy to procure the funding necessary for constructing or buying a building because various financing systems exist now. However, that was not always the case, as we can see from the example of housing. The Government Housing Loan Corporation, which contributed to promoting the culture of owner-occupied houses, was established in 1950. Initially, the service was not as widely available as it is today. Indeed, it was only around the 1960s that private financial institutions started housing financing services.

If enough people cannot procure the funding necessary for construction, the supply of "boxes" cannot proceed, just as if there was a lack of land.

Therefore, in the case of the housing box delivery industry, a business developed before the war combining housing construction and lending services.

For example, in the early Showa period, the Japan Telephone and Building Company (predecessor to the Nihon Denken which does not exist today) sold housing using the monthly sale method, which had previously been used when selling daily necessities ("Denken" No.13, Nihon Denken,[7] 1959). The method was originally based on the so-called "*mujin* way" (meaning, "limitless way" in Japanese) in which people who won a specific lottery could build houses. In the 1950s, a large number of monthly sale housing companies including Taihei Housing, Shokusan Housing, and Nihon Denken were established. At the time, the common practice was to build houses when a third of the money had been paid. Then, the remaining balance, including interest, was paid to the company over the remaining period.

Meanwhile, the Japanese government provided funding for construction in line with policy goals, such as modernizing the construction industry and improving the incombustibility of cities. As will be discussed in detail later, in 1962, a number of prefabricated housing suppliers and manufacturers appeared. These companies relied on technological advances which allowed components to be produced in a factory, unlike the on-site construction methods of conventional housing. After that, the government established a special credit facility within the private framework of the Government Housing Loan Corporation. Further, the government created a system to finance non-flammable prefabricated buildings, specifically steel-frame prefabricated houses.

On a related note, as these systems were being put into practice, the "Factory-Production Housing Review Committee" was established in the Government Housing Loan Corporation. In 1962, approximately 400 houses, across nine different types of houses manufactured by eight companies, were financed and constructed. Two years later in 1964, the "Factory-Production Housing Approval System" was enacted with a range expanded to encompass wooden prefabricated housing as well as concrete prefabricated housing. Since then, the number of prefabricated houses receiving loans under this approval system has steadily increased.[8]

## Carpenters and local housing contractors

From the data presented in the previous chapter, investment in housing has clearly occupied the majority of construction investment since the period of high economic growth in Japan. Since then, local housing contractors have been at the core of the box delivery industry, which is the target of investment in housing.

In the late 1970s when I was a university student, the term "carpenter/local housing contractor" was often used. This term implies that carpenters and local builders could not be clearly distinguished, or simply were not commonly distinguished. Although I used the term "carpenter/local housing contractors" without questioning it, these two are actually quite different. The term "carpenter" is a job title that is assigned to individuals and has a long history dating back to the Ritsuryo law, as discussed in Chapter 1. In contrast, a "local housing contractor" is a contracting business, and moreover, a modern business organization. When searching in "Wikipedia," the word "local housing contractor" does not appear directly in the results. Instead, general contractors dealing mainly with relatively small housing construction projects are called "local housing contractors."

At that time, the term "carpenter/local housing contractor" was used because many of the owners of local housing contractor offices were themselves carpenters. The majority of such owners had apprenticed under a master carpenter after graduating from junior high school, and then had established their own independent office. Even after becoming the owner of a local housing contractor company, many continued to work at construction sites as carpenters. When called an "owner," some would respond, "I am a carpenter," and vice versa. As a result, it was convenient not to clearly distinguish between carpenters and local housing contractors by connecting them with a slash ("/").

However, the situation in modern Japan has changed. The local housing contractor is a local housing contractor, and the carpenter is a carpenter. There are some former carpenters among the owners of local housing contractor offices, but there are also an increasing number of owners, who did not work or train as carpenters.

As an aside, the number of carpenters increased year by year in the period of high economic growth to rise to the hundreds of thousands, as discussed in Chapter 1. As many carpenters became independent after several years of training to establish their own local housing contractor companies, the number of contractors increased tremendously. Although I do not know the exact figure, in the 1980s, there were reportedly at least 100,000 local housing contractors across Japan. Nowadays, even if you order a house from a major housing supplier and manufacturer, or if you ask an architect to design a house, the work is always subcontracted to local housing contractors. Thus, it is no exaggeration to say that local housing contractors are the core of the box delivery industry.

Among local housing contractors, the majority are contractors who are responsible for both the design and construction for conventional wooden houses. In the realm of Architecture, building design is supposed to be done by architects, meaning either designers working independently from the contractor, or designers working for an architectural office, who studied architecture in university or some other educational institution. However, this separation of design from construction is not usually the case in the realm of Building, where local housing contractors offer complete building service from design to finished construction. For example, now just as before, the previously discussed carpenter-turned-owner typically could design, as well as build. Because even inhabitants can design the layout of a house using the tatami-mat system, owners of local housing contractor offices could easily design a house following inhabitant's requests. Thanks to the Japanese-style architectural system based on tatami-mats, it is already the norm to design and construct different houses on an individual basis according to the requirements of specific inhabitants.

Countless local housing contractors play a role in delivering well-constructed, modern "boxes" to people throughout the country and further, providing "boxes" that satisfy the individual requests of each inhabitant. Without question, it is the second phase of open architecture as I refer to it in this book. Ever since I was a student, the world of Architecture has not showed interest in such houses designed and constructed by local housing contractors. However, we should not overlook the achievements made by the world of Building.

The question then becomes, when and why did craftsmen like carpenters change into local housing contractors? Before the war, the "directly managed system" was common, where a homeowner made contracts and paid directly to each worker including carpenters. Under this system, carpenters were merely carpenters. In the period of high economic growth in Japan, the "directly managed system" fell out of favor. Instead, a contract method which put local housing contractors in charge of tasks, like paying each worker, took hold.

In 1999, my laboratory conducted a nationwide survey of local housing contractors. According to the results, among local housing contractor offices founded before 1950, 30% were incorporated between 1945 and 1960, as mentioned in Chapter 1. Assuming that incorporation represents the change from carpenters as craftsman to carpenters as local housing contractors, it appears that that change happened rapidly during the post-war reconstruction period in Japan.

As discussed earlier, in the world of post-war wooden housing, the loan system played a major role in the spread of the "contract method," where the entire construction from start to finish is included in the contract. In fact, financing by the Government Housing Loan Corporation developed, starting in 1950, based on the assumption that such a system exists. Government institutions called for packaging entire housing construction projects and centralizing responsibility.

Actually, the change from the direct management system to the contract system also changed the roles of inhabitants. Not surprisingly, before the war, rented houses were more common. Few people could employ craftsmen and build their own houses. After the war, people could increasingly build their own houses. However, inhabitants began to relinquish the power to manage construction, entrusting the full responsibility to modern companies. The direct result is that as the roles of inhabitants shrunk, the housing construction market expanded with overwhelming force. People who wanted to build a house, but had neither the time nor money to invest, need such an environment where the entire construction from start to finish could be entrusted to someone. As a result, local housing contractors, who could take responsibility for everything, sprung up like buttercups in June.

## The new business of "housing suppliers and manufacturers"

Conventional wooden houses, particularly detached single-family houses, built by local housing contractors, still represent the majority of recent new construction in Japan. However, houses built by large housing companies (referred to as "housing suppliers and manufacturers") do account for around 20 to 30% of recent residential construction. Across Japan, about ten thousand local housing contractors are responsible for over 60% of the design and construction of houses. In contrast, there are only about twenty to thirty large housing suppliers and manufacturers responsible for 20 to 30%. Although the companies offer the same service of building homes from design to finish, their scale of production differs. Small companies, building only several houses per year, have coexisted for many decades with companies that build tens of thousands of houses per year.

The state of housing construction in Japan appears to be in a mysterious coexistence state, especially when compared to other manufacturing industries, such as automobiles. The housing and construction industry is more similar to the restaurant industry. In other words, there are large companies that run countless restaurant locations across the country, as well as small individual stores run by families. The scale of the restaurant does not correlate with the quality of food. In fact, on average, the quality can be regarded as similar, although smaller restaurants tend to have a larger range in terms of quality and price. In this way the coexistence of local housing contractors with large housing suppliers and manufacturers is similar to the state of the restaurant industry.

In the 1980s, when I was a graduate student, the local housing contractor was viewed as a respected senior player in the industry, while the housing supplier and manufacturer was generally considered to be a newcomer. However, as discussed earlier, many local contractors were established after the war, especially in the economic growth period. Thus, with few exceptions, local housing contractors can be seen as the product of a period – around 1960 – that also resulted in the appearance of prefabricated housing suppliers and manufacturers. Both are players in the box delivery industry, contracted to deliver a complete home from design to construction.

Clearly defining the term "housing supplier and manufacturer" is more challenging than "local housing contractor." As mentioned in Chapter 1, in the early 1960s, while conventional wooden housing stagnated, companies constructing homes from panels and components produced in a factory rapidly increased. Such companies shared the characteristic of owning their own factories and became known as "(prefabricated) housing supplier and manufacturers." However, today there are also many "housing supplier and manufacturers" who build houses using conventional wooden construction, as well as platform-frame (so-called 2x4) construction methods. Now even these companies are called "supplier and manufacturer," even though they do not own factories. Instead, the term has come to refer to large companies, which produce and supply housing on a countrywide scale. Actually, the term "housing supplier and manufacturer" is problematic in the first place. Given that the primary business of such companies is to offer a complete service from design to construction, in the same way as local housing contractors, "supplier and manufacturer" does not fully encompass their services, which include design as well.

Regardless of whether such companies own factories or use conventional instead of prefabricated construction methods, the distinguishing feature of a "housing supplier and manufacturer" is the scale of the company's production. The large volume of orders handled by such companies intensively concentrated production and served as the root of this new business model, which emerged in the 1960s. Some factories achieved intensive production through mass production, while others purchased materials from vendors in large volumes. Still other factories standardized and formalized design procedures, as well as worked to improve customer service. These approaches achieved a high degree of efficiency by making products more uniform. In the 1960s, taking advantage of the relative lack of variety, companies pushed customers to accept the limited range of products.

As a matter of fact, prefabricated houses began selling in the early 1960s with only limited options in terms of layout and exterior appearance (see Figure 3.3). Even so, it was extremely difficult to achieve a return on capital investment, such as investments into panel-producing factories. Excluding ready-made houses and condominiums, home buyers in Japan were accustomed to conventional wooden buildings, which could be built according to personal preference using the tatami mat system. As a result, customers demanded more freedom of choice. To increase the scale of factory production, companies had to increase choices in terms of floor plan and exterior appearance. From the late 1960s to the early 1970s, housing suppliers and manufacturers increasingly marketed their products with phrases such as "easy order" and "flexible design" (see Figure 3.4). Although each company has its own system for measuring dimensions and creating Japanese versus Western-style rooms, all the systems were founded on the tatami mat system from the beginning to increase variation in the layout.

The systems of housing suppliers and manufacturers at this time had succeeded in providing customers a degree of flexibility in terms of layout, as well as being able to choose from a range of roof shapes and colors for

*Figure 3.3* The first two-story Model 2B built by Sekisui House in 1964. Source: Sekisui House Co., Ltd.

*Figure 3.4* A two-story "Attic House" model built by Sekisui House in 1979. Source: Sekisui House Co., Ltd.

external wall finishing. In this way, housing suppliers and manufacturers reached the second phase of open architecture, also achieved by local housing contractors. However, housing suppliers and manufacturers did not succeed in reaching the goal of housing in the previous era, namely to make housing widely available to anyone. Using mass production methods, such as those used for the Ford Model T, was expected to result in lower prices for products. However, the price of prefabricated houses in Japan has barely fallen below the price of conventional wooden houses built by local housing contractors. Rather than seeking to lower the price of prefabricated homes, companies sought to guarantee greater freedom for customers.

## The commercialization of housing

From the late 1960s to the early 1970s, major prefabricated housing suppliers and manufacturers expanded their business by ensuring that inhabitants had freedom of choice, consistent with the second phase of open architecture. However, prefabricated housing suppliers and manufacturers were not able to achieve lowering the price of housing, which was the goal of the first phase of open architecture. There are two main reasons that the cost of housing did not decrease. First, having more choices, in terms of exterior finishes and floor plans, directly increased the types of components required and the company's reliance on on-site construction. In other words, the larger number of choices required extra labor and increased costs at both factories and construction sites. The second reason is that there was an increase in labor and costs for sales.

Generally, there is no "salespeople" role in small and medium-sized local housing contractors. In most cases, managers would get the job through their relationships created within a particular geographic region, family connections, and word of mouth. In contrast, "salespeople" account for the majority of employees at major housing suppliers and manufacturers today. Across Japan in local offices and model home plazas, salespeople meet with inhabitants, listen to their requests, present floor plans along with interior and exterior appearances and prices, and manage the signing of contracts. Although specialists and technicians provide home design and cost estimation support, salespeople are the ones in constant contact with owners/clients.

Given the degree of freedom inhabitants have to design the layout and the increased choices of fixtures and interior and exterior finishing elements, the number of meetings with salespeople also increased, along with their workload for making suggestions and corrections. In addition, manuals, personnel training, and quality assurance mechanisms had been carefully prepared. Otherwise, the quality of finished houses would vary widely, resulting in later complaints and problems. It is no wonder that labor and costs increased.

If housing suppliers and manufacturers limit the inhabitant's degree of freedom and choices, labor, cost, and risk will be reduced for factory production and on-site construction, as well as sales. However, then the number of customers will also decrease. How can housing suppliers and manufacturers overcome this fundamental dilemma? The solution clearly appeared in the late 1970s, namely "commercialization."

The word "commercialization" is usually used to mean "making houses to sell on the market." For example, in China, after the Chinese economic reform, conventional company-provided employee housing was replaced by a type of condominium referred to as "commercialized housing." However, in this book, the word "commercialization" is used differently. I use the word "commercialization" to refer to the movement by housing supplier and manufacturers to differentiate themselves from competitors by designing the inner and outer appearance of houses, as well as layout and facilities, in a way that strongly appealed to customers.

A pioneering example, which clearly shows this kind of "commercialization," is the "O Model" sold by Misawa Home[9] (see Figure 3.5). The O Model is a two-story house that offered only four possible layouts, including reversing the home east to west. Simply put, the types primarily differed in terms of having either more or less floor space. The shape of

*Figure 3.5* Misawa Home "O Model" in 1976. Source: Misawa Home Co., Ltd.

the roof did not vary. At the most, there were only three grades when selecting interior and exterior finishing. The limited range of options meant that salespeople only had to meet with owners/clients a few times because almost all prices were already determined. The house utilized a construction method, where large room-sized wall and floor panels were assembled. As a result, having only a few types of panels was sufficient. The home could be produced in a factory, reducing on-site labor demands and resulting in high cost performance. However, the commonly accepted wisdom within the industry was that a home with such a lack of options would not sell well. To compensate for the lack of choices in terms of layout, Misawa Home instead invited owners/clients to explore different lifestyle options and equipped the homes with original components. (See Figure 3.6.) The company began to appeal to customers by creating unique added value. Housing models with limited options had once been called "standardized type." The company achieved "commercialization" by rebranding the homes as "designed type."

Contrary to commonly accepted wisdom in the industry, the homes sold well despite offering only limited customization. No doubt, this had an influence on the industry. By the 1980s, other major housing suppliers and manufacturers increasingly added "commercialized housing" models with some limitations in terms of choices but with distinctly decorated exteriors, exciting suggestions for new lifestyles, and unique original components.

*Figure 3.6* Misawa Home's original room interiors and fixtures from the 1980s. Source: Misawa Home Co., Ltd.

The same approach can be seen in prototypes from the era of modernist architects, such as Gropius[10]. However, the style differed greatly from the dogmatic style of modernism. Instead, home styles began to respond more to market trends. In the world of Architecture in the 1980s, the expression "commercialized housing" was most often used sarcastically, expressing the irritation of architects that market demands more strongly influenced the shape of homes, rather than architectural design intent. In my opinion, the defining difference between the world of Architecture and the world of Building can be understood most clearly in the word "commercialized housing."

The dynamics of the housing market at that time, in the midst of the second phase of open architecture, were not as straightforward as they might have seemed. The prototype approach to construction, which had been adopted in the first phase, was not sufficient to meet the demands in this new era.

## Automated factories

In the 1980s, the types of commercialized houses offered by housing suppliers and manufacturers increased dramatically. Companies established development teams and standardized processes, such as marketing, for commercialization. Increasingly, it became difficult to achieve the original goals of discrimination and differentiation from competitors. With so many different types, customers could no longer determine which product was from which company. In addition, as competition intensified, eventually companies were forced to respond to the conditions of specific sites and to the individual needs of inhabitants. Eventually, the once high degree of limitation was lost. This was the bottleneck of initial commercialized houses. As a result, although the companies achieved some of the aims of the second phase of open architecture, the companies increasingly moved away from the goals of the first phase. To this day, commercialized houses by housing suppliers and manufactures are purchased primarily by owners/clients with relatively high incomes.

However, individuals in the "relatively high" income bracket are relatively more abundant than those in the "high" income bracket, meaning that housing suppliers and manufacturers could achieve a sufficient degree of mass production. Even while mass-producing, the companies adopted a system, which allowed them to respond as much as possible to the individual demands of each inhabitant. This system is called "mass customization." How could companies set prices in the range that customers in the "premium market segment" took seriously, while at the same time improving their ability to meet individual requests? Technological innovations in information processing played a key role.

The intensification of competition over product development led to market segmentation by companies to find their target market. In other words, companies tended to precisely determine the product for development, according to factors such as income level, household size, occupation, age, region, and hobbies. As a result, the types of products offered by each company increased. Given that each product had to have sufficient layout and specification options to accommodate individual preferences and site conditions, many manufacturers dramatically increased the different types of components. The production method, which had been in use until the early 1980s, could not accommodate the sudden increase in components without overly increasing labor demands and costs. Instead, a new production method appeared, which relied on advances in machine technology, including computerized information processing and computer-guided tools and machines.

Let's consider the simple example of a robot. In the 1990s, housing suppliers and manufacturers started to introduce welding robots to their factories. Even if the parts to be welded for each house were different, robots controlled by computers could seamlessly continue their welding work without mistake, working at the similar speed to repeatedly weld the same parts. Therefore, as long as instruction information is well organized in advance, increasing the number of component types does not significantly affect productivity.

Until the 1990s, major housing suppliers and manufacturers produced many of the same component type, stored them in warehouses, and used stored components as they received orders for houses. This conventional method was replaced in some factories by the "production by house" method, where only the necessary components for a specific home that had been ordered were produced. (See Figure 3.7.) Other factories adopted an even more sophisticated method, namely the "assembling-order production" method. In this method, components are produced, according to the order in which they will be assembled at the construction site.

In the early 1990s, I investigated one factory, which in the 1970s had manufactured several thousand different kinds of components. My results revealed that the number of component types under manufacturing control was over 1 million,[11] clearly showing the change in production methods during this time. The shift in production methods helped advance mass customization.

The example discussed above illustrates the impact that information processing technologies had on the prefabricated housing industry. However, conventional wooden houses built by local housing contractors were also impacted during the same period. I am referring to the emergence of automated pre-cutting machines, which automated the processing of wooden post-and-beam joints, such as tenons and dovetails.

Pre-cutting machines, which could create the shape of tenon and dovetail joints with a single cut of a saw, had already been invented in the late 1970s. However, the machines still had to be controlled by carpenters, following guiding lines that they had inked. Inking the guiding lines required as much work as normal cutting processes and had the potential for human errors, as a result of dividing the labor of inking from processing

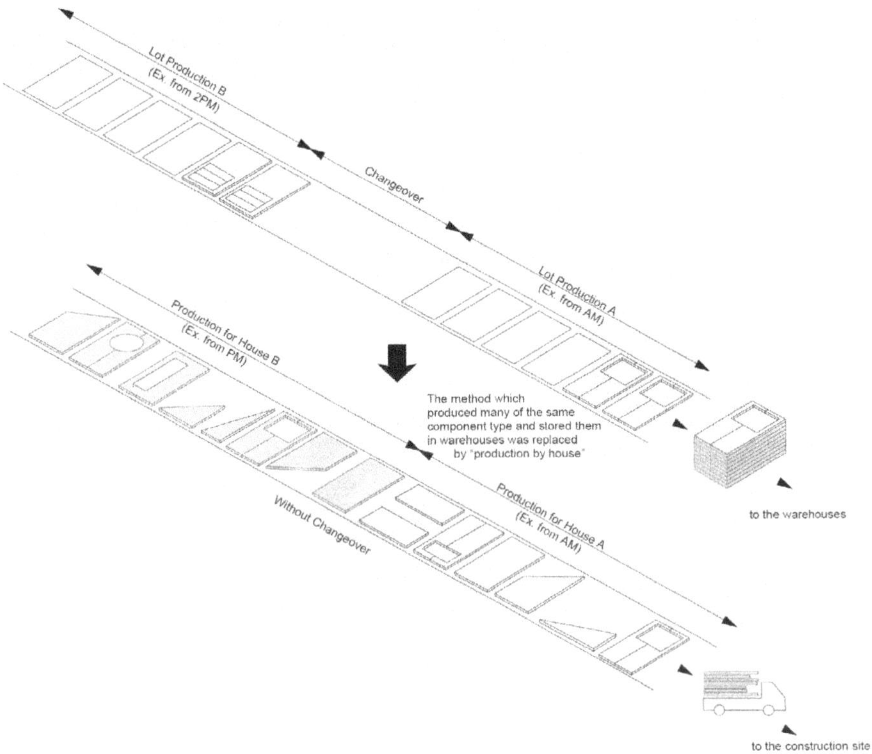


*Figure 3.7* Diagram comparing the conventional "planned production" manufacturing system, where components are stored in a warehouse, with the new flexible "production by house" system

lumber. However, in the 1990s, "CADCAM type pre-cutting machines" (also known as "fully automatic machines") were developed. (See Figure 3.8.) By merely inputting information on a framing plan, showing the positions of posts, beams, and other components, the computer could automatically generate the processing information of each component to control the machine. In other words, it was an automated cutting machine. Due to the shortage of manpower during the bubble economy period around 1990, more and more timber factories and leading local housing contractors equipped themselves with automated pre-cutting machines. At the peak, there were over 900 such factories in Japan.

Small and medium-sized local housing contractors can send simple plan and elevation to pre-cut factories in the area. The factories will then execute the entire process: from procuring and sorting the lumber, to processing the joints, and transporting the processed lumber to the

*Figure 3.8* An automated pre-cutting machine from the 1990s. Source: Miyagawa Koki Co., Ltd.

site. Some factories will even do framing work. Such factories can process lumber much less expensively than the labor costs required for traditional carpentry approaches of inking and manually cutting. As a result, even local housing contractors, who once prided themselves in their commitment to working with their hands, turned to pre-cutting one after another. Readers may still be under the illusion that conventional wooden houses by local housing contractors are built by carpenters hand-manufacturing components in their construction sheds. However, the adoption rate of pre-cutting machines in contemporary wooden houses is at least 80%.[12]

It should be pointed out that the rapid popularization of automated pre-cutting machines is based on the traditional tatami mat modular coordination system. Since the 1990s, conventional wooden houses built by local housing contractors had been industrialized as much as prefabricated houses. This can be included as part of the "mass customization" phenomenon which occurred during this period.

## The activities of salespeople around Japan

The efficiency of mass-customization, at least in terms of producing components, was helped by improvements in information processing technology. However, what about the efficiency of sales costs associated with the early commercialized housing?

The increase in the number of product types, along with the focus on improving the ability to respond to the demands of individual customers and specific site conditions, led to a proportional decrease in sales efficiency. Indeed, compared to commercial-order houses produced in the 1980s, the current annual number of home sales per salesperson is considerably lower.

Among major housing suppliers and manufacturers, some companies deal with apartment buildings for landowners, rather than detached houses for individual residents. In that case, the companies mainly produce apartment buildings composed of several dozen standardized housing units built with the same layout and specifications. In such cases, not surprisingly, the annual number of home sales closed by each salesperson is quite large. Indeed, in 1987, including such apartment building sales, the annual number of sales per salesperson exceeded 10 housing units, according to data in my book *Kougyouka Jyutaku Kou* (*Thought of Industrialized Housing*) (Japanese, Gakugei Shuppansha). However, currently that number barely reaches half the previous level.

In the 1990s, many European and American business people and researchers visited Japan to learn about our country's advanced mass customization industry. I often gave visitors tours around the factories of major housing suppliers and manufacturers. One manager from a British house builder looked around a factory with amazement. He touched a sore point by asking, "Well, how many contracts for houses does a single salesperson close every year?" I clearly remember his response, when I answered, "It's about ten at the most." He nodded, smiling with satisfaction as if to say, "Ah, now I see."

The vast majority of employees at major housing suppliers and manufacturers are salespeople. Thousands of salespeople are employed by each housing company. The personnel costs associated with such a vast network of salespeople are enormous. There are also considerable costs associated with the model houses displayed at display plazas, which support the sales activities of salespeople, as well as the luxurious catalogs produced by companies and public relations with the mass media. Home buyers act as if such facilities and services from salespeople are free. However, all the associated costs are included in the house price. Mass production itself can lower production and procurement costs. However, achieving mass production requires mass sales. The necessity of mass sales increases with mass customization. This is the lesson that we can learn from the experiences of major housing suppliers and manufacturers in Japan. Modernist architects, who were once enthusiastic about the original prototype, could never have anticipated the necessity or difficulty of achieving mass sales that also offer variety.

Setting aside the issue of mass sales for a moment, as mass customization advances, salespeople in Japan should naturally improve in their ability to respond to the demands of individual buyers. Compared to salespeople working in the early days of commercialized housing, which offered only limited design choices, current salespeople must have developed different skills. Thus, while sales efficiency in terms of the number of sales per salesperson is likely to decline, the ability of salespeople to counsel buyers and support homebuilding efforts will certainly improve.

Given my long education as an architect and building engineer, I honestly could not initially understand the necessity of the sales staff of major housing suppliers and manufacturers, nor could I appreciate their skill. I also could not accept the industry myth that the number of salespeople employed by major housing suppliers and manufacturers essentially determines the number of sales. However, listening to talks by leading salespeople from major housing suppliers and manufacturers changed my attitude considerably. Salespeople can tell us about the actual, real stories of people building homes in Japan. These stories capture the diversity of home buyers, the wide variety of motivations they have for building homes, and the challenges and joys they experience in the process. Clearly, salespeople have a close relationship with inhabitants. We could never hear such engaging stories from workers engaged in developing technology or products related to houses.

The challenge of increasing sales efficiency and decreasing sales costs should be further analyzed and considered. Looking ahead to the future, I believe that the skill of salespeople in Japan, forged during the mass customization era, will prove to be an invaluable resource.

## The industry shift from "box delivery" to "place creation"

In this chapter, I discuss changes in the world of Japanese building, focusing on the local housing contractors and major housing suppliers and manufacturers, who helped form the concept of "house" now familiar to us. Specifically, this chapter addresses the early history of the industry, along with changes that occurred during the 20th century. Broadly speaking, the industry developed on the foundation of the tatami mat system, as well as thanks to the extensive existing network of craftspeople in Japan. As the industry approached the second phase of open architecture, companies focused on developing industrialization and information technology, while also mobilizing an army of salespeople to provide exceptional customer service to home buyers. What eventually arose was the box delivery industry with its mission to provide well-built, respectable buildings as promised.

Habraken, an advocate of the philosophy and methodology of the second phase of open architecture, visited Japan several times in the 1980s. His travel writings describe his appreciation of the mass customization methods in Japan. He admired the application of advanced industrialization technologies, which allowed the "box delivery industry" to respond to the needs of individual inhabitants. I feel like that kind of positive impression of the box delivery industry is lacking in the world of Architecture in Japan, which has failed to recognize the unique landscape formed by the world of Building in Japan.

In fact, there is another unique landscape that the "box delivery industry" has provided for us. That is the scenery of our town filled with so many buildings and examples of architecture. That scenery is thanks to direct investments made by the Japanese government over many decades, along with efforts to implement policies to create low interest loans. In addition, citizens have invested heavily. Finally, workers in the box delivery industry have toiled tirelessly, skipping vacations, to help construct that landscape. (See Figure 3.9.)

Historical data shows the unprecedented nature of this landscape. Let's first consider houses as an example. According to data from the Survey of Housing (now known as the Housing and Land Survey) conducted by the Japanese government, there were slightly over 20 million houses

*Figure 3.9* A photograph showing Tokyo in 2005 full of buildings (taken approximately 10km from the center of the city)

in Japan in 1963 on the eve of the high economic growth period. This number was slightly less than the number of households. However, according to survey results in 2013, 50 years later, there are more than 60 million houses in Japan. The number of houses tripled in fifty years. In addition, the survey results showed that the number of houses exceeded the number of households by 8 million. In other words, there are 0.48 houses per citizen, surpassing the ratio of 0.42 in the United States in 2013, which from the perspective of post-war Japan was a symbol of prosperity.

The national investment in "boxes" and the efforts of the box delivery industry over five decades resulted in a totally different landscape.

Although the results are remarkable, I do wonder if we really need 0.48 "boxes" per citizen. The numbers vary depending on the use of the building, but currently more than 8 million houses are vacant (according to the 2013 Housing and Land Survey). Presumably, the population of Japan, along with the number of households, will not increase in the future. As long as the use of "boxes" does not fundamentally change, no more "boxes" are needed in Japan. Although it may be necessary to rebuild deteriorated "boxes," there is no need for the box delivery industry to continue its efforts to increase the number of new buildings.

People may have varying opinions about the design of existing "boxes." There may be complaints that the shape of the "box" is not ideal, or that the interior of "boxes" is overcrowded. Even so, no one can deny from the data above that there is already a sufficient supply of "boxes." Unlike other regions in the world, Japan is not facing a housing shortage. Rather, Japan has the opposite problem. There are too many vacant houses. Of course, there are still other challenges facing the industry, such as the fact that land availability differs dramatically based on price, and the issue of creating housing for the economically disadvantaged remains. However, in light of the enormous number of vacant houses, the real problem seems to be how to use the already existing supply of "boxes."

This means that we should tackle not only the challenge of creating housing for the economically disadvantaged but also the problem of how to use existing vacant houses. How can we fully utilize the richness of the supply of "boxes" to enrich our lives? That is the question facing future generations. Let me attempt to say that more clearly. We need to bring a sense of creativity and joy to the challenge of rearranging and reimagining the superabundant supply of "boxes" into new vibrant "places" for life. After all, these "boxes" represent significant national investment and considerable efforts on the part of the box delivery industry over half a century. I hesitate to use the term "industry" to describe the activities of people working in this area. However, for lack of a better term, I will name it the "place-making industry," since in a sense it follows the box delivery industry.

## Notes

1 "Edo" was the name of Tokyo before the city became the capital of Japan. This term refers to the home layout design module which is primarily used in the geographic region centered around Edo. Typically the center of columns and beams is placed on a grid that is an integer multiple of 3 *shaku* (equal to about 909 mm).
2 Home layout design module which is primarily used in the geographic region centered around the former capital city of Kyoto. Typically columns or beams are placed in a grid with integral multiples of 3.15 Shaku (equal to about 954 mm).
3 This word carries various meanings, but here, the term refers to a tatami mat guest room.
4 A tatami mat room used for meals and family relaxation activities in a Japanese-style house.
5 Jishouji (also known as "Ginkakuji") is a Buddhist temple in Kyoto, famous as a UNESCO World Heritage site. Tougudou in the temple was built in 1486. Located in the corner of the northeast of the building, Doujinsai is a small room, only four-and-a-half tatami mats in size. However, the decorations in the room, including the staggered alcove shelves, writing alcove, and *shoji* windows, are among some of the oldest existing decorations of their kind.
6 Approximately 1.818 meters.
7 Temporarily, it was a leading company that primarily sold conventional wooden houses. In the 1960s, Kakuei Tanaka (who later became Prime Minister) helped manage the company. The company no longer exists.
8 According to the "*The 30 Years of Housing Loan Corporation*" published by the Government Housing Loan Corporation in 1980, the number of factory-produced housing unit construction projects approved by the "Factory Production Housing Approval System" was 22,179 in fiscal year 1965 (of which 3,137 received housing loans), 23,580 (4,548) in 1966, 28,889 (5,373) in 1967, 32,003 (7,914) in 1968, 54,759 (15,270) in 1969, 71,479 (21,017) in 1970, 91,710 (30,759) in 1971, 120,639 (41,124) in 1972, and 152,418 (54,843) in 1973.
9 One of Japan's leading housing suppliers and manufacturers, and established in 1967 by Mr. Chiyoji Misawa. The company mainly builds prefabricated houses, using the wooden-panel method of construction.
10 See Section 2 of Chapter 2.
11 S. Matsumura, *The structure of the world where housing can be made* (in Japanese, "Jyutaku ga Dekiru Sekai no Shikumi"), Chapter 7, Shokokusha, 1998.
12 According to the results of a survey conducted by the National Precut Machine Association of Wooden Housing, by 2013, the percentage of conventional wooden house construction relying on pre-cutting machines had already topped 90%.

## Bibliography

Alexander, Christopher, Ishikawa, Sara & Silverstein, Murray, *A Pattern Language – Towns, Buildings, Construction*, Oxford University Press, 1977 (Japanese version: *Pattern Language – Kankyou Sekkei no Tebiki*, translated by H. Hirata, Kajima Institute Publishing, 1984)

Architectural Institute of Japan, *Kougyouka Kodate Jyutaku Shiryou (Industrialized Detached Houses)*, Shokokusha, 1983

Corbusier, Le, translated into Japanese by Yoshizaka, Takamasa, *Kenchiku wo Mezashite (Vers une Architecture)*, Kajima Institute Publishing, 1967

Fujisawa, Yoshikazu & Matsumura, Shuichi, *Precut Koujou Kikou (Journeys to Precut Factories all over Japan)*, Jyutaku to Mokuzai (monthly magazine Houses and Lumber), Japan Housing and Wood Technology Center, October 1991–April 1998

Herbert Gilbert, *The Dream of the Factory-Made House*, The MIT Press, 1984

Gropius, Walter, *Programme for the Establishment of a Company for the Provision of Housing on Aesthetically Consistent Principles*, Architectural Review, July 1961

Habraken, N. J., *Three R's for Housing*, Amsterdam, Scheltema & Holkema, 1970

Habraken, N. J., *The Structure of the Ordinary*, The MIT Press, 1998

National Home, *Sougyou 30 Nen Kinen (The 30 Years of National Home)*, National Home, 1993

Housing Loan Corporation, *Jyutaku Kinyu Koko 10 Nenshi (The 10 Years of Housing Loan Corporation)*, Housing Loan Corporation, 1960

Housing Loan Corporation, *Jyutaku Kinyu Koko 20 Nenshi (The 20 Years of Housing Loan Corporation)*, Housing Loan Corporation, 1970

Housing Loan Corporation, *Jyutaku Kinyu Koko 30 Nenshi (The 30 Years of Housing Loan Corporation)*, Jyutaku Kinyu Fukyu Kai, 1980

Housing Loan Corporation, *Jyutaku Kinyu Koko 40 Nenshi (The 40 Years of Housing Loan Corporation)*, Jyutaku Kinyu Fukyu Kai, 1990

Daiwa House Industry, *Daiwa House Kougyou no 30 Nen (The 30 Years of Daiwa House Industry)*, Daiwa House Industry, 1985

Jandl, H. Ward, *Yesterday's Houses of Tomorrow – Innovative American Homes 1850–1950*, The Preservation Press, National Trust for Historic Preservation, 1991

Matsumura, Shuichi, *Kougyouka Jyutaku Kou (Thought of Industrialized Housing)*, Gakugei Shuppan-Sha, 1987

Matsumura, Shuichi et al., *Nihon no Jyutaku ga Wakaru Hon (Understanding Japanese Houses)*, PHP Institute, 1994

Matsumura, Shuichi, *Jyutaku ga Dekiru Sekai no Shikumi (The Structure of the World Where Housing Can Be Made)*, Shokokusha, 1998

Matsumura, Shuichi, *Jyutaku to Iu Kangaekata – 20 Seiki teki Jyutaku no Keifu (20th Century Concepts of House-building)*, University of Tokyo Press, 1999

Matsumura, Shuichi et al., *Hako no Sangyou – Prefab Gijyutusha tachi no Shougen (Box Delivery Industry – Talks with Architects and Building Engineers of Prefabricated Houses in the Early Phase)*, Shokokusha, 2013

Matsumura, Shuichi et al., *2025nen no Kenchiku – Nanatsu no Yogen (Architecture in 2025 – Seven Predictions)*, Nikkei Business Publications, 2014

Matsumura, Shuichi et al., *Kenchiku Saisei Gaku (Theory and Practice of Architectural Renovation)*, Ichigaya Shuppan-Sha, 2016

Matsumura, Shuichi, Hirasawa, G. et al., *3D Zukai ni Yoru Kenchiku Kouhou (Building Construction – Learning with 3D drawings)*, Ichigaya Shuppan-Sha, 2014

Miyagawa Koki Co., Ltd, *Miyagawa Koki Hanseiki no Ayumi (The 50 Years of Miyagawa Koki)*, Miyagawa Koki Co., Ltd., 1992

Nihon Denken, *Denken No.13*, Nihon Denken, 1959

Ohno, Katsuhiko, *Gendai Minka to Jyukankyoutai (A Contemporary Folk House and Living Environment)*, Kajima Institute Publishing, 1976

Ohno, Katsuhiko, *Chiiki Jyutaku Kobo no Network (Local Housing Network)*, Shokokusha, 1988

Sakamoto, Isao et al., *Nihon no Mokuzou Jyutaku no 100 Nen (The 100 Years of Japanese Wooden Houses)*, Nihon Mokuzou Jyutaku Sangyo Kyoukai (Japan Wooden Housing Industry Association), 2001

Sato, Kouichi & Matsumura, Shuichi, *The Promotion of Prefabricated Houses by the Government Housing Loan – The Housing Loan Corporation's Contribution to an Improvement in Quality of Japanese Houses*, Journal of Architectural Planning Vol.81, No.722 (pp.841–850), Architectural Institute of Japan, April 2016

Sekisui Chemical, *Unit Jyutaku no Sekai (The World of Modular Housing)*, Sekisui Chemical Co., Ltd., 1990

Sekisui House, *Sekisui House 30 Nenshi (The 30 Years of Sekisui House)*, Sekisui House Co., Ltd., 1990

Sekisui House, *Sekisui House 50 Nenshi (The 50 Years of Sekisui House)*, Sekisui House Co., Ltd, 2010

Uchida Award Committee, *Nihon wo Kaeta Yattsu no Kouhou (Eight Kinds of Construction Methods Which Changed Japanese Architecture)*, Uchida Award Committee, 2002

Uchida, Yoshichika, *Prefab – Kindai Kenchiku no Shuyaku (Prefab – Main Cast of Modern Architecture)*, Kodansha, 1968

Uchida, Yoshichika, *Kenchiku Seisan no Open System (Open System of Building Production)*, Shokokusha, 1977

Uchida, Yoshichika et al., *Jyutaku Seisan No 70 Nendai (Housing Production in 1970s)*, Kenchiku Bunka Journal, Shokokusha, Vol.36, No.414 (pp.37–72) and No.416 (pp.113–142), 1981 April and June

# 4 Connecting with ways of life can give the initiative to the people in the 21st century

## A question inspired by two photography books – has architecture intersected with people's life philosophy?

From the end of the last century to the beginning of this century, when I began to feel that the "box delivery industry" had fulfilled its role, I came across two photography books. One is *Material World: A Global Family Portrait* (Counterpoint, 1994; Japanese version published by TOTO Publishing Co., 1994) from the Material World Project led by Peter Menzel. The other one is *Universe for Rent* (Chikuma Shobo, 2001) by Kyoichi Tsuzuki, who is an editor and a photographer.

*Material World: A Global Family Portrait* is the outcome of a fantastic project in which entire sets of household goods were brought out from the homes of common people around the world and arranged in front of their houses. Then the family members who lived there also came out to be photographed in one picture together with their household goods. It strikingly captures the lives of people from countries representing the middle-range of the thirty countries in the project, such as Sarajevo, Kuwait, Mari, Albania, India, UK, Bhutan, Guatemala, and Japan.

What surprised me was the fact that the photographs of the household goods and the families lined up evoked the living space more richly than the photographs of the buildings. From my architectural education, I had assumed that the "box" was the living space, but I was mistaken. I realized that the living space could be expressed by the inhabitants and their household goods. More than respected architectural photography books, such as *Japanese Folk Houses* by Teiji Ito and Yukio Futagawa, and *Architecture Without Architects* by Bernard Rudofsky, which once led to the reassessment of vernacular architecture, *Material World: A Global Family Portrait* had a greater impact on me during that time. The book also made me think that if the living space could be expressed by streets and household goods, the architecture I had learned and studied was simply an act of forming a boundary of ownership between public streets and private household goods.

The other photography book – *Universe for Rent* – was a national version of Mr. Tsuzuki's photography book *Tokyo Style* published a few years earlier. This amazing photography book included photographs of the interior of several hundred rental apartments across Japan.

Although not previously discussed, apartment buildings, especially Mokuchin (rental wooden low-rise apartment building),[1] were a typical form of residence in modern Japan. After the war, local housing contractors and major housing suppliers and manufacturers built many apartment buildings. The living space of these apartments was typically extremely small compared to owner-occupied houses. In addition, the facilities and finishes were low-grade. There was no system to respond to inhabitants' individual requests about their living space. Thus, I was quite shocked by the diverse and unique living spaces formed in the world of such apartment houses. The photographs in Mr. Tsuzuki's book show that an entire "universe" existed within a 6-tatami mat room, which is about ten square meters. Considering that such apartments were rarely discussed in the world of architecture, I could not help reflecting that architects had been indifferent to the imagination of inhabitants and the strong relationship between inhabitants and household goods, and that we had overlooked the "life" represented by such imagination and connection between inhabitants and goods.

Of course, the chance for me to start thinking that "place" is much more important than "box" was partially related to the fact that the demand for "box" had been fully met. However, in reality, I think the idea was triggered by these two photography books that seemed to ask me as follows: "Has architecture intersected with people's life philosophy?"

It seemed to me that the architecture I knew well had not actually tried to have a special relationship with people's life philosophy, even though it presented itself as dealing with the space of living. There is an example where the action of building itself became a way of life, such as "self-build", but this is a rare exception. Instead, we often find writings detailing the life philosophy by architects, but there are very few architects who talk about their work while referencing the life philosophy of their clients or the inhabitants of their buildings.

Given that enough "boxes" existed already, it was natural that the content of the "box", in other words people's life philosophy, and the "place" where that life philosophy developed, became the target of people's consideration.

## You ought to cross the life philosophy

When looking at the two photography books, I was surprised again by the diversity of people's lifestyles shown in them.

When I was in elementary school before the long summer vacation started, I remember a teacher made me plan a timetable of how to spend every day. That way I could live a regular life even though my school was on vacation. For example, "Wake up at 7 am, from 7:00 to 7:30 am: wash face, calisthenics, from 7:30 to 8:30 am: breakfast, 8:30 to 10:00: study, 10:00 to 12:00: play…".

It may be different depending on generations, but I imagine that you have had a similar experience as well. At the best, we can keep this timetable for the first day, but after the first day, we pass days that have nothing to do with the timetable. I am sure that hearing that, a similar experience comes to mind for you.

Even so, it is reported that as houses were standardized and mass production methods based on standardization developed, the daily schedule of standard adults were prepared in detail and architectural experts worked to standardize the plans of houses following the schedule.[2] This happened, for example, in the Soviet Union, one of the leading countries in home standardization, but it is not limited to the Soviet Union. In the era of mass housing in the 1950s and 1970s in many places around the world, similar standardization was promoted. Compared to children's summer vacations, it is probably easier to create a timetable for working adults, so I imagine that everyone was seriously working on standardization.

Even the marketing that became essential to Japan's commercialization of housing in the 1980s was approached in a similar way. Home manufacturers believed that the plans of houses and way of living could be proposed according to categories of people classified by their main attributes such as age, income, region, and educational background.

Regardless of standardization or commercialization, home manufacturers thought that the portion of people's lifestyle defined by the building in which they lived could be identified almost uniformly by properly classifying people. Thinking about a civil servant or a salaried worker in a modern society during an economic growth period, it may be true that there is little variation in the way people live. However, nowadays, at least in Japan, the situation is dramatically changing.

First of all, the economy is not growing. Nowadays, it is not like previous eras, where companies, which hire people right after graduation from high school or university, continue to grow and employees can continue working there until retirement age without any doubt or insecurity. The scenario where people become economically rich together with companies is a castle in the air. Further, the seniority system that guarantees planning to some extent has been pushed aside by meritocracy. It is no longer an environment where people can live to a retirement age without deeply considering their life philosophy or relying on the Japanese economy and the story of a company when making decisions. It is shifting to an era where people are required to consider and decide their own life philosophy – in other words, an era where people *can* consider and decide their lifestyle by themselves.

In addition, the super-aging society trend in Japan is continuing. Some people now live 90 or 100 years. When people become 60 years old, they have usually worked for about forty years and have another thirty to forty years to live. Moreover, as for the way to live this latter half of life, it is difficult to find a model. People must consider and decide their own life philosophy for this latter half. Put another way, people can consider and decide about the next phase of their lives on their own.

Additionally, there is another societal shift. Given the emphasis in modern society on efficiency through focusing on function, lives of people were functionally decomposed to components such as employment, learning, entertainment, sleep, rest, and meals. Different urban spaces were formed in accordance with each component. Expressions such as "office towns," "factory areas," and "residential areas" symbolize this fact. However, advances in the internet environment have opened up the possibility of working at home. For example, those who left full-time employment to start their own small business can begin working in the town where they live. Also, there is an increase in young people migrating to the countryside to engage in agriculture and forestry for the first time. In this environment, it becomes difficult to continue the approach of decomposing living space based on function.

When following the approach of functionalism, architecture must only intensively consider a specific part of life that has been isolated for that type of architecture. For example, housing is only concerned with bedtime and family relations; school with learning; offices with desk work; factories with production; hospitals with health recovery, etc. Thus, the problems to be addressed by each architectural type remain within a limited range. It is not necessary to consider people's life philosophy, which is a summary of the decomposed parts. Thus, in an era when it is not easy to decompose the lives of people based on functionalism, it is inevitable to interact with people's life philosophy when dealing with architecture. To rephrase more positively, when dealing with architecture it becomes possible to interact with people's life philosophy.

Given that people's life philosophy is considered and determined by themselves, developed over 100 years of life, and impossible to spatially divide, such philosophies are naturally diverse. It can be said that life philosophies are individualized. Beyond attempting to standardize, it is also difficult to make such philosophies the target of marketing. As Habraken once said, "You cannot design the ordinary." Someone's way of living can only be determined by that person. As a result, when trying to create a "place" that embraces people's life philosophy as contents, it is necessary for the person who uses the "place" or lives in the "place" to take initiative by himself/herself. This leads to a new phase of open architecture for the common people.

## Rich resources of space in the 21st century Japan

Enough "boxes" already exist. Such "boxes" could be used to create "places" to encompass people's life philosophy as its content, but what about the quality of the "box" itself? Doubts might be raised about the quality of existing "boxes," such as, "Aren't most 'boxes' too outdated or vulnerable, since they only meet outdated earthquake-resistance codes?" "Aren't they too small, given that many houses in Japan were once ridiculed as 'rabbit hutches'?"[3] Considering such doubts, what is the actual situation?

My conclusion is that most "boxes" currently existing in the 21st century in Japan are sufficient in terms of quality. Thus, it can be said that we should regard these "boxes" as a kind of "spatial resource" with the potential to be used in a wide variety of ways and as "places" where a new way of living can potentially develop.

First, let's begin with the question, "Aren't most 'boxes' too outdated or vulnerable, since they only meet outdated earthquake-resistance codes?" I assure you this is not the case.

Again, as an example, let's consider housing, for which we have an abundance of statistical data. The latest Housing and Land Survey (2013) by the Japanese government shows how many houses were built each year. According to the results, only slightly more than 10% of total houses were built by the year of the Osaka Expo (i.e., by 1970), when the period of high economic growth had reached its peak. Nearly 90% are relatively young "boxes" that have not passed fifty years since their construction.

There may be some people who think, "Can a 50-year-old house be considered 'young'? I have heard that the life span of a Japanese house is only about thirty years." However, in this case, the term "life span" only indicates the number of years from construction to demolition. It does not reflect the age by which a building would become unusable due to aging or deterioration. This point must not be overlooked. As the economy grew, people gained the economic power to rebuild and their demands towards housing increased. Accordingly, many buildings were demolished for reasons such as "the space is too small" or "the amenities are outdated." In these cases, the demolished buildings had not reached their physical life span. Therefore, it is misleading to use the term "life span" to refer to the number of years from construction to demolition. Semantics aside, there is no reason to treat a 40-year-old building as an "old" building close to the end of its physical life span, unless there are significant problems with its design or construction.

Let's return to the Housing and Land Survey results again. Excluding housing for which the construction year is unknown, about 70% of existing "boxes" were built after 1981. The year 1981 is when Japanese earthquake-resistance standards[4] were dramatically altered. Reflecting the change, people know to distinguish the standards by calling the previous standard the "old earthquake-resistance standard" and the standard established after 1981 the "new earthquake-resistance standard." At least 70% of "boxes" are not "vulnerable ones that only meet outdated earthquake-resistance standards." Moreover, even if a "box" was built following previous earthquake-resistance standards, if it is subjected to appropriate seismic diagnosis and required seismic reinforcement, it will not be "a vulnerable one that only satisfies the old earthquake-resistance standard." (See Figure 4.1.)

Next, let's move on to the question, "Aren't most of the 'boxes' too small, as many houses in Japan were once ridiculed as 'rabbit hutches'?" Consider that the size of households living in single-family houses continues to decrease. Therefore, "boxes," which were once too small for the typical family of four or five people, are not cramped at all for current one-person or two-person households. Indeed, it is common to find elderly residents living only on the first floor of their houses, hardly using the second floor with rooms once used for children's bedrooms. Given that cleaning is a major task, there is increased demand to rebuild such houses into smaller homes. In fact on average, the size of existing "boxes" is comparable to the size of newly built "boxes."

For example, according to construction statistics announced by the Japanese government, the average total floor area of houses constructed in 2015 is 82.5 $m^2$ (122.9 $m^2$ for owner-occupied houses[5], 48.4 $m^2$ for rented houses). On the other hand, the total floor area of houses built

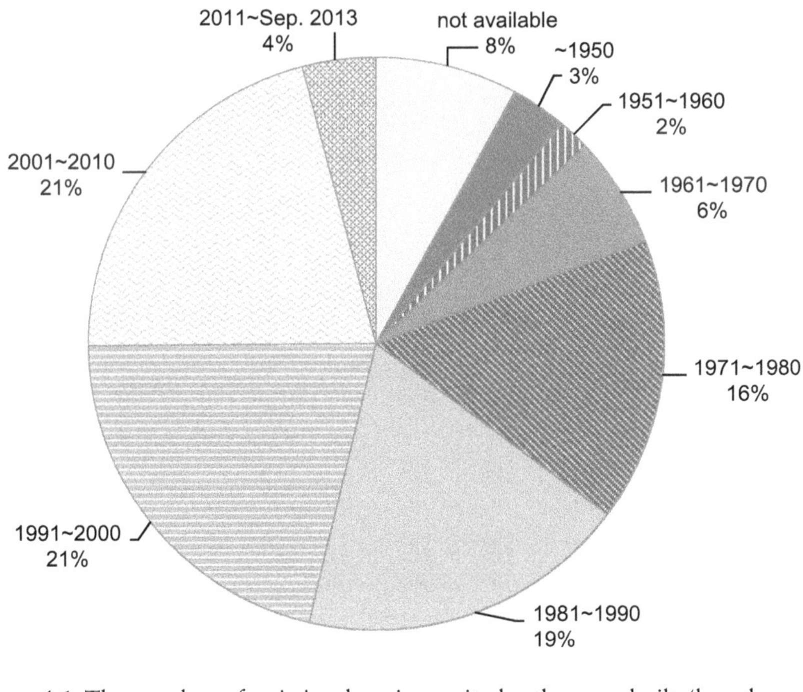


*Figure 4.1* The number of existing housing units by the year built (based on data from the Ministry of International Affairs and Communications)

thirty-five years ago in 1980 is 93.9 m$^2$ (119.4 m$^2$ for owner-occupied houses, 57.0 m$^2$ for rented houses), which is larger than homes built in 2015 on average. Thirty-five years ago, people were building larger houses. People, like myself who lived during the period of high economic growth, tend to assume that the size of newly built houses has increased year by year, but there is no such trend, at least in the past thirty-five years since I graduated from university. (See Figure 4.2.)

To summarize, currently Japan is a "country with abundant spatial resources." So let's not hesitate to tailor such spatial resources, which are abundant and do not have any major deficiencies in quality, into "places" for a quality life. We are living in the moment, when we can say this confidently.

## The frontier opened up by artists

As a surplus of "boxes" emerges, what is the incentive to seize such "boxes" as an available spatial resource and make them into new "places"? I think the economically low barrier associated with utilizing existing boxes is likely the most significant factor.

Around the beginning of the 21st century, I established the Research Team on Conversion (referring to changing the use of buildings) with many of my colleagues in the architectural world. (The official name is the

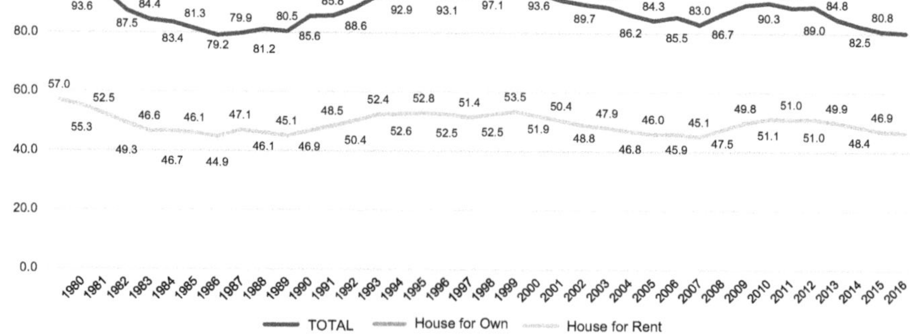


*Figure 4.2* The change in average total floor area of newly built housing units (based on data from the Ministry of Land, Infrastructure, Construction, and Tourism)

"Research Team on Effective Utilization of Urban Space through Building Conversion Technologies.") During that period, the so-called "2003 issue" was a major concern in metropolitan areas. The "2003 issue" was a pessimistic expectation that in 2003, when the redevelopments taking place in Roppongi[6] and Shiodome[7] were completed, the large supply of new office space would result in higher vacancy rates of office buildings, especially in old and relatively inconvenient locations. Indeed, even when we organized the Research Team on Conversion[8] in 2001, the vacancy rate of the office buildings was already on the rise. Therefore, based on our idea to change vacant offices into houses, one purpose of the research team was to devise a way to eliminate legal barriers and reduce technical obstacles involved in such conversions. (See Figure 4.3.)

There are various laws and regulations related to the operation, as well as the construction of new buildings. Many regulations set different requirements depending on the use of the building, for example, as an

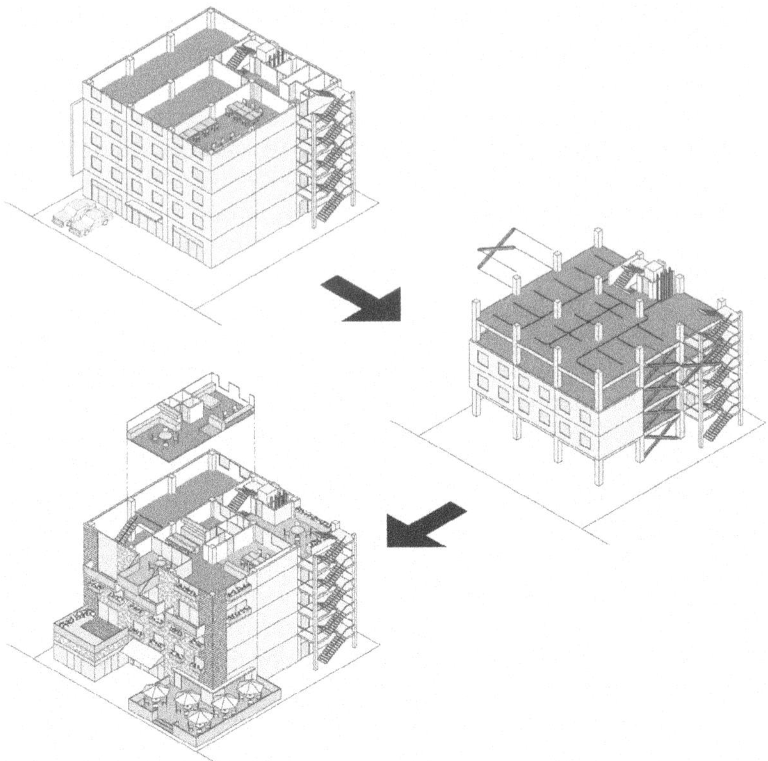

*Figure 4.3* An image showing the conversion of "Offices into Flats" by the Research Team on Conversion in 2001

office, house, or hotel. This is the case with the Building Standards Law and the Fire Protection Law. Thus, from a legal standpoint, it is not easy to change the use of a building. As for technical challenges, since the industry formed with a focus on new construction, the technology to renovate existing buildings was not sufficiently developed or available. Therefore, we decided to tackle it ourselves.

Initially, the purpose of this conversion research was explained in the context of developing ways to make housing more sustainable, especially by breaking away from the easy model of scrap-and-build and avoiding the creation of unnecessary waste. However, I personally considered the purpose of the research to be creating a new form of housing that could replace rental wooden low-rise apartment buildings and maintain the vitality of major cities like Tokyo.

Since the high economic growth period, it was typical for young people who moved from the countryside to major cities to live in rental wooden low-rise apartment buildings. In fact, I was also one of those young people. Such apartments appealed to young people because the apartments were abundant and generally located in relatively convenient areas, yet available at affordable rents due to being small and offering only low quality amenities. In my opinion, rental wooden low-rise apartments played a major role in Japanese architectural history by providing far more living space for low-income people than government-established public housing. These apartments were one of the leaders of modern Japan. However, rental wooden low-rise apartment buildings, the only affordable housing option for young people moving to large cities, began rapidly disappearing from relatively desirable areas. Instead, such apartments were replaced by high-rise non-wooden apartments. Considering that the vitality of major cities like Tokyo is fueled by welcoming low-income young people with hope, talent, and ambition from outside the city, why on earth would we allow the places that house such people to disappear? I simply could not understand it. Therefore, I hoped that converting empty offices into homes without spending too much money could provide an affordable housing option, like the rental wooden low-rise apartment buildings.

In that respect, the pioneering trend of converting warehouses, factories, and light-industry offices into ateliers and dwellings, which occurred in the SOHO district of New York[9] in the 1960s and 1970s, was a very encouraging example. The people driving the trend were young artists who came to New York with confidence in their talent and needed space for their creative activities, but could not live in a decent apartment or afford an atelier on their low income.

As I mentioned before, since the content that is part of creating a "place" is an indication of a person's life philosophy, the creative activities of young artists can also be seen as their way of life. Such artists are different from modern employees, who clearly distinguish between "life" and "work." Artists do not have clear boundaries between activities of "life," "play," and "work." The activities are all combined together as "living" or "life." It seemed natural that such artists would take the lead in changing "boxes" into "places."

In affordable spaces with potential room to expand, young artists could create new lives in which "life," "play," and "work" existed together in complete harmony. This phenomenon had already begun to occur in Japan around 2004, when our conversion research came to an end.

There are many examples but let me introduce only one, the case of Mr. Yasuhiro Hoshina, who resigned from a city planning office to become a textile dyeing artist in Niigata. At the beginning, he started his work in an apartment in Niigata, but he struggled because it was difficult to fit several tanks for dyeing in the small apartment. That reminded him of a coastal settlement that he had previously visited to conduct a community survey when he was a student. He recalled that in the village which had remaining folk houses with thatched roofs, there were empty, unused houses. Of course, such empty houses were not listed on the real estate market. He visited the elder leader of the settlement many times and finally succeeded in borrowing a property with three buildings and a garden. Mr. Hoshina's

*Figure 4.4* Mr. Hoshina's House at Echizen Hama in Niigata Prefecture. Sometimes Mr. and Mrs. Hoshina hold workshops with their artist friends at home. Source: Mr. Yasuhiro Hoshina

enthusiasm and charisma were felt by the community, and he was able to become a member of the village. The monthly rent for the buildings was about 10,000 yen per month. In a once uninhabited "box," Mr. Hoshina's rich way of living is now firmly planted. (See Figure 4.4.)

The elderly people in the neighborhood visit Mr. Hoshina's house every day with gifts of vegetables and fruits. Often, he is asked to help with tasks such as heavy physical work. At that time, Mr. Hoshina stops his dyeing work and casually goes over to help. The year after he started living there, he was nominated as the cultural director of the village and began to work hard on the planning and implementation of events that visitors from outside the village came to enjoy. Mr. Hoshina's friends in Niigata who visit his house are also attracted by the richness of his village life, which cannot be experienced in the city. One friend after another have been moving to vacant houses in the village. It was not only artists who followed Mr. Hoshina. There are civil servants and salaried workers. Mr. Hoshina's story is no longer just the story of one vacant house. The space of the settlement formed by multiple buildings and people's activities has been rediscovered as a resource and the area is slowly being redeveloped as a "place" for living by young people.

## The creativity of users in using existing space

Constructing "boxes" requires expert knowledge and technology. Even when considering only the physical aspects of "boxes," we need knowledge and technology from a wide variety of fields, including knowledge and technology related to foundations and ground, building structures to bear loads from wind and earthquakes, drainage and waterproofing to protect the interior space from rain, fire prevention and fire resistance to prevent the spread of fire, maintenance of a stable indoor temperature environment by controlling influences from the unstable temperature and humidity of outside air, provision of moderate ventilation, durability of various construction materials plus their future improvement and maintenance, health effects of these construction materials, water supply and drainage equipment including the kitchen, toilet, washbasins, bathtub, water heaters, and piping, electrical power and communications systems, air conditioning equipment including heat pumps, ventilation equipment, and ducts, and the future deconstruction, recycling, and reuse of building materials. In addition, it is critical to consider knowledge and technology describing the relationship between aspects of the architectural space, including size, color, and arrangement, and human behavior and perceptions of the space. Of course, we must have knowledge of law and history, as well as knowledge of other topics such as contracts, procurement, and the division of labor in the "box delivery industry." Departments of architecture at universities have tried to accommodate all these kinds of knowledge and technology into their crowded curricula. These areas of knowledge and technology are generally required for the examination to become a Licensed Architect and Building Engineer.[10]

In contrast, what kind of knowledge and technology are needed when using existing "boxes" to create "places"? Expert knowledge and technology related to building "boxes" is required when judging whether an existing "box" possesses sufficient quality or requires repair, or when an existing "box" needs to be renovated to set up a new "place." However, there are many instances where creating "places" can occur without renovating or repairing "boxes." Expert knowledge and technology related to architecture and building have occupied a major position in building "boxes" but are not so essential in the creation of "places" and thus become less of a concern.

The main position in the creation of "place" is not occupied by conventional architectural knowledge and technology but instead by users freely imagining what kind of "place" of living can be created through utilizing a "box." I call this imagination "users' creativity in using existing space" and consider it the core of the future "place-making industry." I think that it is an era in which we expect more from users with creativity rather than experts with knowledge and technological expertise.

When hearing "users' creativity in using existing space," you may recall the use of one-room apartments as shown in the previously mentioned *Universe for Rent* by Mr. Kyoichi Tsuzuki, or Mr. Hoshina's use of a vacant house as introduced in the previous section. However, the size of the target space is not limited. In addition, it is not necessarily the case that only one person becomes the user exerting his or her creativity on the space. It depends on what kind of "place" of living is imagined.

In 2005, just after the conversion research project ended, I had the opportunity to visit a stunning example of conversion in Medellin, Colombia, South America. A huge ruin, about 100 years old, was converted into a "place" of living for economically disadvantaged children and adults. The building, facing a plaza in the center of the town, had been left vacant for many years and become a desolate and dangerous place. Nearby, there was a residential area for low-income people. So an after-school "place" where children could enjoy playing, learning, and interacting with adults was needed. A local NPO serving the community[11] developed "ideas for use" incorporating vague individual demands from the residents. Today, the huge former ruin, the present name of which is Comfama de Aranjuez, is full of vibrancy as a "place" of living for local residents, primarily children.

The facility includes a variety of loosely connected "places," such as a gymnasium and pool where children can play vigorously, a room with publicly available computers for people who do not have access to a computer at home, a corner to provide counseling to pregnant teenagers, and a vocational training facility for unemployed parents. Among the facilities offered, the library impressed me the most.

Although it is quite a large space, the number of books was smaller than I expected. A young man, who told me that he was responsible for setting up and operating this "place," guided me. Like many other young men in the district, he used to be involved with dangerous activities when he was a teenager. Now he proudly explained the importance of the library for people like him in English, saying, "Of course, we have only a small number of books and our collection is not systematic but it is important for children to have books. Children can learn to read and write at school, but they do not have books, a newspaper, or anything to read at home. They have no opportunity at home to apply the reading and writing skills learned at school. However, when they come here, they have such an opportunity. Here, they learn that reading and writing enable them to discover a whole new world. Don't you think this is a wonderful place?" (See Figure 4.5.)

I was touched by his words, which reminded me of the fundamental core of the library as a "place." At the Department of Architecture, I also learned about the planning of libraries, but unfortunately, I do not remember learning about the library as a "place" so deeply connected to real life. I feel I only learned the established system of planning.

"Users' creativity in using existing space" has the power to change a big "box" into a new "place" of living. Actually, a "place," which I am involved with[12] and which I still use frequently, provides one such example. It is "Arts Chiyoda 3331" in Chiyoda Ward of Tokyo. The project transformed a junior high school building with one underground floor and three above-ground floors, which had been closed for almost five years, into an art center with event venues, galleries, small offices, and cafes. It opened in 2010, and in 2013, just three years later, it had become an open "place" of living with as many as 800,000 visitors.

Creation of this "place" was thanks to the creativity of Mr. Masato Nakamura, an artist who continues to play a key role in the facility's management. At the time, Mr. Nakamura was considering the idea of establishing a "place," like an art center where young artists in Japan could gather, exchange, and spread their work to the world. In particular, he was interested in the area between Ueno,[13] which had been the center of the arts since the Meiji Era, and Akihabara,[14] which acquired remarkable recognition for the influence of its creative output on the world. Mr. Nakamura ended up hearing about the closed junior high school, which is located in this area. Since his "ideas for use" were already developed, the project to convert the closed school into an art center quickly proceeded after this fortunate discovery.

In the examples from Medellin and Chiyoda Ward, the existing "boxes" underwent fairly significant renovation. Thus of course, knowledge and technological expertise from architects and general contractors in the "box delivery industry" were part of both projects. However, without "the users' creativity in using existing space" it is likely nothing would have happened.

*Figure 4.5* The library of Comfama de Aranjuez in Medellin

## New trends of migrating to local areas

The migration of people to vacant houses in the country provides another typical setting in which "user's creativity in using existing space" emerges, for example, the previously mentioned case of the artist Mr. Hoshina in Niigata. Migration to the countryside is becoming more and more popular among young people. Such migration can be said to represent their life philosophy. This can be clearly understood by visiting various websites prepared by local governments, which encourage relocation from metropolitan areas.

For example, let me introduce "HIROBIRO Hiroshima Migration Support Media" (www.hiroshima-hirobiro.jp/) operated by Hiroshima Prefecture[15] Regional Force Creation Division and "Hiroshima Living Support Center." The website shows photographs introducing the lives of many people who moved to Hiroshima. Here, Mr. M (Kyoto Prefecture → Hiroshima Prefecture) said: "Since I started to choose my life by myself and walk with my own feet, my world has changed." Mr. N (Tokyo → Hiroshima Prefecture) said: "I took up a new course of life after resigning from being a bureaucrat of the central government. The opportunity to make your life shine does not decrease while you are in the countryside." "Mr. and Mrs. K (Spain/Tokyo → Hiroshima Prefecture): We are a Spanish and Japanese couple, who met in Italy and renovated several 150-year old houses to start a café/bakery. Our commitment to food, as well as artistic and international initiatives, are spreading within and outside the region."

According to the "Hometown Migration Support Center" (an NPO connecting city residents who want to relocate to the country to start a new life with local governments nationwide), the number of inquiries and visitors to the Center in Tokyo increases every year. The number exceeded 20,000 annual visitors in 2015. When the NPO was founded in 2002, it seemed that it was intended to support baby-boomers relocating to the countryside, but now the situation has completely changed. Of the Center's users in 2015, those in their sixties and older accounted for only 16%, about the same percentage of those in their twenties. In contrast, those in their thirties and forties had significantly increased year by year, and when those groups were combined, accounted for over 50% of yearly visitors. (See Figure 4.6.) In addition, the Center asked visitors and seminar participants in Tokyo where they would like to move. The top ten locations in 2015 were Nagano, Yamanashi, Shimane, Shizuoka, Okayama, Hiroshima, Kochi, Akita, Oita, and Miyazaki. Surprisingly, the prefectures of Western Japan far from major metropolitan areas occupied more than half of the top ten.

According to the Center, interest from younger generations clearly increased after the financial crisis in 2008. Further, the prefectures of Western Japan started to rank in the top ten of desirable places to move, after the nuclear power plant accident in 2011.[16] In other words, events that made people rethink their life philosophy appear related to the increase in migration.

According to the explanation of Mr. Kazuo Kasami, Deputy Secretary General of the Center, interest in relocating to rural areas has changed to also include a focus on different ways of working. Mr. Kasami said, "Those who wish to come to the countryside for living quietly and comfortably free from worldly cares account for only 18% of total inquiries. Instead, the number of people who wish to start their own business if

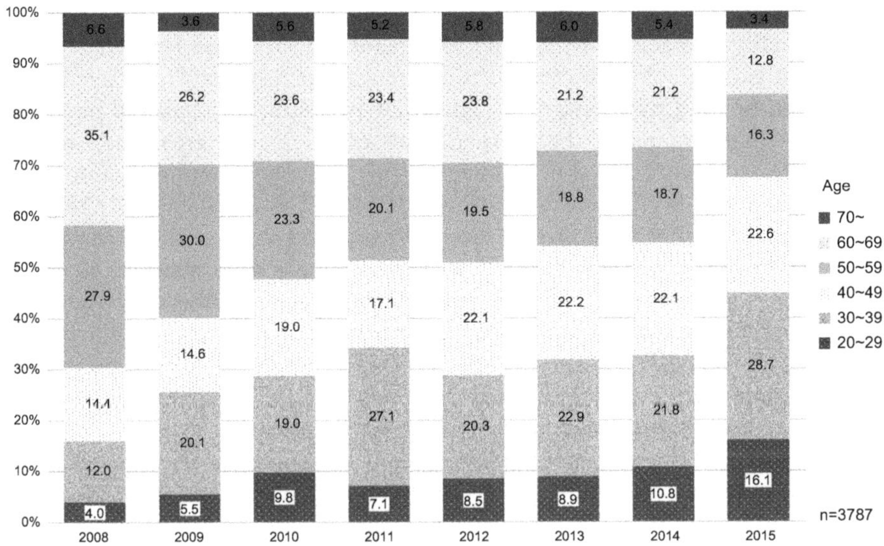


*Figure 4.6* Change in the age of users of "Hometown Migration Support Center"

there are no job opportunities, or who prefer to spend time doing what they really want to do, while pursuing agriculture, rather than to slaving away at a job to earn a living has gradually increased. The first requirement for a relocation site that people mention is 'a nice natural environment,' and now the second is 'job opportunities'."

Efforts to create a new "place" of work through migration are now seen in various parts of Japan. A typical example is the town of Kamiyama[17] in Tokushima Prefecture, which became famous for the trial relocation of Consumer Affairs Agency of the central government in the spring of 2016. In a town, which had been suffering from years of depopulation, new establishments such as an IT company office, a bakery, and Italian restaurants are now located in vacant houses one after another. The main organizer of this movement is the NPO "Green Valley," which has operated the Kamiyama Town Migration Exchange Support Center since 2007. The basic policy of the NPO's former President Nobuya Ohminami is as follows.

"Around 2008, I came up with and began to use the term 'creative depopulation.' In short, it means that we should think about the content rather than being preoccupied with the extent of population decline." Also he explained the originality of their way.

"Although various policies focused on promoting agriculture and forestry have been implemented, there are not many success stories. Instead, I think that if a depopulating town becomes a region which supports diverse work styles, we may be able to form a new region that does not rely solely on agriculture and forestry."

Specifically, residents of the town designate a desired use for each vacant house, for example "this building should be used as a bakery" or "this building should be used by a designer." Then new migrants are recruited based on these designations. Since there are no job offers in the area, they recruit people who already have skills and jobs. This strategy essentially came from reverse thinking. A characteristic effort is a project in 2010 called "Office in Kamiyama." At that time, artists were already frequently visiting the town. As a next step, the town wanted to invite people who worked in fields between art and business, such as video artists, photographers, and graphic designers. They converted a vacant house into an office where such people could stay inexpensively. By creating a "place" for work which previously had no connection to Kamiyama Town, it attracted new residents, who could continue to work while living in the town. (See Figure 4.7.)

The existence of abundant space resources in Japan makes it possible for people to discover a new life philosophy through migration. This phenomenon has the possibility to significantly develop in Japan, especially in the 21st century.

*Figure 4.7* An old house converted into a company's office in Kamiyama (PLAT EASE Corporation). Source: Professor Kouichi Sato

## The life philosophy of "higher quality of life with less living cost"

In 2013, I visited the "Hayakawa Warehouse," an old warehouse turned into an event space, in a town in Kumamoto Prefecture.[18] Afterwards, I visited a quiet old townhouse where a couple was living while remodeling the house by themselves. When I visited, the couple, who moved from a metropolitan area, had been working hard on tasks such as repairing the underfloor and adding insulation to the walls. When they took a break, I exchanged business cards with the couple, Mr. Ikeda and Ms. Ito. I heard that Mr. Ikeda was a website designer and Ms. Itoh was a photographer, but the title on Ms. Ito's business card was "lifestyle adventurer." The title captured their quest on an "adventure" to discover a new lifestyle. The perspective struck me as extremely interesting.

I came back to Tokyo, and later, invited Mr. Ikeda to be a panelist in a symposium. His presentation was wonderful. I was impressed by his clear presentation explaining their passion and appealing practices to live a new lifestyle different from conventional ones, such as the lifestyle of a typical office worker. In particular, I was deeply moved by the term "higher quality of life with less living cost," which described one goal of their lifestyle.

"Higher quality of life with less living cost." From the perspective of their parents' generation (i.e., the baby-boomer generation), the couple's life may appear impoverished and inconvenient, in other words, "a poor quality life that can only spend less living cost." However, Mr. Ikeda said they were enjoying a "higher quality of life." They could work on the renovation of their townhouse at their own pace with occasional support from friends and enjoy the local food. Plus, they could still field job requests from the metropolitan area as before through the internet, but they did not have to be as busy as when they were living in the city.

In response to a question from someone in his parents' generation – "Your lifestyle may be fine for now but what about the future?" – Mr. Ikeda responded harshly. "Your generation lived during a period of societal growth. Thus, you could live day by day without seriously worrying about your life and without concern about your pension. In comparison, our generation has to think more about our lifestyle, since we are living in an era in which we cannot predict the future of society. Don't worry about us."

No doubt, he was describing exactly the situation of his generation. After much consideration, Mr. Ikeda came to the conclusion to pursue "Higher quality of life with less living cost."

I also heard something similar from Mr. Kasami at the Hometown Migration Support Center. He told me that young migrants have a new lifestyle called "multiple jobs." The concept is similar to the "half-farming half-something" lifestyle. Since it is difficult to immediately earn enough from one job after migrating to the area, the approach of "multiple jobs" is a realistic way to earn enough for living by working multiple jobs within one's ability. According to Mr. Kasami, the exact circumstances depend on where you live, but given that food is relatively inexpensive, if you have five different jobs each paying about 50,000 yen a month[19] (e.g., 50,000 yen from agriculture, 50,000 yen from working at a cafe, and 50,000 yen from teaching how to use a computer and internet to local elderly people), you can live comfortably enough.

The "Higher quality of life with less living cost" lifestyle seems sufficiently realistic to achieve. It is not an overstatement to say that the environment of modern Japan with its rich spatial resources offers vast opportunity for such "adventure."

## Necessary soft bonds among weak individuals

Even in Japanese, we use the English loanword "renovation"[20] to refer to the process of altering existing spatial resources and transforming them into new places to live and work. In many cases, the idea at the core of renovation is not related to architectural space, but rather is about everyday living and working in towns. Without a sense of imagination from the user or openness to the real possibility of such a project, the concept of renovation cannot be interesting or become feasible. One advantage of renovation over new construction is that there are already buildings to guide the user. Even if you are not an expert in architecture, you can find a way to get started.

In renovation, we can see a phenomenon where the world of Architecture, once closed off by experts, has opened to users. We can expect renovation to pioneer an era of "open architecture for the people," which is significantly different from the past. I feel this is the fresh contribution of renovation to the Japanese architectural world.

For example, there is an interesting case where a real estate owner demonstrated his creativity. Mr. Jun Aoki of Mame-kurashi Ltd. transformed a rental apartment building with high vacancy rates into an apartment building so popular that it even had a waiting list of hopeful future inhabitants. He achieved this by introducing the option of semi-customized apartments,[21] which allowed tenants to freely choose wall treatments, and of build-out apartments, which allowed tenants to renovate the apartment.

Within architecture ever since the 1970s, architects have aspired to create a rental apartment house, where residents could renovate their apartment freely. In particular, we have frequently discussed the theory and application of SI (support and infill) housing based on Habraken's thought and method. However, hardly any of those applications made it beyond the experimental stage. Remarkably, Mr. Aoki realized a goal that had been pursued for a long time by architects.

So why did Mr. Aoki start such a business? Mr. Aoki said that he came up with this rental system while reviewing his own business model of a real estate owner. The reason why he decided to review such a business model was "NYC, London, Paris & TOKYO rental housing life survey seeking for a loving rental housing"(2010) compiled by Mr. Manjyo Shimahara and his colleague at Recruit Holdings Co.,Ltd.[22]

The report started with a quote from the inspiring texts of Antoine de Saint-Exupéry, "It's the time you spend on your rose that makes your rose so important." Reading this, Mr. Aoki asked himself, "As the owner of this rental apartment, do I love this building? Do the inhabitants love this building?" Then he began to explore a transformation of his apartment building from a "boring rental apartment building" into a "loved rental apartment building." He reached an approach in which inhabitants could actively participate in the process of customizing their space with the full support of the owner. The customization process, which involves intensive communications over materials and construction, encouraged active interaction among neighbors in the apartment building. The relationships which developed among neighbors gave the apartment an additional charm.

In Mr. Aoki's apartment building, renovation of the apartments is achieved by the do-it-yourself efforts of the inhabitants with construction help from neighboring inhabitants. Inhabitants, who become familiar with each other during the construction process, regularly hold a casual party at the outdoor terrace cleverly prepared by Mr. Aoki. Interest in living in the building has developed from friends of inhabitants who attended parties at the apartment, as well as from outsiders, who saw social media posts made by inhabitants. The inhabitants can get to know who lives in the apartment building. Plus the inhabitants and the owner can become friends. This is the building's value as a "place," which is not seen in apartment buildings such as studio apartment buildings where inhabitants rarely communicate. The value of the community created directly leads to a reduction in the vacancy rate and improvement of business performance.

Previously, I talked with Ms. Yuko Nishikawa, a specialist in French literature and author of many books on homes and families, such as the "*History of Literature of Rented Houses and Owner-occupied Houses*" (Saniseido, 1998). I appreciated her idea that given the current situation where one-person households are increasing, loose bonds connecting such "weak individuals" are needed in future living spaces. Mr. Aoki's semi-customized apartments, as well as the shared residences rapidly increasing in metropolitan areas in the last five years, are exactly the new "places" of life that foster such bonds.

Similar to the migration movement of the 21st century, this phenomenon offers the hope that architecture can become a space resource, which is open to people and deeply connected with their life philosophy.

## The freedom of an empty lot

In conventional architectural design, architects carefully think about what activity will occur in the constructed "boxes", for example, "this is a music room, this is a science research room, a staff room, an auditorium ..." and so forth. It is the essence of architectural design to properly plan a room based on what activity will occur there, such as considering the width and depth of the room, the height of the ceiling, the position and size of the windows, the opening and closing method of the windows, the finishing materials and details of each part, the facilities to be installed and their locations, and the like. However, unless the space is used by users exactly as planned, it is meaningless for architects to specially design for each expected use such as music rooms, science research rooms, staff rooms, or auditoriums. This is a serious challenge when constructing new buildings. If a space will not be used as designed, one cannot know the meaning of architectural design.

However, when creating a new "place" for living using vacant "boxes", the situation is different. First of all, vacant buildings and vacant houses are not in use because they are no longer needed for the purpose for which they were originally designed. The essence of creating a "place" as described in this book relies on drawing out the possibilities of a dormant spatial resource under the initial architectural plan of use by users' creativity in using the existing space. This should not be surprising since people's way of living has changed from lifestyles when the building was first constructed. In addition, there is freedom of people and users unconstrained by the intention of the designer.

This freedom is demonstrated in many cases of renovation, but I will introduce just one illustrative example. Like Mr. Aoki of the semi-customized apartment introduced above, Mr. Katsumi Yoshihara[23], an owner of rental apartment buildings, revived his real estate lease business by converting one of his apartment buildings whose vacancy rate had been increasing into a new "place" of living. Mr. Yoshihara established new possibilities for life and work in his rental apartment building, built more than fifty years ago in Fukuoka City,[24] by creating the "Renovation Museum 'Reizensou,'" a "place" where people gathered. Previously the building was an ordinary mid-rise apartment building with similar-sized apartments. Now there is a café selling bagels, a Korean restaurant, a shared office, and more. (See Figure 4.8.) There is also an odd "building manager room" filled with the favorite items of Mr. Sugiyama, who calls himself the "building manager," and a table tennis room, which inhabitants can freely use. How the space resources are being used has developed beyond what the designer originally considered during construction. Considering such examples, the word "freedom" naturally comes to mind for people.

In 2004, during the period when I was promoting conversion research with my colleagues, I received the book *Harappa to Yuenchi* (*Fields and Amusement Parks*) (Ohkokusha, 2004) from the author Jun Aoki[25]. He is an architect and one of my university classmates. The book explained his goal to create architecture like fields without any predetermined use, rather than architecture like amusement parks where the use is already clear. For an architect like Jun Aoki, he wanted to create new architecture

*Figure 4.8* Reizensou of Yoshihara Jutaku in Fukuoka City. Source: Yoshihara Jutaku Limited Company

in the image of a field. For me, any new architecture felt like an "amusement park," while existing spatial resources that underwent renovation like Reizensou seemed like "fields." However, learning that even a classmate like Aoki, who followed a different post-graduation career path, could reach the same conclusion that "fields" are better than "amusement parks," I felt we had reached an era of deeply shared values.

Whatever the case, "fields vs. amusement parks" is an evocative metaphor. The nickname "freedom of a 'field'" nicely captures the user's freedom seen in the process of renovation, through which abundant spatial resources are made into new "places" of living.

If architecture in the 20th century focused first on building amusement parks in various places and then letting each of those amusement parks have their own characteristics, the fact that now we are in an era in which people are looking towards the freedom of "the field" suggests that we have entered a new phase of open architecture for the people.

## The appearance of a new generation

There is another phenomenon, which also made me feel that we had entered a new phase of open architecture for the people. It is the immense popularity of do-it-yourself carpentry and do-it-yourself renovation.

Due to the size and complexity of a building, it is quite difficult to immediately tackle do-it-yourself carpentry at the time of new construction. It is not something that everyone can do. On the other hand, when renovating existing houses, I thought that do-it-yourself carpentry could be enjoyed relatively easily. However, at that time in the 1990s, do-it-yourself carpentry was not prevalent in Japan. I requested a research survey from my friend in the United States, where do-it-yourself carpentry culture had completely taken root. The survey showed how material distribution for do-it-yourself carpentry had developed in the United States of America. My friend requested that I read the report while recognizing the following point. Americans not only renovate their houses with do-it-yourself carpentry, but also do other tasks that Japanese people generally hire someone to do, such as creating complicated documentation related to reporting to government offices, caring for large gardens, and repairing their own cars. Thus, having this do-it-yourself attitude towards an entire life enables do-it-yourself carpentry for home renovation. Considering that Japanese generally leave car repairs to professionals, do-it-yourself would not become popular only in the area of housing. He said that I needed to bear that in mind. I agreed, and thought that do-it-yourself carpentry in renovation of housing would likely not become prevalent in Japan.

Since then more than ten years have passed and when I checked the world of renovation, do-it-yourself carpentry (called "do-it-yourself renovation") was booming. Indeed, in 2015 when I met Mr. Yoshihara, he told me, "in Fukuoka now, even rental apartment buildings, which are a little old and whose vacancy rate have remained high but which allow 'do-it-yourself renovation,' are so popular that people have to wait to live there. Do-it-yourself renovation is trendy and the supply cannot catch up with demand."

In 2015, I also learned of the emerging trend of "charismatic females in do-it-yourself carpentry." Ms. Mari Kume is a representative of the movement. I met her at the 8th Kitakyushu Renovation School[26] event held in 2015. At the time, I was not aware of her popularity. However, at the after party, a manager of a major general contractor's design department mentioned, "I decided to take the do-it-yourself renovation class, since Ms. Mari Kume was teaching." When I confessed, "I am sorry but I do not know Ms. Kume," not only the manager but also other people around me told me about her skill and excellent attention to details. Ms. Mari Kume made the decision to spend her limited living budget on building materials rather than cosmetics. She then she has devised various methods of detailed do-it-yourself renovations, which still managed to meet the requirement of many leases to "return the apartment to its original state."[27] I was surprised that a seemingly ordinary young lady like Ms. Mari Kumi could impress even a veteran designer to say, "Ms. Mari Kume is extremely skilled with details." It seemed that do-it-yourself carpentry was no longer the specialized hobby of middle-aged men with confidence in their renovation skills.

Today, the environment for ordinary people to work on do-it-yourself renovation has developed remarkably. Large do-it-yourself stores, once only common in the United States, now exist in many places in Japan. Like a "toolbox"[28] operated by R Real Estate,[29] an online select shop handling building materials for do-it-yourself renovation also emerged. Information on the practices and enjoyment of do-it-yourself renovation is also spread through social media.

The do-it-yourself renovation phenomenon, in which users take the responsibility of caring for spatial resources and find enjoyment in creating "places," symbolizes the new phase of open architecture for the people. Diffusion of building material distribution through do-it-yourself stores and the formation of collective intelligence through the internet has made it possible. And if a subject which users take initiative to change, or the users' interest is expanding from the interior of their room to their town as a "place" of their living, it can be said that finally we are living in the era of "open architecture for the people."

## Notes

1 Wooden rental apartment buildings built in Japan, mainly in urban areas. Many are two to three stories high. In most cases, the toilet, kitchen, and foyer were not in each room but shared among inhabitants. Often there are no bathing facilities in the whole building. In that case, inhabitants use the public bath in the town. In many cases, each dwelling unit is narrow, around 6 tatami mats in size (about ten square meters). Generally, rent is cheaper than other rental apartments.

2 Hironori Matsubara, "Research on the Transformation of Technology and Façade Expression in Large Panel Flats in Moscow," Master's Thesis at the University of Tokyo, Graduate School of Engineering, Department of Architecture (Collection of the University of Tokyo), 1997.

3 "*cage a lapins*" originally in French.

4 In earthquake-prone Japan, a major portion of the country's Building Standard Law is concerned with earthquake-resistance standards. In June 1981, earthquake-resistance standards were amended dramatically to be more stringent. Therefore, the necessity of earthquake-resistance diagnosis and earthquake-resistance reinforcement is pointed out especially for buildings built according to older standards utilized before June 1981.

5 Such residences were registered as owner-occupied houses at the time of construction. However, after completion, the homes may be used as rented houses.

6 Place name in central Tokyo.

7 Place name in central Tokyo. Prior to 1980 there was a cargo exclusive station, but after that it was redeveloped and is now a district with many super high-rise buildings.

8 From April 2001 to March 2004, this research team received "Subsidies for Industry-Academia-Government Cooperative Innovation Projects" from the Ministry of Education, Culture, Sports, Science and Technology. The author was the research representative and about forty university and corporate researchers composed the team.

9 A representative book dealing with what happened in this area is Sharon Zukin's "Loft Living: Culture and Capital in Urban Change, USA," Johns Hopkins University Press, 1982.

10 In order to contribute to the improvement of the quality of buildings, it was stipulated as a national qualification based on the Act on Architects and Building Engineers (May 24, 1950). There are various categories of licenses, such as First-Class and Second-Class Building Architect and Building Engineer, as well as Wooden Building licenses. To be qualified, an individual must pass each required examination.
11 The NPO's name is COMFAMA.
12 The author is a member of "Kusunokikai," which supports Arts Chiyoda 3331's activities.
13 Place name in central Tokyo.
14 Place name in central Tokyo. It is famous as the center of geek ("otaku") culture.
15 One of the forty-seven prefectures. Located in the western part of Japan.
16 The accident occurred in Fukushima Prefecture in the Tohoku region, due to the 2011 Great East Japan Earthquake.
17 A typical Japanese country town, located in the south of Tokushima City in Tokushima prefecture with a population of over 6,000 people.
18 A prefecture located in the western part of Japan on the island of Kyushu.
19 In 2016, the average monthly income for Japanese people was approximately 350,000 yen.
20 In Japan, the pronunciation of foreign languages is often replaced directly with Japanese syllabary notation; however, the words are often used with a different meaning from the word's meaning in the original foreign language. "Renovation" is used with almost the same meaning.
21 In previous rental housing, inhabitants could not even choose wall treatments, but around 2010, when more flexible rental flats gradually began to appear, this term began to be used for the first time.
22 A Japanese company engaged in services such as recruitment advertisement, temporary staffing, sales promotion.
23 The President of Yoshihara Housing limited company, which manages multiple rental apartment buildings in Fukuoka city.
24 It is the largest city in Kyushu with a population of more than 1.5 million people.
25 1956–present. After graduating from the University of Tokyo, he worked as an architect at Arata Isozaki Atelier and then began practicing independently. An architect representing this generation of Japan.
26 The Kitakyushu Renovation School, which pioneered the move to change the town by renovating vacant buildings and vacant houses and promoting new uses, began in 2011. The eighth meeting was held in 2015.
27 The obligation that the lessor of the room or the building should return the object to the lender at the end of the contract by returning the object to the state at the time of signing the contract.
28 A site that selects or develops building parts and building materials that can be used for renovation and sells them on the internet.
29 A company that manages a site that mediates vacant houses and vacant buildings on the internet. It has been in operation since 2004.

## Bibliography

Aoki, Jun, *Harappa to Yuenchi (Fields and Amusement Parks)*, Ohkokusha, 2004

Habraken, N. J., *Supports – An Alternative to Mass Housing*, Architectural Press, 1972

Habraken, N. J., *The Structure of the Ordinary*, The MIT Press, 1998

Ito, Teiji and Futagawa, Yukio, *Nihon no Minka (Japanese Folk Houses)*, Bijutsu Shuppan-Sha, 1957–1959

Japan Housing Corporation, *Nihon Jyutaku Kodan 20 Nenshi (The 20 Years of Japan Housing Corporation)*, Japan Housing Corporation, 1975

Material World, *A Global Family Portrait*, Counterpoint, 1994 (Japanese version published by TOTO Publishing, 1994)

Matsubara, Hironori, *Moscow no Ohgata Panel Kouhou Jyutaku ni Okeru Gijyutsu to Gaikan Hyougen no Henyou ni Kansuru Kenkyu (Research on the Transformation of Technology and Façade Expression in Large Panel Flats in Moscow)*, Master's Thesis at the University of Tokyo, Graduate School of Engineering, Department of Architecture, 1997

Matsumura, Shuichi, *Jyutaku to Iu Kangaekata – 20 Seiki teki Jyutaku no Keifu (20th Century Concepts of House-building)*, University of Tokyo Press, 1999

Matsumura, Shuichi, *Danchi Saisei (Rehabilitation of Housing Estates)*, Shokokusha, 2001

Matsumura, Shuichi et al., *Conversion Keikaku Sekkei Manual (Conversion Design & Planning Manual)*, X-Knowledge, 2004a

Matsumura, Shuichi et al., *Conversion ga Chiiki wo Kaeru Toshi wo Saiseisuru (Conversion Will Change the Region and Regenerate the City)*, Nikkan Kensetsu Tsuushin Shinbun-Sha, 2004b

Matsumura, Shuichi, *Kenchiku – Atarashii Shigoto no Katachi (Architecture: A New Work Form – from "Box Delivery" Industry to "Place-making" Industry)*, Shoukokusha, 2013

Matsumura, Shuichi et al., *Ba no Sangyo Jissen Ron (Practice of Place-making industry)*, Shokokusha, 2014a

Matsumura, Shuichi et al., *2025nen no Kenchiku – Nanatsu no Yogen (Architecture in 2025 – Seven Predictions)*, Nikkei Business Publications, 2014b

Matsumura, Shuichi et al., *Kenchiku Saisei Gaku (Theory and Practice of Architectural Renovation)*, Ichigaya Shuppan-Sha, 2016

Matsumura, Shuichi, Endo, Kazuyoshi et al., *Kenchiku Seisan (Management and Organization of the Building Process)*, Ichigaya Shuppan-Sha, 2004

Matsumura, Shuichi, Suzuki, Takeshi, and Nishida, Tooru, *Sumai no Risutora (Restructuring of Housing)*, Toyo Shoten, 2010

Nishikawa, Yuko, *Shakuya to Mochiya no Bungakushi (History of Literature of Rented Houses and Owner-occupied Houses)*, Saniseido, 1998

Recruit Holdings, *NYC, London, Paris & TOKYO Chintai Jyutaku Seikatsu Jittai Chousa – Ai Aru Chintai Jyutaku wo Motomete (NYC, London, Paris & TOKYO Rental Housing Life Survey Seeking for a Loving Rental Housing)*, Recruit Holdings, 2010

Rudofsky, Bernard, translated into Japanese by Watanabe, Takenobu, *Kenchikuka Nashi no Kenchiku (Architecture without Architects)*, Kajima Institute Publishing, 1976

Saint-Exupéry, Antoine de, translated into Japanese by Naito, Arou, *Hoshi no Oujisama (The Little Prince)*, Iwanami Shoten, Publishers, 1953

Tsuzuki, Kyoichi, *TOKYO STYLE*, Kyoto Shoin Publishing, 1993

Tsuzuki, Kyoichi, *Chintai Uchuu (Universe for Rent)*, Chikuma Shobo, 2001

*Urban Housing*, Kajima Institute Publishing, September 1972

Zukin, Sharon, *Loft Living: Culture and Capital in Urban Change*, Johns Hopkins University Press, 1982

# 5 The development of the third phase of open architecture

## Visualizing the vast availability of space resources, in order to promote active discussion and understanding by the public

To summarize, during the first phase of open architecture, industry experts had strived to create well-designed prototypes and mass produce such designs in order to provide "boxes" where a wholesome, modern life could be lived. Although progress was made towards that goal, leaders of the second phase of open architecture realized the importance of incorporating the needs of people as well as local regional differences, into the design of such "boxes." These factors had been overlooked during the first phase of open architecture. Leaders of the second phase of open architecture rejected the focus on "modernity," which had preoccupied industry experts in the first phase. Instead, the second phase was marked by an attempt to adapt to market changes such as a push for variety and choice. Currently in 21st century Japan, the third phase of open architecture has begun. People now create "places" to enrich their own lives, using the existing supply of "boxes," technological advances, and wisdom accumulated during the previous two phases.

The key differences between the third phase of open architecture and the second phase are: (1) that architecture develops in direct connection with people's life philosophy and (2) that the key players in the field of architecture are the inhabitants, not architectural professionals. That naturally leads to the question: what role then do architectural professionals play? This chapter will attempt to address this question.

Third phase open architecture widely encompasses all the various actions involved in creating "places" of living. This era is unlike the earlier two phases of open architecture, where industry experts clearly defined the goals of architectural development. It is also unlike the second phase, which focused on achieving open architecture through the specific method of mass production. Instead, I propose that the third phase of open architecture encompasses a variety of creative acts undertaken by many people around Japan. Given the variety represented in this third phase, I will not summarize the results of my research in terms of either goals or production methods. Instead, I will focus on people's "manner" of creating new living "places" using existing "boxes." Generally, choosing a method requires having clear goals. However, "manner" does not assume that goals have been clearly predefined, instead it can arise through feedback with human activities.

The following seven sections outline the approaches of this new wave of industry experts.

First, when people attempt to create a "place" for a new way of living, it is not immediately obvious where or how to effectively utilize the supply of "boxes" which already exists. Thus, it is critical to help the public visualize the condition and location of potentially available space resources in the city.

As an excellent example, consider the town management company "Kitakyushu Yamorisha" (www.yamorisha.com, Japanese only) created for the Kokura area of Fukuoka prefecture. To create the map, the members of Kitakyushu Yamorisha investigate all the vacant buildings, rooms, and houses which are located within walking distance of the Kokura downtown area. This area used to be the central commercial area in the city, but within recent years, has declined significantly. The members then plot the location of empty spaces on a town map using pictures. The map includes many properties which are not in the conventional real estate market. As a result, the map is a valuable resource for locating potentially usable space resources, both for people within and outside the neighborhood.

In addition, the map includes detailed data about the building, such as built year, how it was previously used, seismic specifications, included facilities, and building owner and rent, all of which are investigated by Kitakyushu Yamorisha. The map makes it possible for a potential buyer with creativity and vision to locate an appropriate existing "box."

With a map visualizing the vast space resources available in their neighborhood, people can easily imagine how they could utilize those resources. From there, they can discuss their ideas, share with others, and hopefully realize their dream.

## Sparking and directing users' creativity to utilize existing space

The second approach is to spark users' creativity to imagine new ways to use existing spaces, and direct that resulting creativity.

As an example of such users' creativity in using an existing space, I will use the previously discussed case of Masato Nakamura, who converted a vacant middle school building into an art center, 3331 Arts Chiyoda (www.3331.jp/en).

A select group of people may exist, who could apply the degree of creativity that Mr. Nakamura demonstrated in reimagining the existing space. However, while many people have the potential to be creative, the skill may be dormant. It needs somebody or something, perhaps the right opportunity, to awake and guide their creativity. Mr. Nakamura signed a contract with local authorities in the Chiyoda ward to rent the entire building, which was quite large. He showed his plan to convert the building into an art center. He also invited people, who were interested in developing their art-related work in the area. The actions of Mr. Nakamura attracted many people and stimulated their creativity in using the existing spaces. Now the variety of events held in the space exceed even what Mr. Nakamura imagined. The art center has become the "place" of vivid life and work.

In addition, it is important to note that Mr. Nakamura rented the whole building not only for his own use, but for other people to use as well. In fact, Mr. Nakamura included the condition that people who he had never met could use the space, as part of the lease.[1] As a result, even people who had not located their own space resources could gain access to the space and have an opportunity to be creative in using the existing space.

As another example of users' creativity, consider the actions taken by George Maciunas[2] and Fluxus[3] members who helped artists move into vacant buildings and warehouses in the SOHO (South of Houston Street) area of New York in the 1960s. These pioneers created a cooperative for artists interested in using or living in available spaces in the area. Plus, they created a system to allow people to rent the entire building, which is usually difficult for individuals.[4] The organization stimulated and guided the creativity of many users in using existing spaces.

Creating structures to organize users' creativity can be helpful when dealing with large space resources, which are typically difficult for individuals to rent by themselves. In addition, making organizations to gather and disseminate information can be useful for relatively small space resources scattered around a town. Recently, a number of such structures have been created, including a website providing space resource information to people planning to migrate to towns with many vacant houses and which are eager for new residents.

Providing this kind of information is obviously aimed at organizing users' creativity in using existing spaces. Behind such systems are creative people, with their own imagination about how to use existing spaces. Without systems, users' creativity in using existing space cannot be connected with space resources to create new living "places."

What kind of systems have been created? I learned about one system – the Wakayama Way[5] – from Mr. Kazuo Kasami, who works at the Hometown Migration Support Center (www.furusatokaiki.net/Japanese only). ("Wakayama" is the name of a prefecture in Japan.) The "Wakayama way" is a public–private partnership. "One-stop service staff" stationed at each local authority in Wakayama prefecture offer complete consultant services, from finding properties to moving. Afterwards, private companies establish a "host council," which supports migrants. Under this system, this council interviews migrants to evaluate whether they are suitable for the location and then shows them possible homes. The system also provides a template for the leasing contract. Further, the council offers real estate agencies, as a supporter to broker the deal.

## Sharing information related to experiences creating "places"

The third approach is sharing information. As previously discussed in Chapter 4.8, the new renting options of "semi-customized apartments" and "custom build-out apartments" gave inhabitants the freedom to modify the interior finishes of their rental units. These new options overturned a condition typical in most rental contracts, which required renters to return the apartment to its original condition, even if the inhabitants had modified the interior in some way. Giving inhabitants the freedom to modify the rental units addressed an untapped feeling of "I want to do it myself!" It also cleverly brought out and helped organize users' creativity in using existing spaces.

As an aside, many such DIY renovation attempts were circulated, for example through social media channels, showing the enjoyment of DIY and showcasing the ingenious designs which resulted from such efforts. The information could be shared with people who wanted to attempt a DIY project themselves and served as a demonstration of users' creativity in using existing space. The spread of information helped spur the rising popularity of DIY renovation.

The importance of sharing information can also be seen in the migration trend of moving to rural and mountain areas. People who have already moved to rural areas publish information, such as how they remodeled once vacant houses which they bought or were renting, what kinds of local foods and drinks they enjoy, who they spend time with, and what kind of activities they typically do. That information is then further shared by others, which helps people to envision their future life if they migrated. For example, people might think, "Nice! That arrangement could apply to my situation" or "Now I can imagine what my life would be like if I migrated to the countryside like them." The information can inspire people who want to utilize their own creativity to transform an existing space but have not done so because of concerns about possible risks.

*A Pattern Language* by Christopher Alexander attempted to open the closed fortress of "space," which had been treated by architectural experts as the exclusive domain of architects. The book attracted attention during the second phase of open architecture. Now, in Japan, the philosophy of *A Pattern Language* has begun to be applied to the sharing of knowledge and the creation of collective intelligence related to place creation.

As an example, consider the social welfare organization "Bushi-En" established in Ishikawa Prefecture.[6] The president of the organization, Mr. Yoshinari Ohya, and all his staff are experts in welfare issues but amateurs in the field of architecture. However, they were the ones who renovated an abandoned temple in a small town into an open-use community space, which anyone from adults to children could freely enjoy. (See Figure 5.1.) Of course, some professionals were involved in constructing the space, but the staff of Bushi-En conceived of the entire concept for the renovation, even though they had no training in architecture. Their design is appealing with no boundaries separating the different types of spaces, which range from elderly welfare facilities to employment support centers for disabled people to recreational facilities like restaurants and public hot springs where anyone can gather. This kind of mixed-used space is rarely designed by architectural experts. The staff of "Bushi-En" even thoughtfully considered and worked to improve small details, such as furniture layout, the design of seating areas, and the flow between interior and exterior spaces.

After their experience, they used *A Pattern Language* as a method of consolidating opinions when they designed a new village-style hub called "Share Kanazawa." From their previous renovation project, the "Bushi-En" staff already had experience with conceiving designs to renovate existing

*Figure 5.1* The abandoned temple of Saienji was converted from a Buddhist temple into a welfare facility in Komatsu City in Ishikawa Prefecture. Source: Professor Kouichi Sato

spaces. However, for this project, they read Alexander's *A Pattern Language* and selected "patterns" they liked in order to convey their vision for the space to the architectural designer. In terms of opening architecture to the people, *A Pattern Language* is still highly innovative as a "language." However, within traditional architecture, the ideas of the book are now rarely discussed. Instead, amateurs of architecture whose creativity had been awakened by renovation projects use the book as "language" just as Alexander may have intended.

Sharing knowledge related to place arrangement is an important means of harnessing the user's creativity in using existing spaces to reimagine existing space resources. I am extremely pleased to see how the accomplishments of the second phase of open architecture have continued to have an impact.

## Forming a community of allies to act all around the world

The third phase of open architecture has just started. Therefore, there are many possibilities, which are still unknown. To develop those possibilities, it is important to create a stimulating discussion amongst like-minded people, including people who have already started creating "places" for a new way of life, and people who want to start such projects. In other words, the "manner" of advancing the third phase of open architecture is through forming a community of allies to act all around the world.

In terms of my own efforts, my team set up the HEAD (Home & Environment Advanced Design) Study Group in 2008. Our group included the architects Yasumitsu Matsunaga and Sotaro Yamamoto, as well as Mr. Yoshitsugu Shimizu, an advocate of the modern version of "Yamori" (a kind of facility and area manager in Edo period) and Mr. Hiroshi Nagaya, a businessman. We aimed to overturn the current state of the architectural world. In 2010, we asked three architects and pioneers of creating "places" through renovation, namely Manabu Shinbori, Yoshihiko Oshima, and Masataka Baba, to establish a Renovation Task Force in the HEAD Study Group. That task force held the first renovation symposium in Osaka followed by a symposium in Kagoshima. I met many people at events organized by the HEAD Study Group during this time. For example, I met Mr. Ryo Yamazaki, an up-and-coming community designer at that time, the architect Yohei Shimada, who started a "Yamori" business in Kitakyushu, Mr. Manjo Shimahara and Mr. Tomohito Yabe, both marketers who worked to connect the renovation world with real estate businesses, Mr. Hitoshi Kinoshita, a pioneer in town development, and Mr. Hirofumi Uchiyama, who was working to nurture renovation as a new business.

There was more excitement for the renovation symposium than we expected. Shortly afterwards in 2011, we organized the first "Renovation School" workshop in Kitakyushu. As a group, we believed that the creation of new "places" could not be achieved solely through the approaches of architecture, nor solely through the efforts of people from real estate. Instead, we were inspired to organize the event in order to nurture new players to create "places" through renovation. Professor Mitsuhiro Tokuda from the Kyushu Institute of Technology, and Mr. Shimada, who grew up in Kitakyushu, were both eager to collaborate. Mr. Oshima, Mr. Baba, Mr. Uchiyama, and Mr. Shimahara also enthusiastically attended the four-day workshop.

There are two interesting points about the renovation school. The first is that many of the business proposals conceived during the four-day workshop for remodeling vacant houses and empty buildings were actually implemented. In Kitakyushu, the workshop was held twelve times in total by March 2018, and sixteen projects were commercialized by 2015. (See Figure 5.2.)

Secondly, the event attracted a diverse range of people of varying ages, backgrounds, and occupations, but all were engaged in creating new "places" through renovation in various locations around Japan. For example, I met Tomonori Kuraishi, Tsuyoshi Hirose, and Kei Miyamoto, who were involved in helping small businesses become established in a hundred houses and rooms, which had once stood vacant in Nagano City (home of the famous Zenkouji Temple). In addition, I met Koichiro Ichiki from the NPO Atamista, who was actively working to promote renovation in Atami City (well-known in Japan for its hot springs). In this way, networks of people who were tackling similar problems across various cities were brought together, forming a network of practitioners who were creating "places" through renovation. This network lead to the planning and launching of renovation workshops in many cities around Japan. Ultimately, in 2015, workshops were held in over thirty places throughout the country. (Currently the company Renove-Ring, which specializes in holding renovation workshop events, has taken over the work of the HEAD study group in overseeing all the events.) I am amazed by how much the movement has grown in only five years. I cannot help feeling that interest in creating "places" through renovation is rapidly expanding and spreading across Japan.

Importantly, both the instructors and the participants of renovation workshop events were not necessarily individuals from the field of architecture. In fact, the majority of instructors and participants had no background in architecture. Why did the events attract non-architectural experts? The concept of creating a "place" through renovation forms the core of these workshops. However, that idea is not a special idea from architecture, but rather a broader idea about living and working in urban environments. In order to create interesting ideas for creating a "place" through renovation, which can actually be realized, it is critical to consider both the perspective of the user and the feasibility of the project. One advantage with renovating existing spaces is that

*Figure 5.2* A photograph taken at the closing party of the 8th Kitakyushu Renovation School. The man who wore glasses with the white hair reflected at the left side of the photograph is the author. Source: Kitakyushu Yamorisha Co., Ltd.

unlike building new construction, the existing buildings can serve to guide the user. Therefore, even if you are not an architectural expert, it is easy to get started with renovation.

Suggesting that the "forging of relationships to act" formed the foundation of this movement might sound like an exaggeration, especially in the closed world of architecture. However, when using existing space resources to create a new "place" for living, the importance of encountering new people and exchanging information cannot be overlooked. My experiences at the renovation workshop events clearly demonstrate this.

## Achieving sustainable town management

People from the world of architecture – of which I am a typical example – tend to be emphatic about the important contribution their own specialty makes to buildings. In addition, most of them complain that ordinary people do not seem to appreciate the significance of their work. For example, experts in earthquake resistance usually want people to evaluate buildings based on how well the buildings can withstand earthquakes, while experts in energy efficient and zero-energy buildings want people to be interested in the building's insulation. Similarly, architectural design experts, when they see the exterior of buildings designed according to the preferences of ordinary people, may wish that people would improve their sense of aesthetics, in order to appreciate "true" architecture. While I understand that this is a natural tendency, it also strikes me as self-centered. It seems that architects tend to focus solely on themselves, while looking down on ordinary people.

One day, along with some of my colleagues from architecture, I read part of a real estate manual on how to determine the price of condominiums. In terms of criteria used to evaluate the price of a condominium, the manual included factors like the location and the surrounding environment. However, in terms of architectural features, the manual only included features like whether the exterior wall was tiled or not. Reading this, we all became angry and thought, "This is precisely why the architecture of condominiums does not improve." However, when ordinary people choose an apartment where they would like to live for a long time, it is only natural that they consider the location and surroundings to be important factors. If we criticize their focus on non-architectural features, it only shows that our values are not aligned with the common thinking of home buyers. As architects, we have failed to integrate the actual way that people live into our value system. Without doubt, the location of the apartment and the surrounding environment will greatly affect the way people live there after relocating. However, admittedly the finish of the building, for example, whether the exterior wall is tiled or not, may have little effect on the quality of people's lives.

After all, human beings live in the space created by the town. We do not live just in buildings. So far, I have used the terms "box" and "space resource." You, as the reader, might have thought that I am focusing only on the creation of a "place" inside a building. However, both "boxes" and the surrounding town space together form a "place" for a new way of life, providing a place where the activities of people can occur to create a whole way of living. If only a specific space inside of a building is designed to be an excellent "place" but shared space outside the front door and in the wider neighborhood are not improved, an enjoyable and rich life can never be achieved. Recognizing that fact, a number of people around me have increasingly dared to use the expression "renovation machizukuri" (renovation town planning).

Indeed, all the pioneers from the world of renovation have pointed out the importance of sustainably managing the town space. If only a single vacant house is renovated to become a new "place" for life, the town space, as a whole where we live, does not change much. In addition, a large-scale redevelopment, which tears down many old "boxes" all at once and replaces them with one big building, has a major impact for a short period but little to no long-lasting impact. In other words, such approaches do not allow the town space to respond dynamically to changes over time. In order to create a sustainably vibrant "place," it is better to gradually implement the creation of "places" through small renovation projects. This way, new places can accumulate over time in the town space. This idea spread among people, who began to use the expression "renovation town planning" to highlight the importance of the process of slowly renovating the entire town space. Just as the process of living itself is not the final result but an unfolding process, creating a new "place" for life is an ongoing and never-ending process.

Recognizing the process nature of renovation, it is important that the act of renovating space resources to create new "places" for life and work does not end with a single building but rather continues in the town space.

At the Renovation School, in order to provide vacant houses and empty buildings as practice cases for the workshop, the event organizers negotiated with building owners in advance, especially impressing upon them the significance of their buildings. In addition, the owners were invited to the final presentations on the last day of workshop to exchange ideas and discuss the proposals. (See Figure 5.3.) Thus, the people living in the area could be part of the entire discussion. If the owners decided to allow their vacant houses and empty buildings to be used creatively by new users to reimagine the existing space, it would lead to sustainable management in the town space. I, along with the Renovation School members, firmly believed so.

## Teamwork between businesses and organizations

When I imagine how the various projects to create new "places" utilizing space resources accumulate in the town space, I am fascinated by the way that those spaces slowly spread and become intertwined with the activities of that town. As an example of the ties, which can develop among people conducting a variety of activities around a town, let's consider the case of the Monzen-machi area in Nagano City.[7]

Currently, in Monzen-machi (home of Zenkouji Temple[8]) in Nagano City, many new shops and workplaces in old vacant houses and buildings are opening one after another. In 2010, Nano Graphica, a small organization focused on local theater production and editorial design, published a booklet titled *Suggestions for living in Monzen, Nagano City*. (In

*Figure 5.3* At the final presentation of the Kitakyushu Renovation School. Source: Kitakyushu Yamorisha Co., Ltd.

Japanese, "monzen" refers to the area in front of a temple.) The booklet includes photographs to show visually the lives of the people who moved to the old buildings in the Monzen-machi area around Zenkouji Temple. At the same time, a completely separate group of people, who were involved with running various shops and offices, formed an LLP[9] organization to rent a 50-meter long vacant factory building. In the building, which was almost 100 years old, the group started a new way of living.

Ms. Tamami Masuzawa, leader of Nano Graphica, also lives with her family in an old town house, which is about 100 years old. In addition, she runs a cafe, as well as a planning and editorial office from the same building. She was inspired to start living there after she saw many old houses begin to be destroyed. Although Ms. Masuzawa had once seen those houses as merely a part of the scenery of the town, she realized how significant the houses were to her and her own life. She urged the owner to at least let the public see the inside before demolition. Walking around inside the old town house before demolition sparked a thought inside her head. She realized, "this building can still be used!" Then she moved into the building. After that, she published a series of booklets with the mission to communicate the richness of life in Monzen. The booklets are available for sale in cafes and shops around Nagano City. Tourists can pick up the booklets and perhaps be inspired to think, "we can live here like this." However, a series of booklets alone was not enough to encourage people to immigrate to the area and start living in Monzen. (See Figure 5.4)

At the same time, there was an LLP that started renting a vacant factory building in the area. The enterprise included Mr. Tomonori Kuraishi, in charge of a real estate and construction business, as well as various people from architecture design offices and editorial offices. Together, the group

*Figure 5.4* "Nagano Monzen Gurashi no Susume" (*Suggestions for Living in Monzen, Nagano City*). Source: MY ROOM Co., Ltd.

wanted to use this project as a model to encourage people to come and use space resources in the town, such as vacant houses and buildings, to start new ways of living and working.

Eventually, a partnership began to take shape between the efforts of Ms. Masuzawa to publish her booklet *Suggestions for living in Monzen* and the LLP led by Mr. Kuraishi. Since Mr. Kuraishi runs a real estate business, he is always looking for owners who are willing to rent their vacant houses and buildings. He regularly organizes tours of vacant houses, attracting people who are considering moving to the town and who may have the creativity to reimagine existing spaces. Not surprisingly, NANO GRAPHICA joined this tour effort.

These new partnerships that developed among various people attempting projects around the town represented a turning point for the city. A new team took shape. Further, the "Monzen life" lifestyle inspired many people, who began moving to Monzen-machi from all around Japan. Even as Japan faces a declining birth rate and aging population, the Monzen-machi area blossomed into a vibrant "place" for life and work. Within just five years, over eighty new small businesses have been founded in the town. Moreover, these people and their activities continue to create new "places" for life and work. Their efforts are loosely tied together to dynamically influence and change the town space.

A similar case can be seen with the R Real Estate Group[10], which was founded in the Nihonbashi area[11] of Tokyo and has since grown into a nationwide brand.

The company had its start, when Mr. Masataka Baba, an architect, began looking for a centrally located, convenient, and reasonably priced space to rent for his own office. Eventually, after negotiating with the building owner, he was able to rent a two-story warehouse, which had been vacant, and launch his architect office. Through that process, he discovered many building and warehouses in the area, which were vacant but not publicly available on the real estate market.

From there, he started a blog showing photographs of vacant buildings in the area, which were not listed on the real estate market but were potential space resources that could stimulate users' creativity in using existing space. Visits to his blog increased rapidly with a flood of comments like "I would like to live in this kind of building" and "I also want to make a warehouse like this the base of my work."

Mr. Baba realized the business potential of his blog and founded his company, along with friends who knew about real estate distribution. The company, called "Tokyo R Real Estate," provides a new online real estate distribution system connecting space resources with people who want to apply their creativity to reimagine existing spaces. Similar to Nagano City, the Tokyo R Real Estate team includes people with experience from various different industries. The new life and work of young generations, who moved into the area, transformed the town space, which used to have many back offices of wholesale stores, into a vibrant and exciting place.

## Open architecture for the people

At the beginning of this book, I wrote about the state of the field of architecture when I entered my university's department of architecture. Until then, many people in Japan had been educated in architecture, just as I would also be educated. To this day, that has not changed.

Architectural education started in Japan, after the Meiji Restoration (1868),[12] when the Japanese government began promoting modernization. One government effort included adopting European-style architecture by establishing the Department of Architecture in 1877 within the Engineering College (Kobu Daigakko), now known as the Department of Architecture at the University of Tokyo. In 1879, there were just four graduates: Kingo Tatsuno,[13] Toukuma Katayama,[14] Tatsuzo Sone,[15] and Sichijiro Satachi.[16] (Kingo Tatsuno is still widely known as the designer of the Tokyo Station and the Bank of Japan.) Today, the number of architecture departments in Japan exceeds 100 with over 10,000 graduates every year. Many of those graduates worked hard all around the country, as members of the "box delivery industry." As of the end of September 2015, the total number of registered architects, as defined by the 1950 Act on Architects and Building Engineers,[17] had risen to 360,000 first class architects,[18] 750,000 second class architects,[19] and 17,000 timber construction architects.[20] (These totals include both living architects as well as those who have passed away.)

While it might not be a concern of the general public, I cannot help wondering, what is the new role for these architectural experts? Especially with the start of the third phase of open architecture, what exactly should all these architectural experts do? At the very least, there is no doubt that we need to considerably adjust our attitude.

Related to the issue of attitude, let's look back at the mindset of architects in the early stage of architecture. Looking at the mission statement of the Architects and Engineers Association, as well as the lyrics of the "Song of Architect," the mindset of that era becomes clear. Both were written in 1955. Their contents are as follows.

> The Mission Statement of the Architects and Engineers Association (1955): 1. The architecture we create is the finest art form, created for the happiness of humankind. 2. We, as architects, should strive to be pioneers leading the development of society. 3. For the advancement of its members, this association must have the utmost solidarity.
>
> (The official website of Japan Federation of Architects and Building Engineers Associations, www.kenchikushikai.or.jp/about-our-society/koryo_kaika.html)

The mission statement clearly reflects its writing in 1955, especially in its focus on architecture as an art form and by its encouragement of architects to become leaders of society. The lyrics of Ichizo Inoue's "Song of Architect," which won first place in a competition, are as follows.

1) The hammer sounds, sharply roaring in the clear sky of the century. We are mighty. And we will defend the happiness of our brethren. We are architects.
2) We will surpass the progress of the era to foster a new culture. We will hold high our ideal to build ever-lasting peace. We are architects.
3) Our mission of construction will forever serve the young, growing Japan. We pledge to refine this technology together and make great strides into tomorrow. We are architects.

From the song, the aim of architects is clearly the happiness of their comrades, eternal peace, and promoting construction in Japan.

Contemporary architects cannot possibly adopt a similar mindset, in the face of the third phase of open architecture. First, the subject of architecture is no longer the art of architecture. Architecture may be an art from in a way. However, the subject of architecture has shifted to the entirety of people's lives and activities happening in a new "place." As architects, our role is not to guide people's philosophy of life, nor is our objective achieving the happiness of only our comrades. Further, our mission is not limited by nationality. Of course, achieving everlasting peace remains important. However, the original mission of construction work after the war in Japan has largely been fulfilled.

In 2013, I published *Architecture: A new work form from "box delivery" industry to "place-making" industry* (in Japanese). After that, I held a series of meetings with fifteen pioneers leading renovation town planning projects. I wanted to ask their opinion about whether a traditional architectural education could prepare people to work in the renovation and renovation town planning fields. One opinion expressed stood out as particularly persuasive to me. The opinion was that, of course, being an expert in one field is important. However, unless one also becomes knowledgeable in other fields, in other words becomes a "multilingual" expert, success can never be achieved. They all recognized that if education still focuses on traditional architecture, there is no hope for succeeding with renovation.

With its accumulation of knowledge and rich culture, architecture is an excellent field for intellectual stimulation. However, the ideal of being an expert of that accumulation of knowledge has faded and become rather old fashioned. Therefore, after being trained in architecture, one must return to thinking about the user as the key player in the creation of new "places" and first consider the inhabitant's philosophy of life.

Currently, in the third phase of open architecture, the main theme has shifted from constructing new buildings to creating a "place" of life and work through using existing space resources. The main focus is the user of the space. The question then becomes: how do architectural experts become aware of their roles? Many people feel that the so-called architectural profession must be overhauled. However, there are many arguments, which once appeared in the second phase of open architecture that can now be discussed without any connection to political intentions. Those arguments give us a better clue about what might develop in the future.

First of all, let's consider the opinions of Habraken, who published *You cannot design the ordinary*[21] and tried to divide the residential environment into "support" and "infill". Habraken insisted that dwelling is an action. Therefore, architects cannot design it. In addition, he proposed that the role of architects is like a gardener. Gardeners are not able to create plants themselves but they are able to manage the environment to help the plants grow well. In the same way, architects are not able to create housing but are able to manage the environment to help housing develop. In other words, architects should "strive to be a gardener." This can be considered an important "manner" in the third phase of open architecture.

Adopting Habraken's perspective leads us to the questions: how should we go about cultivating "place" creation using spatial resources? And what kind of environment is best suited to that process?

The first step is a series of actions. We must determine the necessity of improving space resources and then provide methods to improve those resources. Professional knowledge is necessary to diagnose buildings, repair deteriorated parts, effectively implement seismic retrofitting, and improve environmental performance. Even inhabitants can participate in this process to an extent. To return to the concept of the architect as a gardener, this first step is equivalent to identifying whether a plant is diseased and then appropriately treating with fertilizers and chemicals. In terms of construction, professional skill is necessary because DIY by inhabitants cannot address all the problems. However, unlike new construction, each renovation project is usually only a small unit. Therefore, it is preferable to employ multi-skilled workers, who can handle the diagnoses and overhaul of both design and construction.

The second step is collecting and editing existing technology and knowledge. This process is exemplified by the *Whole Earth Catalog*. Nowadays, printed materials are less widely used. However, the importance of effectively distributing information about technology to inhabitants has not changed, and is equivalent to soil improvement by a gardener.

The third step is supporting "place" creation by creating a system of materials, technologies, financing systems, and government policies. For example, consider the open system, Turner's idea for creating housing in developing nations included not only materials and technologies but also financing methods and government policies. This step corresponds to supplying proper nutrients and water by a gardener.

The fourth step is similar to Alexander's *A Pattern Language*, namely providing a kind of linguistic system concerning the contents of space to be set up. One might ask, what activity by a gardener corresponds to this step?

These are merely examples of the potential new role for architectural experts, which were inspired by the discussions I cited in this book. If the concept of "aiming to be a gardener" is more widely understood, various roles will be created and generated during the development of the third phase of open architecture.

The traditional architectural community clearly does not fit the era of the third phase of open architecture. Consider a quintessential architectural photograph, which architectural experts have no doubt seen many times. Typically, these photographs are taken before delivery, in other words, before people start living and working in the building. The furniture, which conveys the people's lifestyle, may even be removed for the photograph. The existence of this type of photograph symbolizes the way in which traditional architecture is disconnected from people's lives. This style of architectural photography developed naturally because many architectural masterpieces (like Villa Savoye, designed by Le Corbusier and later nominated as a World Heritage site) were usually unoccupied. In other cases, architects became famous without ever building anything but purely based on their drawings for "unbuilt" theoretical projects.

However, such architectural photographs no longer make sense in the era where existing space resources are connected with users' creativity in using existing space. The focus is not the structure but rather the contents embedded in it. Of course, a photograph of the bare structure of space resources can still serve to stimulate users' creativity in using the space. In other cases, however, the photograph has no meaning because the most important element, namely the contents of the space, has been omitted.

Let me introduce an example of a photograph, which symbolizes the third phase of open architecture. The photograph shows "Tamamusubi Terrace," which was originally built as middle-height public housing. The 50-year-old facility stood vacant, before being renovated by three business operators. These five buildings were part of "Tama-daira Danchi," a pioneering project of large-scale residential developments led by the Japan Housing Corporation, which was founded in 1955. There are various reasons why these five buildings are the only ones that remained from the original project, while the other buildings were rebuilt. The Urban Renaissance Agency[22] (successor of the Japan Housing Corporation) subleased these five buildings to businesses recruited to conduct new projects. The three business operators mentioned above were the ones who met the requirements to sublease the buildings.

A business operator rented two buildings and launched a rental share house business for young people, another one rented one and launched a rental house business with vegetable gardens for couples, and the last one rented two and launched rental housing for elderly people with day services. If a photograph were taken without any people, the photographs would only convey "the buildings are updated compared to before." For example, the exterior paint on the 50-year-old building had been updated. But the essence of the project would be lost. Instead, when I asked the team to send pictures, they provided the images shown as Figure 5.5. These pictures show how the new contents (i.e., "people's lives") are embedded in the old structure (i.e., the "box").

When stimulating "place" creation and directing the creativity of many people to use existing space, the overseeing business operators must focus on enriching the contents. In other words, management, especially in early phases, should strive to spark the possibility that the space develops into a vibrant and dynamic living "place." In the case of the housing revitalization project, one employee of the business operators who managed the two

*Figure 5.5* One of various human activities at the Tamamusubi Tarrace. Both of the new inhabitants and other people living in the surrounding estates enjoy autumn events organized by the new inhabitants and the management companies. Source: Rivita Co., Ltd.

buildings offered to become a resident in the share house. That employee is actively engaged in helping to expand the possibility of the contents. For example, the employee hosts informal meetings for share house residents. Former residents, who lived there several decades at the time when the Japan Housing Corporation managed the buildings, are also invited. The new inhabitants and former residents can meet and network. The hardware does not change, but the content is continuously changing to become more fun and more vibrant. This dynamic vibrancy cannot possibly be captured by a traditional architectural photograph.

Another clear example is the Arts Chiyoda 3331 project, which I previously mentioned. Mr. Nakamura, the artist who launched the project, established the operation company "Command A" to manage the art center, along with Mr. Yoshitsugu Shimizu, who is an advocate of the modern version of Yamori (traditional area manager). Together, they plan and hold art exhibitions and various live performances in the large event space on the first floor. In addition, they frequently hold meetings with the people who joined the "place" as building tenants, as well as local graduates from when the building was once a junior high school. As I mentioned, as of 2013, 800,000 people visit a year. If they considered their work finished, when the renovation of the 30-year-old school was completed, it likely would never have flourished in this way. Even worse, it might never have even survived as a "place" at all. Efforts which continuously change the contents to be more fun and more appealing, create the "place."

The process of arranging space resources into a new "place" of life and work never ends. Architectural experts are now facing the challenge of whether they can join the efforts of enriching contents, rather than merely focusing on the structure. Such efforts can be summed up as, "Embedding the future of life and work in the town." In other words, creating the future is an ongoing process.

## Notes

1 A contract in which a business operator rents all the rooms of a rental building and sublets each room to tenants.
2 1931–1978. An American contemporary artist.
3 The avant-garde art movement of the 1960s led by George Maciunas. The term is also used to refer to the related organization.
4 Sharon Zukin, *Loft Living: Culture and Capital in Urban Change, USA*, Johns Hopkins University Press, (1982).
5 A prefecture in Western Japan located adjacent to Osaka.
6 A prefecture located in the northern part of Central Japan.
7 The prefectural office city of Nagano prefecture located in the central part of Japan.
8 A Buddhist temple in Nagano City. Over 6 million people visit each year.
9 An acronym which stands for "Limited Liability Partnership."
10 4–10.
11 The name of a place in central Tokyo. There are many shops and restaurants in the area, which have been operating for many decades, including the first department store ever built in Japan.

12 In the late 19th century, the process of political and social transformation, which contributed to the collapse of the Edo shogunate domain structure. The transformation was the origin of the centralized nation of Japan and helped spur the formation of Japanese capitalism. The transformation ended with the establishment of the new Meiji government in 1868.
13 1854–1919. In 1884, after Professor J. Condor of the Department of Architecture, he became the first Japanese professor at the Imperial College of Engineering (now known as the University of Tokyo, Faculty of Engineering). He built many buildings as an architect, including Tokyo Station and the Bank of Japan.
14 1854–1917. The architect well known for his masterpiece Akasaka Palace.
15 1853–1937. An architect who left behind many architectural works, including an office town in front of Tokyo Station in the Marunouchi area.
16 1857–1922. An architect. After working at various government agencies, such as the Ministry of Industry and the Ministry of the Navy, he worked for the NYK Line company.
17 See Chapter 4.
18 See Chapter 4.
19 Ibid.
20 Ibid.
21 Ibid.
22 Urban Renaissance Agency is a public organization, created by merging the Japan Housing Corporation (founded in 1955), the Land Development Corporation (founded in 1975), and a department of the Regional Development Association (founded in 2004). With recent changes to the public housing system, the agency no longer undertakes new construction. Instead, it is focused on redevelopment and rebuilding. A main focus of the agency is managing its supply of over 700,000 rental housing units.

## Bibliography


Alexander, Christopher, Ishikawa, Sara & Silverstein, Murray, *A Pattern Language – Towns, Buildings, Construction*, Oxford University Press, 1977 (Japanese version: *Pattern Language – Kankyou Sekkei no Tebiki*, translated by H. Hirata, Kajima Institute Publishing, 1984)

Matsumura, Shuichi, *Kenchiku – Atarashii Shigoto no Katachi (Architecture: A New Work Form – from "Box Delivery" Industry to "Place-making" Industry)*, Shoukokusha, 2013

Matsumura, Shuichi et al., *Ba no Sangyo Jissen Ron (Practice of Place-making industry)*, Shokokusha, 2014

Matsumura, Shuichi et al., *Kenchiku Saisei Gaku (Theory and Practice of Architectural Renovation)*, Ichigaya Shuppan-Sha, 2016

Nano Graphica, *Nagano Monzen Gurashi no Susume (Suggestions for Living in Monzen, Nagano City)*, Nano Graphica, 2009

Turner, John. F. C. et al., *Freedom to Build: Dweller Control of the Housing Process*, New York: Macmillan, 1972

*Urban Housing*, Kajima Institute Publishing, September 1972

*Whole Earth Catalog*, Stewart Brand, 1968–1972

Zukin, Sharon, *Loft Living: Culture and Capital in Urban Change, USA*, Johns Hopkins University Press, 1982

# 6 Open architecture ahead – to play with vacant buildings

## Renovation as art

I explained a little about Arts Chiyoda 3331 in previous chapters, but I would like to summarize it here once again. Arts Chiyoda 3331 is a well-known renovation project that created an art center from a junior high school in Chiyoda Ward, which had closed. The center now attracts 800,000 visitors every year.

Japanese media, such as newspapers and TV, have coined the phrase "the empty house issue"[1] to describe the problems caused by the increasing number of empty houses multiplying in Japan. However, houses are not the only issue. There are also lots of former business buildings, factories, and school buildings standing vacant all around Japan.

With creativity and a proactive attitude, those empty spaces can be used in a way to entertain people, like Arts Chiyoda 3331. Thus, I call those empty spaces "spatial resources," implying that the empty buildings are in fact a precious resource in Japan. Indeed, Japan is in the stage where the country can be called a nation with abundant spatial resources.

Previously, I mentioned a key player in the Arts Chiyoda 3331 project – Mr. Masato Nakamura – an artist and professor at the Tokyo Art University. His work in the Arts Chiyoda 3331 project skillfully demonstrated that seemingly abandoned and useless spatial resources have great potential. Toward the end of 2017, I received an unexpected phone call from Mr. Masato Nakamura. He said, "There is a contemporary artist that I would like you to meet. Also, I want you to see his work." Mr. Nakamura was referring to the artist Mr. Yusuke Nishimura. It turned out that Mr. Nishimura is not only an artist but also a specially appointed associate professor in the painting department of Tokyo Art University. Mr. Nakamura asked me to meet Mr. Nishimura in Kiryu City[2] of Gumma Prefecture, an area located about 100 kilometers north of Tokyo. Since I was curious about Mr. Nishimura, I researched his work. I found out that he held an exhibit of his work at Arts Chiyoda 3331 in the winter of 2015. The title of his exhibit was *To have a conversation.* Mr. Yuto Fujioka, the curator of the exhibit, wrote the following about the exhibit:

> Honey displayed in all four corners of the room filled the whole space with a sweet smell. The honey served to remind visitors of the long history of humans eating honey since ancient times, evoke the image of bees as vehicles for pollination, and subtly imply the presence of intangible air and the cycle of the ecosystem. Mr. Nishimura observed the changes happening to the honey itself, as well as the phenomena caused by the presence of the honey, such as the behavior of insects who were attracted by the honey. Within this multi-layered conversation process, Mr. Nishimura is observing the microscopic world from the macro level of consciousness.[3]

Apparently, a lot of honey was poured directly on the floor of the exhibition room. That was part of Mr. Nishimura's work of art. I could not help wondering how an artist, like Mr. Nishimura, who converts "conversation" into art found himself in the small rural city of Kiryu City. However, Mr. Nishimura must be interesting for Mr. Nakamura to introduce him to me. I figured for the time being, I would just go and meet him. So, I headed to Kiryu City on a sunny Sunday in January.[4]

I found Mr. Nishimura's art studio in a surprisingly conspicuous place. Seeing the saw-tooth-roof building reminded me of the time during my childhood when I visited a factory managed by one of my friend's family. I felt nostalgic. Under the roof is the space, where Mr. Nishimura has been working on renovation for over a decade, along with Mr. Hiroyuki Yamazaki, the owner of the building, and Ms. Rie Ishii, Mr. Nishimura's partner.

Given its history as a flourishing manufacturing area, producing silk fabric products, Kiryu City still has many former factory buildings. A distinguishing feature of the factories is their saw-tooth-roof design. This design, comprised of a series of ridges, was a common design for factories in the past, providing a large roof surface area to take advantage of sunlight to light the interior of the factory. Kiryu City is well known for the many saw-tooth-roofed factory buildings which still exist. A number of former factories, which offer a large interior space within easy reach from the city center, have been renovated into shops and cafes that attract young customers.

I expected that Mr. Nishimura's work as a contemporary artist would be one of those renovation projects to make use of a former saw-tooth-roofed factory building. However, as soon as I went inside, I realized that my expectation was completely wrong. In the first place, the "use" of the building, which is supposed to connect people and the building, did not exist. Instead, the relationship between people and the building had been organized in a way that felt natural, yet was clearly intentional, into a space, or rather into a boundless time.

The owner of the building, Mr. Yamazaki, closed the building twenty years previously, about a decade before Mr. Nishimura started his renovation project. After being closed, the building was no longer a working factory and stood there silently. For a decade, Mr. Yamazaki struggled with his mixed feelings of hope and nostalgia, as he tried to decide how to deal with the building and fabric-making machines, which once hummed busily in the factory. He had not been able to bring himself to demolish the building, despite knowing that he probably should. Then, one day, Mr. Yamazaki met the contemporary artist Mr. Nishimura. Mr. Yamazaki asked Mr. Nishimura what he should do with his saw-tooth-roofed building. From there, they started their joint project.

For the decade since then, their work helped release Mr. Yamazaki from his mixed feelings towards the fact that he shut down his business. Together, they collaborated to work on the saw-tooth buildings, which had previously stood untouched, yet undemolished. In the process, they empathized with each other and uncovered aspects of the building that Mr. Yamazaki never expected. Like an archeological dig, it required both mental intelligence and physical labor. The discovery of a valuable object would shift the direction of the digging project. Mr. Nishimura, as an artist, did not alter his purpose of overall direction of the project. However, the project was completely different from the typical construction project, which is executed towards a set deadline with a clear plan and concept for the use of the building. Usually, renovating a building of this size would be completed in about a year. However, even after a decade, the renovation project had not produced a clear direction for the future.

Ten years ago, in that dark space filled with broken machines, they undertook their first project, namely to repair the fabric-making machines and bring back the sounds which had once filled the building. To do that, Mr. Yamazaki had to make a number of new parts that the broken machines were missing. In the end, they also had to throw away some machines, which even after great efforts to fix and revive the machines could not be repaired.

After listening to the voices of the machines, they disassembled them, revealing a very open and brightly lit space beyond their imagination. Sunlight streamed through the tall windows on the east side of the saw-tooth roof, creating a moment like a Rembrandt painting. Apparently, while working on the building, the three of them experienced miraculous scenes like this many times. After that, Mr. Nishimura continued his efforts to reshape the relationship between people and space, as well as uncover new discoveries. At the same time, the joint project among the three of them, led by Mr. Nishimura, kept going.

The process of cleaning the floor felt like searching for evidence that humans and machines once worked together in that space. The team of three spent as much time as they needed to gently remove layers of greasy dirt on the floor. Eventually, as if the floor was trying to communicate something, the original wood pattern appeared with old scratches showing where workers used to walk. When they demolished part of the wall, a panorama of a rainbow over the river embankment located next to the building property suddenly appeared in front of them. After that, they demolished an old shed between Mr. Yamazaki's house and the saw-tooth-roof building, creating a new pathway to the factory bringing fresh air inside.

Only the three of them experienced these entire series of events. Other visitors to the building over the past decade only had the opportunity to experience a specific moment in the evolution of the building. Of course, you can share a moment with someone by interacting with him/her but it is impossible to share one's entire life experience with someone else. The building was the same. Now I could only see the building in its final state. I could not possibly experience everything the group of three had felt while working on the building over the past decade. For example, I watched a video of the three of them polishing the building's floor. I saw a level of care absent from typical construction projects, where workers destroy and haul away old floors simply because the floor is old and needs to be demolished. The thoughtful action of these three was fundamentally different.

Mr. Yamazaki explained to me, "There are many large buildings with saw-tooth roofs, showing that Kiryu City was once home to large fabric corporations. In fact, many smaller fabric manufacturers, housed in small saw-tooth-roofed factories like ours, were the true base of Kiryu City."

After leaving Kiryu City, I felt that the aim of Mr. Nishimura was to transform his ordinary saw-tooth-roofed building located in an ordinary town owned by an ordinary person into a spiritual ground where the past, present, and future fused into a single moment.

## "Play" realized in the country of rich space resource

I opened this chapter by jumping into a discussion of the current trends in the art scene. However, the real reason why Mr. Nakamura introduced me to Mr. Nishimura was that he wanted to know how a professional from the architectural industry, like myself, would view Mr. Nishimura's artwork. I had the opportunity to talk at length with Mr. Nakamura and Mr. Nishimura at a symposium organized after my visit to Kiryu City.[5] The following is a summary of our conversation:

From the perspective of someone in the construction industry, Mr. Nishimura's activity would no doubt be considered "renovation" because Mr. Nishimura is modifying an existing building. At the same time, however, it is completely different from a typical "renovation" because there is no expectation for completion, no defined purpose or use, and no deadline by which it must be finished. In the construction industry, most renovation projects are just "business" to satisfy the given purpose based on specifications provided by customers. On the other hand, Mr. Nishimura's activity is a more enriching and human type of "personal entertainment."[6] By "personal entertainment," I do not mean "casual playing" like children do. I certainly understand that Mr. Nishimura and his team take the project very seriously. However, I would be so bold to say that their project is a kind of "personal entertainment" but not necessarily "business" per se. Mr. Nishimura's art work in Kiryu City made me realize that in this era where there is an abundant stock of available buildings in Japan, you do not need to be an architectural expert to "play" with architecture.

For me, this realization proved unexpectedly significant. I had understood that many currently unused, empty houses and buildings can in fact be put to use. From this understanding, I had referred to the stock of empty buildings in Japan as a "spatial resource" rather than using negative expressions like "Japan's empty house issue," which are favored by the media. The success of Mr. Nishimura's "personal entertainment" project demonstrates that Japan is currently blessed with a great wealth and abundance of spatial resources. Indeed, the very fact that Japan has an abundance of spatial resources enables this kind of "personal entertainment."

As soon as I came up with the concept that the abundance of spatial resources in Japan enables this kind of "personal entertainment," I began to recall many recent examples of such activities by consumers.

One example is a renovation workshop called "Minami Boso DIY Eco-Renovation" (https://mb-republic.com/satoyama-life/). Workshop participants work to upgrade insulation, taking empty old houses with insulation problems, such as having gaps around the door, and turning them into living spaces where new residents can stay warm even during cold winters. Like a sports club, the workshop creates positive forward momentum, motivating not only future residents of the homes but also other people to join the renovation activity. I argue that this project is not a "business" but rather a form of "personal entertainment." (I will describe this project in more detail later.)

Another example are projects by Ms. Mari Kume, who is a leading figure among female DIYers (http://magichappiness.blog.jp/). Shortly after she married and moved in with her husband to a worn out, dated public apartment building, her husband took her to a home improvement store. That visit inspired Ms. Kume to start her own DIY projects. She came up with many ideas to temporarily renovate their apartment with removable materials, so that the apartment could be returned to its original state when they moved out. She began to publish online about the progress of her DIY renovation projects, sharing her unique approach and lessons she learned. She attracted a great deal of attention. When I met her a few years ago, she had already risen to become a leading figure among female DIYers. I remember that she told me that when she had to choose between buying remodeling materials or make-up products, she would always choose to buy materials to renovate her and her husband's apartment. Her passion comes from the fact that her DIY renovation projects are "personal entertainment" for her. Thanks to her reputation, many house-related companies have now approached her about collaborating. Her activities are increasingly becoming a "business." However, the original motivation for her work was purely for "personal entertainment."

The last example I would like to introduce is the "Renovation School" movement (https://re-re-re-renovation.jp/schools/). This project started in 2011 in the Kitakyushu City of Japan. Since then, it has grown dramatically. Now, you can find a "Renovation School" event happening somewhere in Japan nearly every week. The school brings together people from all over Japan of varying ages and from many different professional backgrounds. At the events, students work in groups to develop detailed business proposals of how to put empty buildings to use. Given that many plans do become actual businesses, one might wonder if this activity should really be considered a form of "business." However, after joining the last meeting, where students present their plans to residents of the town, and also witnessing the volunteer spirit of many of the participants who pay their own transportation to the events, I hesitate to call this a "business." I believe the project is rightly considered "personal entertainment."

Most people in the architectural industry, myself included, tend to consider the utilization of existing buildings (i.e., remodeling, renovation, and real estate management) as the same category as the construction of brand-new buildings undertaken zealously when there was an insufficient supply of spatial resources. As a result, architectural professionals tend to see the utilization of empty buildings as a form of "business." However, I insist on calling such activities "personal entertainment" because it feels more fun and exciting when we view these activities as "personal entertainment" rather than mere "business." Further, even if there is some connection to the industry or marketplace, we cannot help but feel a greater sense of potential by considering it a form of "play."

The question then becomes: whose "personal entertainment" is it? The answer is that it is everyone's personal entertainment, whether they are architectural experts or not. Generally, building brand-new buildings is too much work and too complicated to allow it to be "personal entertainment" for non-experts. The notable exceptions are traditional Japanese tea rooms, which were once constructed in the past, and small sheds, which have recently become a popular form of "personal entertainment." Building brand-new buildings requires too much expertise for non-experts to be able to create safe and comfortable indoor spaces. However, modifying existing buildings, such as making the space more interesting or comfortable, allows even non-experts to actively get involved. Therefore, the action of modifying existing buildings is more likely to be a form of "personal entertainment," rather than the construction of new buildings.

When I attend housing industry meetings and committee meetings organized by the government, I often hear unenthusiastic research reports, such as "the market for remodeling and renovation is not growing, despite great efforts to promote it." As long as those people consider remodeling and renovation to be "business," treating it the same as building new buildings, this lack of enthusiasm will not change. I would recommend that they dare to consider remodeling and renovation a whole new industry, which can promote and support "personal entertainment" befitting a nation with abundant spatial resources.

In spite of the opinion I just expressed in this chapter, I would like to acknowledge that I used to view remodeling and renovation as a new trend but still as a form of "business." This perspective can be seen in the industrial discussions that I present in my publication, *Architecture: A New Work Form – from "Box Delivery" Industry to "Place-making" Industry* (in Japanese: *Kenchiku – Atarashii Shigoto no Katachi*, Shoukokusha, 2013). In Chapter 5 of this book, I did come to the realization that existing spatial resources will be increasingly utilized by non-architectural experts. However, I did not yet realize that these activities could be a form of "personal entertainment." Now, I am certain that the concept of using empty houses as "personal entertainment" will flourish in the future.

## Frontier opened by Japan

All around Japan, one can find previously unused spatial resources transformed into spaces for living a comfortable life. As I discussed before, in the process of creating these spaces, the concept of renovation as "personal entertainment" often appears regardless of the exact purpose or scale of the project. Why is this so? It is because the spatial resources were simply sitting there with no purpose and without being used by anyone. As a result, no one is upset if the resources are used boldly, even for the personal entertainment of the person undertaking the renovation. This leads to the question, why have these spatial resources been neglected for so long? I propose that the only reason is that it is impossible to demolish them.

Let's consider Hashima Island (also known as "Battleship Island")[7] located in Nagasaki. This island provides a prime example of the phenomenon that buildings in Japan remain standing, despite having no purpose and not being actively used, simply because they cannot be demolished. On the island, there are a number of buildings built between 1910 and 1970 from reinforced concrete. Together, the buildings once formed a complex with housing and schools, as well as health and welfare facilities. However, the site was abandoned in 1974, when the coal mine on the island closed and the last remaining group of residents moved away.

A decade ago, I visited this uninhabited island for research. I was amazed to see many buildings, now abandoned, which originally had been built very densely together. Right next to where the boat docked and I disembarked, I found a former school building, seven stories high and made of reinforced concrete. The ground underneath the building had been weathered by high waves over the past forty years. Many of the once invisible concrete piles, which had been buried underground, now stood exposed. When I timidly peeked inside a former company-owned apartment building located next to the school, I discovered evidence of life from 1974. There were rooms with abandoned televisions and pieces of furniture, no doubt left behind when the owners of the homes moved away from the island.

Eventually after passing many company-owned apartment buildings, I reached a former commercial area with movie theaters, shops, and various public service buildings. I could imagine these buildings having been necessary, when the island was at its peak with a population of 5,000 people, frequently commuting by boat to the neighboring islands. At the top of the tallest hill on the island, I even found a shrine. Of course, there were also facilities related to the former coal mining industry as well. For example, a large bath facility remains on the island. The building has three bathtubs, once used in order for workers coming from the undersea tunnels to cleanse all the coal dust from their bodies. Seeing the facility, one can imagine how mining work used to be done in the past.

The oldest buildings on the island are the former apartment complexes, built by companies for housing their employees. Construction was completed in 1916, making the buildings over a century old. As far as I know, these buildings are among the top five oldest remaining examples of reinforced concrete architecture in Japan. At the time the apartment buildings were built, reinforced concrete represented state of the art technology. However, after decades of being exposed to salty wind and occasionally to salty water carried by high waves, the reinforced concrete buildings have aged, like an illustrative example from an architecture textbook.

In 2001, a company in the Mitsubishi Group, which had managed the coal mine, transferred ownership of the island to Takashimacho Town (which is now part of Nagasaki City). Without any influence from the transfer of ownership, the ruins continued to stand for forty years. Ultimately, in 2015, the ruins were registered as a World Cultural Heritage site, specifically as representing one of the "Sites of Japan's Meiji Industrial Revolution: Iron and Steel, Shipbuilding, and Coal Mining." With this status, the buildings will not be demolished for a long time. In a few years, it will be half a century since the buildings have been abandoned. During that time, the cast-off shells of the majestic Meiji era have been transformed into a tourist destination as a World Cultural Heritage site.

Why have the buildings on Battleship Island not been demolished? As outsiders, we cannot know all the internal factors. I did hear rumors that former residents, who grew up on the island, along with other supporters fought to preserve the buildings. Let's consider cases similar to Battleship Island. Typically, unless there is the clear plan for generating revenue, the costs of demolition cannot be justified. As a result, few companies are willing to step up and take over managing the land. In addition, usually there are no major issues caused by leaving the buildings undemolished.

In this way, the buildings on Battleship Island demonstrate the general situation of abandoned buildings in Japan. Of course, there are also some unique factors surrounding Battleship Island, specifically that all the residents had left the island and that as an island, the place was quite isolated. However, aside from these unique factors, most available spatial resources in Japan today share similar reasons to Battleship Island for why the buildings have not been demolished.

All around Japan there are many buildings that cannot be demolished, not only unique places like Battleship Island, but many ordinary places as well. Thanks to that, Japan has become a country rich with spatial resources.

Around Japan, one can find many unused buildings left for similar reasons as the buildings on Battleship Island, namely because the abandoned buildings cause no real problems and there is no clear path to generating revenue with the property. A visitor to Japan might think the buildings have been preserved because there is public support for keeping the buildings as cultural assets or historical objects. However, that is not the case. Many of the undemolished buildings are just ordinary buildings.

One underlying factor contributing to the increasing number of empty buildings in Japan is the weakening of conventional local industries. For example, on Battleship Island, the closure of the coal mine resulted in many abandoned buildings. Similarly, in Kiryu City, the waning silk industry left behind many empty saw-tooth-roofed factory buildings. In some exceptional cases, the ruins of such once flourishing local industries are recognized as World Heritage Sites. However, in most cases, the industries simply weaken and eventually disappear. Also, often the empty buildings and houses left behind are not sufficiently old to recognize them as cultural assets. Unless new businesses rise up to take the place of the previous industries, those empty buildings and houses will remain abandoned, despite their potential as space resources. I propose that we need new stories provided by new people to breathe new life to the buildings. However, in most cases, the buildings remain empty and lifeless.

It might be possible that even after local industries fade, certain towns demolish old buildings, which no longer serve any purpose, and construct new buildings. However, this depends on the population of the town increasing to generate greater consumer activity, ensuring a sufficient revenue stream from the new buildings. Few towns fit this model, meaning that the demolition of old buildings to make way for new construction is not financially viable in most places. Yet another factor underlying the large number of undemolished building is the super-aging and ever-decreasing population in Japan.

It is widely known that Japan has the highest percentage of elderly people in its population,[8] compared to the rest of the world. That percentage only continues to increase. For many decades, the average life span of Japanese women has been longer than women in any other country in the world.

Further, in terms of overall population, Japan appears to be the only country among developed countries facing the problem of a shrinking population. The decrease in Japan's population, coupled with the increasing number of elderly citizens, naturally leads to decreased demolition and rebuilding activities.

Further exacerbating the situation is the history of vigorous construction by the "box delivery industry," which continuously built new houses and buildings for the nearly half a century after the period of high economic growth in Japan. As a result, there is an enormous stock of buildings. In particular, there are many buildings, which were built too recently, to consider them as "historical."

Just as local industries faced a turning point in their business, the population in Japan began to decrease. At the same time, the number of elderly citizens reached an unprecedented level, which had never been recorded in any other country in the world. It is no wonder that Japan was not able to demolish so many ordinary and not especially old buildings, even though the buildings were empty. Currently, no other country faces this problem. However, it is predicted that many countries will eventually become like Japan. The birth rate will decline leading to an increase in the elderly population and a decrease in the overall population. Also, like Japan once did, there are many countries experiencing economic growth driving the rapid construction of new buildings. Thinking that way, Japan could be seen as a pioneer. In the future, many other countries will eventually experience similar phenomena to what Japan is currently experiencing.

Authors of business-related articles often refer to "challenges faced by developed countries." These "challenges" may never be resolved, nor should we necessarily try to resolve them. Rather I believe that we should understand "challenges" as "circumstances" encouraging us to search for and create new ways of life that address these challenges. Although there might not be many current successes that we can share with the world, we should focus on expanding our international network and friendships in order to share whatever knowledge might be useful to others. We should not focus only on our position as a pioneer and become too fixated on trying to leverage our experience for future international business. Japan stands at the gate to a never before seen world. We are living in a fascinating era.

## We cannot play with cultural heritage

Historic buildings are common examples of buildings that cannot be demolished. The buildings on the Battleship Island, which were registered as a World Heritage site, are no doubt cultural heritage assets. In the case of cultural heritage buildings, rather than saying we cannot demolish them, we should think that we are purposefully protecting them.

Under the Law for the Protection of Cultural Properties, the Agency for Cultural Affairs in Japan defines buildings, which fall into the category of tangible cultural assets, as follows:

> "a tangible form that possess high historic, artistic, and academic value to Japan"
>
> (quoted from the website of the Agency for Cultural Affairs in Japan: www.bunka.go.jp/english/policy/cultural_properties/introduction/buildings/)

Tangible cultural properties designated by the Japanese government consist of National Treasures, Important Cultural Properties, and Registered Cultural Properties. There are 255 National Treasures (284 buildings in total), 2,480 Important Cultural Properties (4,959 buildings – some are also designated as National Treasures), and 11,772 Registered Cultural Properties (as of August 1, 2018. Source: www.bunka.go.jp/english/policy/cultural_properties/introduction/number/). In addition to Tangible Cultural Properties designated by the Japanese government, there are also Tangible Cultural Properties designated by prefectural and local governments. These properties are also subject to protection under the law.

To be registered as an Important Cultural Property, a building must meet the basic requirement of being more than 50-years-old. In addition, the following three conditions must be met:

1) The building must contribute to the country's historical landscape
2) The building must serve as a good structural model
3) The building cannot be easily duplicated

In my opinion, the description of these three conditions is vague. It strikes me as challenging for an individual to correctly judge whether a building meets these conditions or not. However, the requirement of being 50 years old or over is clear. Many of the buildings in Japan were built in or before 1968. Thus, the buildings are already at least 50 years old. Across Japan, the majority of spatial resources being worked on as part of renovation projects satisfy the requirement. Being registered as a Cultural Property would bring advantages, such as subsidies for repairs and tax reductions. However, the designation would also restrict structural modifications and changes to the building's appearance.

In this book, I use the term "ordinary buildings" to clearly distinguish those buildings from Cultural Properties. Unlike buildings registered as Cultural Properties, people can freely use and modify ordinary buildings. In other words, ordinary buildings allow for the freedom of "play." Ordinary buildings also represent spatial resources which have not been demolished. I would be so bold to say that these are spatial resources with which we can freely play. We cannot do that to protected Cultural Properties.

Let's consider a few more examples of "ordinary buildings," which were mentioned in previous chapters – uninhabited houses in Kamiyama Town in Tokushima Prefecture, unused former wholesale stores in Nihonbashi area in Tokyo, vacant former factories and townhouses in Monzenmachi Town in

Nagano City in Nagano Prefecture, 40- to 60-year-old rental apartment buildings in Fukuoka City in Fukuoka Prefecture, abandoned temples in Ishikawa Prefecture. All of these properties are quite old and are a part of local history. However, one cannot confidently say that these properties contribute to Japan's historical landscape, or that the buildings serve as good structural models. Also, it does not seem too difficult to duplicate those buildings.

When readers of this book read "utilizing old buildings," I think most people would likely think of preserving and utilizing cultural assets, which are considered to be historically valuable. Therefore, the image of spatial resources tends to be limited to culturally and historically valuable properties. Of course, those buildings are spatial resources. However, I want to emphasize the potential of "playing" with ordinary, abandoned buildings, which are abundant around Japan.

Related to this common misconception, I recently heard an interesting story from Mr. Ishii. In his thirties, Mr. Ishii turned an empty building in Ukiha City[9] in Fukuoka Prefecture into a book café called "Minou Books & Cafe." I had the opportunity, along with Professor Takeshi Suzuki and Professor Kouichi Sato, to interview Mr. Ishii. The interview was featured as episode #47 in a series of interviews exploring "lifestyle perspectives" on the website "Dwelling Web – Lifestyle, dwelling, and town" run by The Japan Federation of Housing Organizations. (The website is available only in Japanese.)

In the center of Ukiha City, there is the Preservation District for Groups of Historic Buildings. Here is a description of the area from the official website of Ukiha City:

> The Chikugo Yoshii Preservation District, located close to the center of Yoshiicho Town in Ukiha City, is the landscape along the Sainokigawa River and Minami River with a series of firmly built plastered townhouses and grand mansions. After a devasting fire in 1869, thatched townhouses fell out of favor, replaced by tile roofing and plastered townhouses. By the Taisho era, at the peak of Japan's economic growth, the landscape looked practically the same as we can see it today. In the Preservation District, about 250 of properties including such traditional buildings, gardens of mansions, and trees along the river are protected.
>
> (The official website of Ukiha City, www.city.ukiha.fukuoka.jp)

The beautifully preserved old landscape with a long row of buildings is indeed spectacular. In contrast, Mr. Ishii's book café, although located in the center of Ukiha City, is not on the street with the traditional buildings. The café is on the first floor of an ordinary looking building, which used to be a seafood store. Mr. Ishii chose a non-cultural asset type of spatial resource. Explaining his choice, Mr. Ishii said, "The Preservation District is intended to preserve the area's heritage but I feel that it has become a place in which we cannot generate new things." Mr. Ishii's words captured my attention.

Spatial resources, which are considered cultural assets, cannot be demolished and are carefully protected and preserved. This means that the buildings have little freedom. Using the expressions that I have introduced in this book, we can describe the situation as, "not being able to 'play' with them like we can do with ordinary buildings." In my opinion, spatial resources, which are recognized as cultural assets, are unlikely to deliver new ways of living. Mr. Ishii's words were straightforward, yet sounded ironic.

Inheriting continued cultures, instead of creating new ones, would be an appropriate purpose of protected spatial resources such as cultural assets. However, even in Preservation Districts, activities inside the buildings do not necessarily get inherited. A post-town area on the main street is an example. Post-towns were needed when walking was the only form of transportation for most people. Today, the function of post-towns got obsolete. Some buildings in post-towns have been transformed to bed-and-breakfast places, however, in most cases those buildings are being used as small cafes and small shops.

It is very rare for any spatial resource, whether it is a cultural asset or an ordinary building, to be used again for its original purpose. By definition, becoming empty and unused means any activity in the property has ceased. There are some limited cases, where members of younger generations revive an activity, which once went extinct, by restarting it. However, in most cases, entirely new stories, entirely new activities, and entirely new purposes are born in those spatial resources, as was the case of Mr. Ishii turning a former seafood store into a book café.

In the majority of cases, when spatial resources are renovated, the original activity is not continued in the space. Residents who have lived in the area for many years need to understand this fact. Without this understanding, a new story, which everyone can share, will never be born. Buildings themselves do not change shape. However, the life, work, and play of people in the town continue to change. Forgetting this basic fact will lead to unnecessary conflict in the town.

## In Asian countries

Previously, in the section about "being a pioneer," I mentioned that we should focus on expanding our international network and friendships in order to share whatever knowledge might be useful to others. In fact, in neighboring Asian countries, instances of people "playing" for their personal entertainment with the existing stock of buildings have begun to appear.

First, let's consider the case of Shanghai in China. In 2016, I visited this enormous city, after not having visited for almost ten years. Not surprisingly, I saw the city had changed in many ways since my previous visit. In the Pudong area, an astonishing number of high-rise buildings had been constructed, including the tallest building in China, the Shanghai Tower.

The scale of development in Pudong surpassed anything that I could have imagined ten years earlier. Just before the Shanghai Tower officially opened, I was allowed to visit the 118th floor. I enjoyed seeing an expansive panorama of the city. I was so high that I could even look down on the Shanghai World Financial Center built by the Mori Building Company, which had attracted a great deal of attention ten years ago. The view brought into focus the dynamics of "development" currently happening all around China.

However, if you to leave this building and walk in the old neighborhoods of the city, you can also feel that in other parts of the city, the way of life in Shanghai is turning in a different direction from this kind of advanced development. During my visit to Shanghai, for the first time, I visited two neighborhoods, which have become famous enough to be found in tourist guidebooks, namely 1933 Old Millfun and Tianzifang.

The former was once a slaughterhouse built in 1933 from reinforced concrete by a British architect. The space has a somewhat mysterious feel partially because of the design of the building, which emphasizes the hardness of the concrete material, as well as the layout of the building peculiar to a slaughterhouse. Now, the space is filled with shops, cafes, restaurants, and event spaces catering to a younger crowd. The building has taken on a new kind of liveliness.

The latter example of Tianzifang is an area of brick Lilong housing, typical of modern Shanghai urban housing. Artists have taken over some buildings, turning them into ateliers and galleries since a little over a decade ago. Other buildings have been transformed into stylish shops and restaurants creating a lively shopping area. The transformed neighborhood is bustling enough that pickpocketing has become a concern.

Shanghai is also home to the Xintiandi district, which was a popular tourist destination ten years ago. The district is a redeveloped Lilong area, which combines modern construction with the flavor of older Lilong buildings. The two places I visited during this trip to Shanghai are markedly different from the Xintiandi district. Both 1933 Old Millfun and Tianzifang have been developed in a way that utilized the existing, original space resource. Seeing these two places, I felt that a new era of utilizing spatial resources has also begun to take root in Shanghai.

In Taiwan, you can also find some interesting developments.

At the closing party for the 8th Renovation School held in Kitakyushu, I met Professor Jui-Pi Su from Tunghai University in Taichung. In the 1990s Professor Jui-Pi Su studied in the architecture program at the University of Tokyo, where I work. When we met at the Renovation School event, I asked him why he was attending the closing of the Kitakyushu City "Kokura-Uo Machi" project. He answered that he was curious to see what kind of activity happened at a Renovation School event, so he decided to attend himself in order to experience it.

Like parts of Japan, the central area of Taichung where Professor Jui-Pi Su lives has also started to decline and there is an increase in the number of empty buildings. Professor Jui-Pi Su began to wonder how those spatial resources could be used. He established the "Taichung Downtown Recreative Foundation" project in one of the empty buildings in the town center. According to Professor Jui-Pi Su, the project has faced many issues, including challenges of business management. As a result, it is not progressing smoothly. In a desperate effort to salvage his project, he decided to attend the Renovation School in Kitakyushu hoping to learn how to succeed in utilizing spatial resources.

His presence at the event demonstrates the increasing globalization of our world, which has been brought about by the current internet age. Before the 21st century, no one in Taiwan could have known about a minor event happening in Japan, like this Renovation School. I imagine he learned about the event from videos of past Renovation School events, which are posted on YouTube. With rudimentary Japanese ability, the videos could be interesting and could attract many people from outside Japan. In more extreme cases, even if you understand absolutely no Japanese, modern translation software could enable you to watch and understand the videos to some extent.

In 2015, I organized the "Conference for Making Renovated Towns" in collaboration with Professor Mistuhiro Tokuda, an associate professor from the Kyushu Institute of Technology. At the first gathering held in Osaka City, I invited Professor Jui-Pi Su and asked him to present about renovation activities currently being undertaken in Taiwan. He presented even more examples than I could have imagined, leading us to launch the second gathering of the conference in Taiwan in 2016.

On the first day of the convention, all the participants rented bicycles and toured examples of renovation projects in the center of Taichung and nearby areas. We saw old city office buildings turned into galleries and cafes. Our group visited the central atrium in the former Miyahara Ophthalmological Clinic, which is a historical building from the period of Japanese rule[10] that has been transformed into an upscale ice cream shop. We also saw other projects, which utilized ordinary spatial resources. For example, we visited the Green Ray and Shen Ji New Village where small shops and restaurants had been created on the lower level of old government employee residences, which offered lots of empty rooms. In the center of the city, an empty building has been turned into a hotel. We stayed there. Also, the office for Professor Jui-Pi Su's "Taichung Downtown Recreative Foundation" project is in a former vacant building right above a shop on the first floor.

Before anyone knew it, we had passed the entire day touring around the city on our bicycles. With a unique motivation and purpose for each project, the number of projects to transform spatial resources into new places for living was impressive. When people in the architectural world think about Taichung, the first thing to come to their mind is no doubt the National Taichung Theater designed by Mr. Toyoo Ito. I am sure that architectural experts would think about the city as a place where buildings designed by international architects are being built one after another. At the same time, although less flashy, there are also many renovation projects to "play" with existing buildings being undertaken in the older central part of the city. A visitor to the city can see two opposing movements developing within one city. It is truly a modern spectacle, or rather should I say that it is a very modern landscape in Asia.

Next, traveling to the south of Taichung, one can find Chiayi City, the closest town to the Alishan National Scenic Area. This part of Taiwan is the production area of Taiwan cypress, which was used in the past in Japan to build the Meiji Shrine,[11] Kashihara Shrine,[12] Yasukuni Shrine,[13] and Todaiji Temple.[14] The 2016 second Renovation Conference also included a tour of this site, where Professor Cheng-Che Chen at Nanhua University, another international graduate of the University of Tokyo graduate program, had collaborated with students on interesting, housing-related renovation projects.

In Chiayi City, a wooden prison left over from the era of Japanese occupation has become a local tourist attraction as a historic building. However, there are actually more than a hundred wooden houses remaining in the area, which were built as staff dormitory facilities. With the closure of the prison, such facilities have become unnecessary. Some buildings are still inhabited but most have become empty, unused spaces.

Professor Chen originally researched architecture history. While recognizing the value of the former dormitory buildings, he sought to create a new place, which would attract young people to live and exchange ideas and would help foster new businesses. In this way, utilizing the area, in an economically viable way, would help to preserve the area.

The buildings are already old wooden structures. Beyond that, the buildings were constructed in a subtropical area, where wood quickly deteriorates. The condition of the buildings would make them unusable, no matter their location. He has been proceeding with renovation slowly by collaborating with students and graduates of his architectural department. The slow pace means that the project cannot be compared to a typical business renovation project. Rather, the project is closer to the serious "personal entertainment" of Mr. Nishimura in Kiryu City, which I introduced at the beginning of the chapter.

Professor Chen envisions a future where the older spatial resources could drive the creation of new local industries in Chiayi. Specifically, he is focused on a new lumber industry, based on the connection with Alishan as a wood production area. Discussions and projects in Japan related to renovation and the future of the regional lumber industry have been inspiring him. He told me that looking to the future, he expects more and more opportunities for exchanging ideas.

Among the professors from Japanese universities who participated in the "Conference for Making Renovated Towns," some of them have already started educational exchange with Professor Chen's lab. Specifically, there were also a number of people who started workshops at renovated wooden houses. I focused on exchanging ideas with other Asian countries through the "Conference for Making Renovated Towns." Young people were already working to achieve those aims. I feel a great sense of hope seeing their passion.

## Conclusion – hope is being cultivated

Let's return to Japan with its abundance of spatial resources. I previously discussed the "DIY Eco-Renovation" project, as an example of work undertaken for personal entertainment. One of the first events held was a workshop called "Minamiboso DIY Eco-Renovation" (https://mb-republic.com/satoyama-life/). The architect, Mr. Masayoshi Takeuchi, played a key role in the workshop, along with Ms. Miori Baba. Ms. Baba is the director of the non-profit organization Minamiboso Republic, and in fact, enjoys living in two places herself.

Although this is not a popular opinion to express, if I am honest, I would say that I am not so drawn to topics like "eco-friendly," "energy conservation," "low-carbon emission," "climate change," "sustainable life-style," and "natural living." Of course, I understand that modern society considers these to be important concepts. However, at least as a researcher, I have steered away from focusing my research on these trendy themes.

That being said, even a contrarian like myself could not help feeling moved by the presentation of Mr. Takeuchi, when he presented the work of his "Minamiboso DIY Eco-Renovation" project. No doubt, Mr. Takeuchi, as both an architect and as a citizen of modern society, often talks about and discusses the importance of the concepts that I raised earlier. Amazingly, when he introduced the "Minamiboso DIY Eco-Renovation" project, he did not mention any of those words even once. This immediately grabbed my attention.

For example, Mr. Takeuchi told the story of a person who bought an old private house on the Boso Peninsula[15] of Chiba Prefecture. Being quite outdated, the house had many openings, which made it unbearably cold in the winter. The low price of the property lured the owner into buying the house. Ironically, to make the house comfortable, a professional contractor would no doubt charge millions of yen (equivalent to tens of thousands of dollars) to improve the insulation of the house. The house was particularly expensive to renovate because it had a larger floor space than the average, newly built house. The owner could not possibly pay that much for the repair. Hearing this, I am sure you are curious about what happened in the end. In a country like Japan with abundant space resources, one can actually imagine this kind of episode happening. Rather than giving up, the owner found an unexpected way to turn the problem into an activity for personal entertainment. Since hiring a professional would be expensive, the owner decided to somehow tackle the project herself, along with her friends. Of course, being non-professionals, the owner could not expect a professional quality job. Still, the owner ambitiously aimed to create a warm, snug home that could withstand the winter by spending only several hundred thousand yen (equivalent to several thousand dollars). The bold aspiration of the home owner inspired Mr. Takeuchi and his colleagues to join the project.

Mr. Takeuchi realized that countries with abundant spatial resources must have a lot of people facing similar challenges. He decided to hold a workshop in this house, introducing DIY renovation, which he had previously attempted at the Renovation School. People, who were aware of the problems of insulation and uncomfortably cold houses, attended, as well as others who were excited about the idea of trying their hand at improving the performance of insulation. In the end, a crowd of more than ten people joined the workshop. Mr. Takeuchi was joined by a specialized craftsperson, who helped teach the course. At first, the participants attended a lecture on the basics of insulation. Then, they were divided to learn various specialized tasks, including cutting, pasting, and scraping. In the end, everyone joined a party celebrating the completion of the project.

Later, when I researched more, I found out that Mr. Takeuchi was asked to be part of the project by Ms. Miori Baba, a writer who splits her time between two homes. I found out that is why details of the project, as well as the workshop, had been published on the internet (https://style.tokyu-resort.co.jp/dual-area-life-14, in Japanese only). It felt like a breath of fresh air, when I listened to Mr. Takeuchi's experiences and reading Ms. Baba's report and heard no mention of abstract ideas like "eco-friendly," "low carbon emission," and "sustainable lifestyle." They did not approach their work like a professional baseball player, practicing intensely every day. Instead, their work was like a game of pick-up baseball, where friends gather to play just for fun. This refreshing feeling is the same one from a game of pick-up baseball. Currently Japan has an abundance of spatial resources, including empty houses. Those spatial resources are like freshly mowed fields, inviting people to enjoy playing baseball. It may be just an empty field, or a proper baseball field in a park.

The experiences of Ms. Baba and Mr. Takeuchi through the "Minami-boso Eco-Renovation" project show us that the abundance of spatial resources allows for "play." I feel inspired to call for "Becoming a society that plays with the stock of buildings." Of course, in Japan, the population will continue to shrink, the birth rate will continue to decrease, and the number of elderly citizens will continue to rise. Let's not lose sight of the hope, which comes from entering an era where Japan will be a mighty country blessed with spatial resources. I feel the era coming, and I see that hope beginning to be cultivated in Japan. The hope springs from the richness of architecture, which emerges when architecture is opened to the people.

## Notes

1 According to data announced in 2013 by the Japanese government, Japan has more than 8,000,000 empty houses. This number includes homes where the contact information of the owner is difficult to obtain, as well as homes which are not being maintained at all and thus falling into dangerous disrepair. Given such circumstances, empty houses tend to be seen as a serious problem for the local community, rather than seen in a positive light. In particular, media outlets in Japan have started to refer to the number of empty houses as Japan's "empty house problem." As a result, the general public has developed a negative image towards empty houses.
2 A city located in the eastern part of Gunma Prefecture with a population of approximately 110,000 people. The city is known for being the site of the ancient origin of the silk industry in Japan.
3 An excerpt from the exhibition pamphlet (published by Arts Chiyoda 3331) for Mr. Yusuke Nishimura's exhibition "For a dialogue with the land – Things that memorialize its action, the place we live and time" The exhibit was on display from March 1 to March 31, 2018.
4 A quote from me about Mr. Nishimura's art, which appeared in the exhibition pamphlet described in footnote 3 above. The quote has been slightly edited here for the purpose of this book.
5 On March 24, 2018, a symposium was held at Art Chiyoda 3331 titled "Yusuke Nishimura, Shuichi Matsumura, and Masato Nakamura – The Spirit of the Field: Traversing between Architecture and Art." A panel discussion from that symposium can be watched on YouTube. Please note that the video content from the event starts from 27 minutes. (www.youtube.com/watch?v=WaAutqPWO3U)
6 This word is used with the same meaning as the concept of "play" discussed in "homo ludens" by the Dutch historian Johan Huizinga (1872–1945).
7 From the Meiji era to the Showa era, Hashima Island flourished thanks to coal mining in the ocean. The area once had greater population density than Tokyo. However, since the closure of the mine in 1974 and the departure of the final residents from the island, Hashima Island has been uninhabited. In 2015, the International Council on Monuments and Sites (ICOMOS) designated the island as a World Cultural Heritage site representing "Meiji Japan's Industrial Revolution Heritage-Iron, Steel, Steelmaking, Shipbuilding, and Coal Industry." The following website offers a guide for tourists to the island (https://travel.at-nagasaki.jp/en/what-to-see/47/).
8 According to the "2018 White Paper on the Aging Society" published by the Cabinet Office of Japan, in 2015 the percentage of people age 65 years and older in the total population (i.e., the "aging ratio") was 26.6% in Japan, 21.1% in Germany, 19.6% in Sweden, 18.9% in France, 18.1% in the UK, and 14.6% in America.
9 A city with a population of less than 30,000 people, which is located in the southeastern part of the Fukuoka Preference in Kyushu.
10 This refers to the period of time from April 17, 1895, when Taiwan was transferred to Japan from the Qing Dynasty by the Shimonoseki Treaty, until

October 25, 1945, when Taiwan was returned from Japan to the Republic of China by the Potsdam Declaration.

11 A shrine built in 1920. This shrine, which is located in Tokyo, is devoted to the worship of Emperor Meiji and his wife, Empress Shoken.

12 A shrine, located in Kashihara City in Nara Prefecture, which is dedicated to the first Emperor of Japan, Emperor Jinmu, and the Empress.

13 A shrine built in 1869 and located in Tokyo. It celebrates the soldiers who fought for the government and ruling courts during the civil war in Japan following the Meiji Era.

14 A temple located in Nara City in Nara Prefecture. It was built by order of Emperor Shomu in 743, as a temple to protect the whole country of Japan.

15 A peninsula facing the Pacific Ocean on the southeastern side of the Kanto region (which includes Tokyo). It occupies a major part of Chiba Prefecture.

## Bibliography

Huizinga, Johan, *Homo Ludens*, (Japanese version, translated by Motoichiro Satomi), Kodansha Co., Ltd., 2018

Matsumura, Shuichi, *Kenchiku – Atarashii Shigoto no Katachi (Architecture: A New Work Form - from "Box Delivery" Industry to "Place-making" Industry)*, Shoukokusha, 2013

All other references are from websites or exhibition pamphlets and shown in the text.

# Index

Note: page numbers relating to figures are given in *italics* and notes by n, followed by the note number


1933 Old Millfun 149
"2003 issue" 97
2011 Great East Japan Earthquake 114n16

Act on Architects and Building Engineers 114n10, 129
Act Establishing the Japan Housing Corporation 47
Act on Public Housing 47
added value 78
affordable housing 98
Agency for Cultural Affairs 145–146
aging population 5, 128
Akasaka Palace 135n14
Akihabara 102
Akiyama, Tetsukazu 54
ALC wall panels 18
Alexander, Christopher 3, 58–60, 119, 121, 132
Alishan 151
Aoki, Jun (architect) 110
Aoki, Jun of Mame-kurashi Ltd. 108–110
apartment buildings 42, 109; public housing 29, 140; reinforced concrete 16, 143; rental properties 91, 98, 110, 112, 113n1, 114n23; sales figures 83; "support" 48; *see also* condominiums
apprenticeships 25
appropriate technology movement 57
"architect builders" 59
Architects and Building Engineers, Act on 114n10, 129
Architects and Engineers Association 129
Architectural Association School of Architecture 55
architectural design 19, 36n3, 36n6, 109–110; commercialization 79; "places" 121; sustainable town management 124; vernacular architecture 42–43; *see also* design and construction
architectural education 90, 129–130
architectural experts/professionals 129, 131, 132, 134, 140–142, 151; communities of 123; "places" 119–120; space resources 116, 141; vacant buildings 7; ways of life 92
architectural photographs 53, 90, 132, 134
*Architecture without Architects* 44, 90
*Arts & Architecture* magazine 53
Arts Chiyoda 3331 project 5, 102, 134, 136
Asahi Kasei Corporation 24
Asian countries 7, 148, 152
assembling-order production 80
assembly line method 1
Association for Factory-Produced Housing 9–10
automated processes 79–82

Baba, Matsataka 121–122, 128
Baba, Miori 152–153
Bank of Japan 129, 135n13
"Basic Plan for Industrialization of Housing Construction" 32

Battleship (Hashima) Island 142–145, 154n7
Bemis, Albert F. 9, 36n4
Bertalanffy, Ludwig von 46
birth rate 128, 145, 153
block masonry construction 11
Boso Peninsula 152
box delivery industry 129, 145; arrival of 3–6; basis of 68–71; creativity of users 100, 102; shift to "place creation" 84–86; suppliers/ manufacturers 73; ways of life 90
Brand, Stewart 3, 57–58, 61n27
bubble economy 17, 81
build-out apartments 108, 119
building components *see* component types
Building Engineers, Act on 114n10, 129
building owners 117, 125, 128
Building Standard Law 11–12, 18, 37n16, 113n4
built-on-demand housing 28
Bushi-En 119–120

CADCAM type pre-cutting machine 81
capital investment 17, 74
carpenters 33–35; construction units 29, 31; floor plans 66; local contractors 70–73, 82; machinery 80; organizations 45; "play" 7; PRECON 15; skills 43; Ukeoi contracts 25–27
centralized housing 55
"Chanoma" 65
Cheng, Cheng-Che 151
Chiayi City 151
Chinese economic reform 77
closed systems 4, 56
cold-formed steel 18–19
collective intelligence 60, 119
Comfama de Aranjuez 101, *103*
"Command A" 134
commercialization 15, 27–28, 76–79, 92
commercialized housing 77–79, 83–84
community surveys 99
component types 4, 16, 19, 27, 43, 45, 53, 80
computer-guided tools and machines 80
concrete houses 10
condominiums 3–4, 29, 57, 74, 77, 124; *see also* apartment buildings; commercialized housing
Condor, Josiah 36n7, 135n13
construction industry 4, 73; "Basic Plan" 32; "box delivery" 68, 70; companies involved in 19; "play" 139; Ukeoi contracts 25
construction starts 18, 29
contemporary folk houses 3, 49
contents of the space 132
contract method 25, 38n29, 72; *see also* Ukeoi (turn-key) contracts
contractors 3–4, 26–27, 31, 70–76; apartment buildings 91; architect relationships 54; "box delivery" 84, 102; carpenters managing 45; charges 152; female designers 112; impact of technology 80–82
"conventional methods" 29, 53, 80
conventional wooden constructions 74
conversion 96–99, 101, 110
Corbusier, Le 2, 10, 36n5, 46–47, 61n10, 132
cost performance 55, 78
craftsmen society 35
creative depopulation 105
creativity of users 100, 102
Cultural Affairs, Agency for 145–146
cultural heritage 145
"Current and Future Prospects of the Housing Industry" 32
customization 21, 78–80, 82–85, 109

*daiku* 33–34
Daiwa House Industry Co., Ltd. *21*, 25, 27
Daiwa House Type A 25
deforestation 10
degree of freedom 4, 76–77
"demilitarized zone" 50
*Den-ken Chiku* 45
Department of Housing and Urban Development (HUD) 33
depopulation 105
design and construction 19, 25–26, 59, 71, 73, 131; *see also* architectural design
"designed type" homes 78
detachable units 48
detached houses 17, 34, 83
dimensions: exterior 19; measuring systems 74; rules governing 66; standard guidelines 51, 53
"dining-sleeping separation" theory 47
direct management system 26, 72

DIY (do-it-yourself) 6, 13, 59, 109, 111–113, 119
DIY Eco-Renovation 140, 152–153
DOCOMOMO JAPAN 37n12, 37n17
Dom-ino 47
dome method 58
Dymaxion Dwelling Machine 52, 58, 60n8, 61n17

Eames, Charles and Ray 3, 52–54
Eames House 52–54, 61n18
earthquake-resistance codes/standards 94–95, 113n4
"easy order" system 20, 74
economic growth 2, 31, 68, 73, 145, 147; *see also* high economic growth
economic reform, China 77
economically disadvantaged people 55, 86, 101
"Edo Module" 65
education, architectural 90, 129–130
Eishin Gakuen Higashino High School 62n31
elderly people 100, 108, 133, 144
empty buildings/houses 125, 140–141, 144, 150; increasing numbers 136, 153, 154n1; "play" 7, 147; renovation 122, 136; utilization 99, 142; *see also* vacant buildings; vacant houses
empty space 117, 136
Engi Law 34
Entenza, John 53

factory-produced components 32
factory-produced elements 16
factory-produced housing 9–10, 31–32
Factory-Produced Housing Approval System 13
Factory-Production Housing Review Committee 70
farmland, release of 17
field surveys 45
financial crisis 5, 17, 104
financial resources 55
financing system 4, 27–28, 69, 131; *see also* funding; investment
fire protection 13–14, 98
fireproofing 10, 13, 15
first class architects 129
Five-Year Housing Construction Plan 32
flexibility 4, 16, 19, 74
flexible design 74
floor panels 78
floor plans 4, 19, 24, 43, 47, 61, 66, 74, 76
Fluxus 118
folk houses 3, 43–44, 48–50, 60n6, 99
Ford, Henry 1
Ford Model T 1, 76
freedom to build 3, 54, 56–57
freedom of choice 4–5, 50–53, 56, 74, 76
freedom from system 3, 52–54
Fujioka, Yuto 136
Fukui, Yukichi 23–24
Fukuoka City 110, *111*, 114n23, 147
Fuller, Buckminster 46, 52, 58–59, 60n8, 61n17, 61n29
functionalism 43, 93
funding 43, 69–70; *see also* financing system; investment
Funo, Shuji 54–56
*fusuma* 66
Futagawa, Yukio 43, 90

gardeners 131–132
general contractors 31, 39n38, 71, 102, 112
General Headquarters (GHQ) 2, 8n1
General System Theory 46, 56
GHK *see* General Headquarters
"Ginkakuji" 66, 87n5
Goto, Kazuo 15, 37n10
Great East Japan Earthquake 114n16
Great Kanto Earthquake 13
Green Valley 105
Gropius, Walter 2, 46, 79
"Group of Traditional Buildings" 45
"Guidelines for Promoting the Housing Industry" 32
*Gunkyo* 3, 54–59

Habraken, N. John 3, 46–48, 50, 52–55, 57, 66, 85, 93, 108, 131
"half farming half something" 107
hand-manufacturing 82
Hashima (Battleship) Island 142–145, 154n7
HEAD (Home & Environment Advanced Design) Study Group 121–122
Hebel House 24
height limit of buildings 18, 37n16
high economic growth 5, 15, 42, 45, 145; customers and 69–72, 86;

government/industry initiatives 25, 33; ways of life 94, 96, 98
high-incomes 79
high-rise apartment buildings 42
"higher quality of life with less living cost" 107–108
Hirose, Tsuyoshi 122
Hiroshima Migration Support Media 104
Hitchcock, Henry-Russell 44
Home & Environment Advanced Design (HEAD) Study Group 121–122
Hometown Migration Support Center 104, *105*, 107, 118
Hoshina, Yasuhiro 99–101, *99*, 103
household goods 90–91
"houses as commodities" concept 57
housing components *see* component types
Housing Corporation 4, 47, 61n11, 132, 134, 135n22; government/industry initiatives 9–10, 16, 24, 32, 37n11, 37n14
"Housing with Industrialized Components Applied" 32
housing industry 31–33, 38n36, 42, 61n23; "box delivery system" 3, 4; meetings 141; prefabricated houses 24, 80
housing investment 31, 68, 70
Housing and Land Survey 85–86, 94
Housing Loan Corporation 12–13, 16, 27–28, 69–70
Housing Project Union (HPU) 54
housing shortage 9–10, 31, 35n2, 47, 86
housing starts 29, 31
housing suppliers and manufacturers 42, 91; customer inclusion 70, 73–80, 83–84, 87n9; government/industry initiatives 19–21, 25, 27–29, 31, 38n22, 38n28
HPU (Housing Project Union) 54
HUD (Department of Housing and Urban Development) 33, 39n37, 39n38

Ichiki, Koichiro 122
Ichiura, Ken 9–10, 36n5
ICOMOS (International Council on Monuments and Sites) 154
Imanishi House 44, *44*, *45*
Imperial University of Kyoto 36n6
Imperial University of Tokyo 10, 36n3, 36n5, 36n7, 36n8
"Important Cultural Property" 44, 60n6, 60n7, 146
Inaba, Shingo 26
incombustibility 36n8, 70
individual demand 79, 101
industrial productivity 1
industrial products 48, 53
Industrial Revolution 1
industrialization 2, 4, 36n7, 47–54; customers and 84–85; government/industry initiatives 15, 17, 32–33
industrialized building production 43
industrialized housing 21, 32–33, 83
infill 4, 48, 50, 52–53, 57, 108, 131
information processing 79–80, 83
information sharing 6, 7, 119–121
infrastructure 11, 28, 69, *69*, *96*
intermediate technology 57
International Council on Monuments and Sites (ICOMOS) 154
"international style" 43–44
investment 17, 31, 48, 68–70, 74, 85–86; *see also* financing system; funding
Ishibashi, Nobuo 38n28
Ishimoto, Tokusaburo 23–24
Ishiyama, Osamu 3, 47, 54, 61n12
Isozaki, Arata 114n25
Ito, Teiji 43, 60, 90
Ito, Toyoo 151

Japan Academy 60n2
Japan Building Center 28
Japan Federation of Housing Organizations 147
Japan Housing Corporation (JHC) 16–17, 32, 37n11, 37n14, 47, 61n11, 132, 134, 135n22
Japan Housing Finance Agency 12
Japan Nitrogen Fertilizer Company 23
Japan Telephone and Building Company 70
Japanese Folk Houses 43, 48–50, 90
Japanese-style architectural system 72
Japanese-style wooden buildings 67, *67*
JHC *see* Japan Housing Corporation
Jishouji Temple ("Ginkakuji") 66
job opportunities 105
Johnson, Philip 44

Kahn, Lloyd 58
Kamiyama Town 105–106, *106*, 146
Kasami, Kazuo 104, 107, 108, 118
Kashihara Shrine 151
Kasumigaseki Building 18
Katayama, Toukuma 36n7, 129
*ken* 66
"Kenchiku" 42, 142
Kenmochi, Isamu 61n16
Kenmochi, Ryo 3, 51–52, 61n16
Kikkaikan Building 56–57
Kinoshita, Hitoshi 121
Kiryu City 136–137, 139–140, 144, 151
Kitakyushu Renovation School 112, 114n26, *123*, *126*
Kitakyushu Yamorisha 117, *123*, *126*
Kobayashi, Akio 25
Korean War 18
Kozai Club 19
Kume, Mari 112, 140
Kuraishi, Tomonori 122, 127–128
Kurashiki Rayon 36n6
Kyo Module 65
Kyoto Institute of Technology 23
Kyushu Institute of Technology 122, 150

land 4, 6, 11–13; availability 86; man-made 31; managing 143; policy 17; role of 69
large-sized panel construction 17
law: Building Standards 11–12, 18, 37n16, 113n4; Engi Law 34; Ministry of Construction 11–13, 32; Public Housing 12, 16, 47; Ritsuryo law 71
Law for the Protection of Cultural Properties 145
leasing contracts 119
Levittown 52, 61n17
Licensed Architect and Building Engineers 101
life philosophy 5, 90–93, 98, 104, 106–109, 116
life span 48, 94, 144
lifestyle 48, 54, 58, 128, 132; customer inclusion 78; government/industry initiatives 12, 17; twenty-first century 91–92, 107–108, 110; vacant buildings 147, 152–153
"lifestyle adventurer" 107
light-gauge (cold-formed) steel 18–19, 22, 24, 27
Light-Gauge Steel Construction Association 19
Lilong housing 149
*Limits to Growth* 42
LLP organizations 126–128
loan system 72
local builders 2, 25–28, 71
local craftsmen 45, 54
local housing contractors 3–4, 45, 54, 91; carpenters 70–73, 82; customers 70–74, 76, 80–82; government/industry initiatives 31
Long-Term Plan for Industrializing Housing Production 32
low cost housing 53
low-income people 98, 101
lower price, mass production 76
lumber industry 151

Maciunas, George 118, 134n3
"manner" 7, 117, 121, 131
manufacturers *see* housing suppliers and manufacturers
market segmentation 79
mass consumption 56
mass customization 79–80, 82–85
mass housing 3, 16–17, 47–48, 55, 57, 92
mass production 42–43, 46–47, 53, 61n11, 61n17, 116; customer inclusion 74, 76, 79, 83, 92; government/industry initiatives 19, 28, 33–34; lower price 76
mass sales 83–84
Massachusetts Institute of Technology 38n26
master carpenters 25–26, 71
Masuzawa, Tamami 126, 128
*Material World: A Global Family Portrait* 90
Matsunaga, Yasumitsu 121
Matsushita Electric Works 38n23
Matsushita Group 24
Matsushita, Konosuke 22, 38n23
Matsushita Number 1 model 22, 25
Medellin, Colombia 101–102, *103*
Meiji Restoration 129
Meiji Shrine 151
Menzel, Peter 90
meritocracy 92
"Micro House" *21*, 25, 27
Midas, King 46

migrants/migration 5–6, 103–107, *105*, 109, 118–119
Minami Boso DIY Eco-Renovation 140, 152
Ministry of Construction 11–13, 32, 38n37
Ministry of International Trade and Industry 32, 38n36
Ministry of Land, Infrastructure, and Transport 28
Misawa, Chiyoji 87n9
Misawa Home 77–78, *77*, *78*
mixed-used space 120
Miyamoto, Kei 122
model home plazas 76
model houses 33, 83
modernist architects 2, 79, 83–84
modernity 2–3, 116
modernization: of architecture 33, 35, 42–45, 53, 58; of society 1, 129
modular construction 48, *67*
modular coordination 4, 82
modular units 21, *51*
Mokuchin apartment buildings 91
Monsanto Company 24, 38n26
monthly sale method 70
"mujin way" 70
multilingual experts 130
multi-skilled workers 131
multiple jobs 107
Muromachi period 66
Museum of Modern Art in New York 44

Nagano City 122, 125–126, *127*, 128, 134n8, 146
Nagaya, Hiroshi 121
Nakamura, Masato 102, 117–118, 134, 136–137, 139
Nano Graphica 125–126, 128
National Home Project 24
National Treasures 146
new construction 43, 45, 98, 108, 112, 123; customers 68, 73; government/industry initiatives 17–18, 32
new towns 16, 37n11, 37n12, 37n13
Nihon Denken 70
Nihonbashi 128, 146
Nippon Steel Sumikin 37n18
Nishikawa, Yuko 109
Nishimura, Yusuke 136–140, 151, 154n3–5
Nishiyama, Uzo 47, 61n12
Nobe, Koichi 54
non-architectural experts 122, 142
Non-Flammable City 14
nuclear power plant accident 5, 104

O Model (Misawa Home) 77, *77*
Ohminami, Nobuya 105
Ohno, Katsuhiko 3, 47–54, *51*
Ohya, Yoshinari 119
oil crisis 17, 20, 42, 68
oil shocks 43
on-site construction 28, 33, 70, 76, 77
one-person households 109
online real estate distribution system 128
open architecture: future 136–155; phases 1–8, 116–135
open markets 50
open system 4, 51–52, 56, 131
"Operation Breakthrough" 32–33, 38n37
ordered houses 17, 21
"ordinary buildings" 146, 148
Osaka Expo 94
Osaka Prefecture 37n12, 60n6
Oshima, Yoshihiko 6, 121–122
owner-occupied houses 6, 12, 69, 91, 95–96, 113n5

packaged houses 27–28, 57
Panasonic Homes Corporation *22*, 24
panel-type houses 9–10, 24
*Pattern Language* 3, 58–60, 65, 119, 120–121, 132
personal entertainment 139–142, 148, 151–153
philosophy of life 5–6, 130
photographs, architectural 53, 90, 132, 134
Pilot House Building Technology Proposal Competition 32–33
"place" 5–7; architectural experts 119–120; design 121; third phase development 117–119, 128, 130, 133–134; ways of life 91, 93, 100–102, 105–106, 109–110, 113
place arrangement 121
place creation 84–86, 119, 131–133
place-making industry 5–6, 86, 101
planning module research 24
plastic houses 23–24, 38n26
platform-frame construction 74
"play" 99, 148, 151, 153, 154n6
population: aging population 5, 95, 128, 144; country towns 114n17; decline 7,

135; Gunma Prefecture 154n2; Hashima Island 154n7; of Japan 35, 86, 143–145; new towns 37n11–13; urban inhabitants 31, 144
post-and-beam joints 80
post-and-beam structure 9, 19, 50
post-towns 148
postmodernism 42
postwar reconstruction period 26, 72
pre-cut components 9
pre-cutting machines 80–82, *82*, 87n12
precast concrete construction 13, 19, 32
PRECON 13, *14*, 15–16, 37n10
prefabricated houses 2–4, 13, 18–20, *21*; emergence 21–25, *22*; suppliers/ manufacturers 25–29, 31–32, 42, 45, 70, 73–74, 76, 80, 82, 87n9
prefabricated housing industry 24, 80
"Premos" 10
price of housing 76
production: scale of 21, 73; "weather chart" 29, *30*
"production by house" 4, 80, *81*
productivity 1, 4, 31, 80
"Promoting Standardization in the Housing Industry" 32
Protection of Cultural Properties Act 45
prototyping 46–47, *53–54*, *58*; customers and 79, 84; government/ industry initiatives 9–10, 19, 22, 25; space resources 116; vernacular architecture 43
public housing 4, 11–13, 16–17, 29, 36n3; apartment buildings 29, 140; government-established 98; industrialization 47; mass production 61n11; Urban Renaissance Project 132, 135n22
Public Housing Law 12, 16, 47
public-private partnerships 118

"Quanset Huts" 24

R Real Estate Group 113, 128
"rabbit hutches" 94–95
rapid economic growth 2, 68
RC (reinforced concrete) flats/ apartments 16–17, 143
ready-made houses 74
ready for sale houses 17
real estate market 5, 99, 117, 128
Recruit Holdings Co., Ltd. 109
registered architects 129
Registered Cultural Property 146
"Reizensou" 110–111, *111*
release of farmland 17
renovation 5–7, 119–123, *123*, 125, 130–131, 134; as art 136–139; vacant buildings 140–142, 146, 149–153; ways of life 102, 107–113, 114n20, 114n26
renovation *machizukuri* (renovation town planning) 125
Renovation School 112, 114n26, 121–122, *123*, 125, *126*, 141, 149–150, 153
rental apartments 18, 91, 108–110, 112, 113n1, 114n23, 146
rental contracts 119
rented houses 6, 72, 95–96, 109, 113n5
Research Team on Effective Utilization of Urban Space through Building Conversion 97
Ritsuryo law 71
robots 80
room-sized (wall and floor) panel 21
Roppongi 97
Rudofsky, Bernard 44, 90

Saint-Exupéry, Antoine de 109
sales efficiency 83–84
salespeople 4, 76, 78, 83–84
Satachi, Sichijiro 36n7, 129
Sato, Kouichi 147
saw-tooth roof 137–139, 144
Sawada, Mitsufusa 15, 28–29
scale of the company's production 74
Schumacher, E. F. 42, 57
second class architects 129
seismic diagnosis 95
seismic reinforcement 95
Sekisui Chemical Co., Ltd. *20*, 22–23, *23*, 25, 38n22, 38n24
Sekisui Heim M1 *23*, 48, *49*, 50, *51*, 61n14
Sekisui House Co., Ltd. *20*, 24, *75*
Sekisui House Type A *20*, 22, 24–25
self-build 6, 56–60, 62n30, 91
semi-customized apartments 108–110, 119
"semi-industrialized housing" 32
seniority system 92
Shanghai 148–149
share houses 133–134
"Share Kanazawa" 120

shared residences 109
sharing information 7, 119–121
Shimada, Yohei 121–122
Shimahara, Manjyo 109, 121–122
Shimizu, Yoshitsugu 121, 134
Shinbori, Manabu 121
Shiodome 97
*shoji* 66, 87n5
Shokusan Housing 70
Showa period 70
SI *see* support and infill
"Simple Concrete Structures" 10
skyscrapers 18, 42
slum improvement 55–56
*Small Is Beautiful* 42, 57
social welfare organizations 119
SOHO district, New York 98
Sone, Tatsuzo 36n7, 129
"Song of Architect" 129–130
Spaceship Earth concept 58
spatial resources 5–6, 94, 96, 108, 110–111, 113; architectural professionals 116, 141; empty spaces 140–142, 144, 146–154; place creation 131
SPH (Standard of Public Housing) 17
standard design method 16–17, 28
Standard of Public Housing (SPH) 17
standardization 65, 92
Standardized Component Building System 51, *52*, 61n16
standardized housing units 83
"standardized type" 78
steel-frame prefabricated housing 18–20, 24, 70
steel structures 2, 17–19, 22
stored components 80
Styrofoam 59
Su, Jui-Pi 149–150
subsystems 50, 52, 53
super-aging society 5, 93, 144
super high-rise apartment buildings 42
suppliers/manufacturers *see* housing suppliers and manufacturers
"support" 4, 48, 50, 131
support and infill (SI) 4, 48, 108
sustainable management 124, 125
Suzuki, Takeshi 147
"system" 2–3, 43, 46–54, 56, 65–67
System B 25
system dynamics 46
systems approach 46
Taichung 149–151
Taichung Downtown Recreative Foundation 150
Taihei Housing 70
Taihei Industry 15
Taiwan 35n2, 149–151, 154n10
Taiwan cypress 151
Takashima, Naoyuki 54
Takeda, Yonekichi 26
Takeuchi, Masayoshi 152–153
Tamamusubi Terrace 132, *133*
Tanabe, Heigaku 13, 15–16, 37n9, 37n10
Tanaka, Kakuei 87n7
tatami mats 47, 65–67, 72, 74, 82, 84, 87n3–5, 91, 113n1
tatami module 5, 65–66, 68
*Tatemono* 42
Tatsuno, Kingo 36n7, 129
technological innovation 79
Tianzifang 149
timber construction architects 129
Todaiji Temple 151
Tokuda, Mitsuhiro 122, 150
Tokyo Institute of Technology 15, 37n8
Tokyo metropolitan government 37n13
Tokyo R Real Estate 128
Tokyo Station 129, 135n13, 135n15
*Tokyo Style* 91
Tougudou Doujinsai 66
town management 117, 124
Toyo University 54, 61n22, 61n25
Toyoda, Kiichiro 15
Toyota Housing Corporation 24
Toyota Motor Corporation 15
Toyota T & S Construction Co., Ltd. 15
Tsuzuki, Kyoichi 90–91, 101
turn-key (Ukeoi) contracts 2, 25–28, 38n29
Turner, John F.C. 3, 55–56, 58, 131

Uchida, Genkou 31
Uchida, Yoshichika 43, 45, 51–52, 60n2, 61n14, 61n16, 65
Uchiyama, Hirofumi 121–122
Ueno area 102
Ukeoi (turn-key) contracts 2, 25–28, 38n29
Ukiha City 147
UNESCO World Heritage sites 87n5
universalization 42
*Universe for Rent* 90–91, 101

University of Tokyo 23, 27, 36n3, 36n7, 43, 60n1, 60n2, 61n14, 61n16, 65, 129, 135n13, 149, 151
"unselfconsciousness" 3, 54
Urabe, Shizutaro 10
Urban Building Law 11, 37n16
Urban Renaissance Agency 37n11, 37n13, 132, 135n22
"users' creativity in using existing space" 101–102, 118–119, 128, 132

vacancy rate 97, 108–110, 112
vacant buildings 7–8, 110, 114n26, 117–118, 128, 136–155; *see also* empty buildings/houses
vacant houses 5, 86, 118–119, 122, 125, 128; ways of life 100–101, 103, 105–106, 110, 114n26
vacant offices 97
value system 124
"vernacular" 2, 42–45, 47, 58
vernacular architecture 42–45, 48, 65, 90
village life 100
Volumetric District System 37n16

"Wakayama Way" 118
wall panels 16, 18–19
War Damage Reconstruction Institution 10–11
Watanabe, Toyokazu 54
Watanabe, Yasutada 33–34
weak individuals 108–109
"weather chart of house production" 29, *30*
Western Japan 65, 104, 134n5
*Whole Earth Catalog* 3, 57–58, 62n30, 131
wooden architecture 33
wooden buildings/houses 3, 58–59, 151–152; customers 66–67, *67*, 71, 73, 74, 76, 80, 82, 87n7, 87n12; government/industry initiatives 10, 13, 15–16, 19–20, 26, 28–29, 31
wooden low-rise apartment buildings 91, 98
wooden prefabricated housing 70
working at home 93
World Cultural Heritage sites 143, 154n7

Xintiandi district, Shanghai 149

Yabe, Tomohito 121
Yamamoto, Sotaro 121
Yamazaki, Hiroyuki 137–139
"Yamori" 121, 134
Yasukuni Shrine 151
Yawata Iron & Steel (Co., Ltd.) 18, 24
Yokoyama, Gennosuke 25, 38n30
Yoshihara, Katsumi 110, *111*, 112, 114n23
Yoshimura House 44, *44*
Yutaka Pre Con 15

*zashiki* room 65–66
Zenkouji Temple 122, 125–126
zero-energy buildings 124

For Product Safety Concerns and Information please contact our EU
representative GPSR@taylorandfrancis.com
Taylor & Francis Verlag GmbH, Kaufingerstraße 24, 80331 München, Germany

www.ingramcontent.com/pod-product-compliance
Ingram Content Group UK Ltd.
Pitfield, Milton Keynes, MK11 3LW, UK
UKHW022124190926
475702UK00013B/1636

*9780367785086*